# The St. Louis Irish

# The St. Louis Irish
## An Unmatched Celtic Community
by William Barnaby Faherty, S.J.

Missouri Historical Society Press • Saint Louis

Distributed by University of Missouri Press

Published in the United States of America by the
Missouri Historical Society Press
P.O. Box 11940, St. Louis, Missouri 63112-0040

Library of Congress Cataloging-in-Publication Data

Faherty, William Barnaby, 1914–
    The St. Louis Irish : an unmatched Celtic community / by William B. Faherty
      p. cm.
    Includes bibliographical references (p.   ) and index.
    ISBN 1-883982-39-1 (cloth : alk. paper) – ISBN 1-883982-40-5 (pbk. : alk. paper)

    1. Irish Americans – Missouri – Saint Louis – History.
    2. Irish Americans – Missouri – Saint Louis – Ethnic identity. 3. Saint Louis (Mo.) –
History. 4. Saint Louis (Mo.) – Ethnic relations. I. Title: Saint Louis Irish.

    F474.S29 I64 2001
    977.8'660049162—dc21                                   00-069920

Distributed by University of Missouri Press
Design by Robyn Morgan
Printed in the United States by Edwards Brothers Printing

∞ the paper used in this publication meets minimum requirements of the ANSI/NISO
Z39.48-1992 (R 1997) (Permanence of Paper).

Cover illustrations: Courtyard walls, St. Michael's Catholic Church, St. Louis.
Photographs by David Schultz © 2000. Missouri Historical Society Photograph and
Print Collection.

    02  03  04  05    5  4

# Contents

# Foreword

Almost every St. Louisan claims some Irish ancestry around March 17, and perhaps on a Saturday night at McGurk's Pub on the near south side. The music, the merry toasts, the stories and the poetry, the lyrical myths, the immigrant's poignant longings, and even the bloody history of the land of Ireland—indeed the whole romance of being Irish—speaks to something in each of us and catches us in a certain sparkling rhythm and rhyme.

The reality of being Irish in St. Louis is even more intriguing, and Father William Barnaby Faherty's work and research on the story of this "unmatched Celtic community" enriches the story of us all.

St. Louis is a place of many stories, of numerous colors and accents and high and low sounds, a veritable chorus of narrative voices. The lilt and cadence of the Celtic tones is heard throughout our regional narrative, mingling with the French and German, the African and African American, the Indian, the Asian, and many more. In discerning and exploring this particular strain in our intricate heritage, we do not diminish the whole story but rather expand and enhance it.

Story and place are inseparable, for what is a story without a place to anchor it? Irish hands helped to build this town on the river, and—among the diversity of voices and the multiplicity of perspectives—the stories of the Irish community have helped to create this place that we call St. Louis. To tell the true story of our place we must acknowledge and encompass all the voices that have contributed to the narrative chorus. We must listen to and retell the stories that connect us, the experiences in common that foster trust and obligation. Our consciousness of our history must be inclusive, so that we can recognize and understand a common interest in our past and in our regional memory, and our stories will oblige us to examine what we have done well and what we can do better. Our personal narratives will vary, so our story must expand and allow us to explore our differences and examine the qualities and the experiences that we share with the St. Louis Irish and with the rest of our region past, present, and to come.

So many of the streets and buildings that the early Irish in St. Louis saw, inhabited, built have been abandoned and obliterated, in some cases for good and valid reasons yet in others through indifference and disregard. The almost mythical Kerry Patch has had several boundaries through its St. Louis peregrinations, and its specific geographical dimensions have often been under question and scrutiny.

The exact location of Kerry Patch doesn't matter. It is the place that matters, a place that although its physicalities have been lost or altered is buttressed and preserved with the stories that have formed and transformed its people into an intrinsic element of our city and our region. You will find so many of them here.

At the risk of fortifying the Celtic stereotype, I will say that the Irish are fine storytellers, William Barnaby Faherty assuredly among them, and I hasten to acknowledge the competency of this fine storyteller as a writer and historian and stalwart St. Louisan. It is a pleasure to include Father Faherty and *The St. Louis Irish* in the publications of the Missouri Historical Society Press.

—ROBERT R. ARCHIBALD

# Preface

During the first fifty years after the Louisiana Purchase, the village of St. Louis gave a more cordial welcome to Irish Catholics than any place in the world, including the city of Dublin itself. Several factors influenced this welcome. First, the French were a hospitable group of people. Secondly, they shared the Catholic faith with a good percentage of the Irish newcomers. Thirdly, St. Louis was the commercial center of the vast midland empire and numerous in-coming Irish were skilled in merchandising. English penal law kept all Irish, Catholic and Protestant, from manufacturing. English landlords owned more than 90 percent of the arable acreage throughout the island. As a result, commerce was the only economic avenue open for the average Irishman. Many excelled in this field.

Since the Irish met only a hostile reception in the already established business communities on the eastern seaboard, they chose the unfrozen economic atmosphere of the vast midwest territory. To this open land came the Mullanphys and the O'Fallons, the Bradys and the McKnights, the O'Connors and the Campbells, the Thorntons and the Christys in early American days. They prospered. Once established, they did not forget the newcomers moving into the area. Even before Missouri became a state, Irish merchants started the Erin Benevolent Society to help others. The Irish intermarried with the French as well as the Anglo-Americans. John Mullanphy's daughters married officers in the United States Army. Harriet Brady married Ferdinand Rozier, a successful Creole merchant. John Little of County Down married a member of the prominent Chouteau family. These French-Irish marriages were typical of others.

A series of events spawned the Irish immigration to the area. Less than four years after the founding of St. Louis in 1764, an Irish regiment of the British Army patrolled the area of Cahokia and other villages on the east bank of the Mississippi River. In a secret treaty, King Louis XV of France gave the west bank of the river to the king of Spain. A few years later, King Charles IV of Spain came to realize that a great number of his troops in the New World were Irish, and he learned that Catholics from Maryland, many of them of Irish ancestry, were moving into the area. To take care of the spiritual needs of his Irish soldiers and the settlers from Maryland, King Charles sent a Dublin-born priest, Father James Maxwell, to Upper Louisiana. He soon became a major frontier leader, materially and spiritually.

The Irish who came invited relatives in the homeland. Father Maxwell's nephew, Hugh Maxwell, for instance, came at his uncle's invitation. Anthony Doyle, a farmer on the rich acres of Florissant Valley near St. Louis, wrote to friends and relatives in Ireland of the glories of the area.

Every day was market day for the merchants, Irish or not, in the central Mississippi Valley. Farmers began to plow the rich acres of southern Illinois. Traffic expanded on the rivers, especially after 1817 when the first steamboat arrived in St. Louis. River towns grew. Travellers headed west. St. Louis merchants supplied these people. Further, they provisioned the soldiers at Fort Snelling in Minnesota, Fort Madison in Iowa, Fort Smith on the Arkansas River, and Fort Atkinson on the Missouri and Fort Bellefontaine and later Jefferson Barracks on the Mississippi.

Roving missionaries, French and Irish, occasionally visited the little village. In 1818 Territorial Bishop Louis William Du Bourg took up residence in St. Louis. He brought with him Vincentian priests from Italy, Religious Sisters of the Sacred Heart from France, and invited Jesuit missionaries from Belgium. All of these religious groups soon welcomed Irish members. Du Bourg also began an academy for boys that became St. Louis College in 1821. Patrick Sullivan taught classical languages there, more than a half century before an Irish Catholic was welcome on the faculty of University College–Dublin or University College–Cork.

The Daughters of Charity, many of them of Irish background, came to open a hospital in 1826. Mercy Sisters, exclusively of Irish background, came a few years later. They, too, opened hospitals as well as engaged in other charitable activities for the poor.

In 1827 another group of successful Irish St. Louisans formed the Missouri Hibernian Relief Society to help their fellow Irish who wished to emigrate and those already in St. Louis who were in need. James Seeley was the first president, William Piggott, secretary. In 1840 second-generation Irish Americans, under the leadership of Christopher Garvey, began a Society for the Diffusion of Alms. James P. Barry, John Timon, and John T. Mitchell belonged to this group. They assigned one man to look after the needs of the poor in each ward of the city. In 1841 Judge Luke Lawless presided at the first meeting of a fourth group, the "Friends of Ireland." They elected John O'Fallon president, with Judge Lawless and businessmen Edward Walsh, James Clemens, Jr., and John P. McNeil vice presidents. They, too, assigned representatives to look after the needs of people in every ward of the city.

In 1845 St. Louisans started the first unit of the St. Vincent de Paul Society in America, an organization that emphasized "hands-on" charity. While its first president, Dr. Moses Linton, of Anglo-American background, was a convert from Protestantism, and the first spiritual director, Father Ambrose Heim, an immigrant from Alsace, the society numbered a large percentage of Irish members in its personal concern for the poor. The secretary, Judge Bryan Mullanphy, mayor of the city and son of the area's first "millionaire," personally aided poor people in a variety of ways. Eventually his entire fortune went to immigrant aid.

By the time the refugees of the Famine—men and women with no urban skills and little training for city life—arrived in St. Louis in the late 1840s, the Irish were already well-established, both the wealthy merchants like Edward Walsh and John Thornton, and the small shopkeepers who clustered on the near northside around St. Patrick's Church.

Those "Famine Irish" who were resourceful enough to reach St. Louis usually came through New Orleans and up the river by steamboat. They accepted the help of relatives or of the benevolent societies while they found work loading or unloading steamboats at the levee, laying tracks for the railroad to the west, digging clay in the pits at Cheltenham a few miles beyond the city limits, baking bricks at the numerous kilns that helped make St. Louis a brick city, or planting trees at Henry Shaw's country home that became the Missouri Botanical Garden a short time later. Others settled on farms in neighboring rural communities, such as O'Harasburg or Tipton in Illinois, and Florissant in Missouri, where their relatives who had already established themselves in those communities welcomed them.

A negative image prevailed of the "Famine Irish" in other cities. Historians spoke of them as a "wretched lot of culturally and technologically impoverished peasants," "pioneers of the American urban ghetto," "involuntary, non-responsible exiles," and "pitiful spectacles of manhood." Such descriptions never fit the Irish in St. Louis.

At least two earlier historians realized that St. Louis had its own unique image. In his *History of Missouri*, David March called St. Louis "the chief Irish Settlement in the United States." In a story of the Irish in Ireland and America, *To the Golden Door*, George Potter wrote, "The Catholic Irish enjoyed a status of equality in early St. Louis denied them in the East." No historian challenged either writer.

During those early American years, the St. Louis Irish could rightly claim recognition as a Celtic community unmatched anywhere in the world.

# Acknowledgments

Thanks go to many individuals: to Ed Cody and his associates in the Galway–St. Louis Sister-City Committee; to Joseph B. McGlynn, Jr., and Patrick Donnelan and other members of the St. Patrick's Day Parade Committee; to George Clough and his associates in the Ancient Order of Hibernians; to Dr. Emmet Larkin of Chicago University; to my students NiNi Harris, Claudia Voulgaraikas, Jay Neis, and Harry Kelsey; to Rose Feurer, Northern Illinois University, an expert in labor history; to Daniel "Duke" McVey of the AFL–CIO; to Sharon Kinney Hanson and Tere Rios Versace; to Mary Struckel who typed this manuscript and its revisions; to Nancy Merz who appraised it at each step; and to many who helped with the research: among them Brother Michael Grace, S.J., Loyola University Archivist; Mary Seematter of the Carondelet Historical Society; Mr. and Mrs. Stan Prater with the 8th Missouri Infantry Re-enactors; Ruth Menard of Ruma, Illinois, with the "Old French Settlements"; John Waide, Randy McGuire, and Christy Harper of the Saint Louis University Archives; Miriam E. Joseph of the Pius XII Library; Sister Teresa Maria Eagan, C.S.J., at the Archdiocesan Archives; Noel Holobeck and Kate Sathi of the Saint Louis Public Library; Mary Ellen Davis at the Mercantile Library; Sister Mary Louise Gordon of Visitation Convent; Sister Charline Sullivan of the Sisters of St. Joseph; Sister Genevieve Keusenkothen, D.C., archivist of the Daughters of Charity; Sister Elizabeth Farley, R.C.S.J., and Sister Catherine McMahon, R.C.S.J., archivists of the Society of the Sacred Heart; Bernie Lewandowski and Mary Dahm of the Historical Society of St. Louis County; Paul Winslow, labor historian; Kevin Madden, writer for the Labor Advocate; Sarah M. Springer, archivist of the George Meany Memorial Archives in Silver Springs, Maryland; Glen Holt, director of the St. Louis Public Library; and the members of the St. Louis Genealogical Society, whose work was extremely valuable in locating the early Irish residents.

# Ancestral Areas of Pre–Civil War Immigrants to the St. Louis Region

McGlynn
O'Donnell

Cummings
Dillon
Rankin
Montgomery
McAnulty
Campbell
Lowry

McGenis

White
Burns

Murphy
Tiernan

Little

Gilfillian
MULLANPHY

Dougherty

THORNTON

McKnight

Dowling
Gilhuly

Matthews
Moloney

Donnelly
Hayden
Dowling

McGovern

O'Hara

Higgins
McDermott
Loughlin

**Dublin**

Kavanauugh
McDonough

Byrne

O'FALLON

Duggan
Dolan

Hanlon

Charless

Faherty

McLaughlin
Donovan

Byrnes

Bolton

Bonacum
Ryan  Feehan

O'Sullivan
Nolan
Carroll

Conner
Rochford

Cleary
Lynch

Hennessey     Lillis

O'Shea
Madden      Ryan

Doyle
Murphy

Drew

O'Leary    O'Brien
Brady   Fitnam
Fitzgibbons

Connor    Lee

♣ **Famous St. Louisans
from the Dublin area**
Rev. James Maxwell
Judge Luke Lawless
Edward Walsh
Archbishop Peter R. Kenrick
Mother Mary D. P. Bentley, RSM
Rev. John B. Bannon
Canon O'Hanlon

# Two Centuries of Irish Chronology (1798–1998)

1798    "Year of the French"—revolt of the United Irishmen, led by Protestant lawyers, Wolfe Tone and Thomas Emmet, aided by a French Army; suppressed with cruelty by Lord Cornwallis.

1800    Act of Union—dissolved Irish Parliament. Irish Protestants represented in English Parliament.

1829    Catholic Emancipation—Daniel O'Connell took his seat in Parliament.

1840s    Irish Famine—hundreds of thousands starved to death. Equal numbers sought homes elsewhere.

1847–48    "Young Ireland Party"—insurrection in Tipperary.

1869    Disestablishment Act—ended forced support by Catholics of the Protestant Episcopal Church in Ireland.

1871    "Home Rule Party" founded by Isaac Butt. Charles Stewart Parnell assumed leadership when elected to Parliament in 1875.

1886    First Home Rule Bill—defeated.

1893    Second Home Rule Bill—passed by Commons; rejected by Lords.

1914    Home Rule Becomes Law—Ulsterites under Sir Edward Carson threatened Civil War; Home Rule postponed until after the European War then in progress.

1916    Easter Rebellion—ill-advised outbreak brought brutal retaliation.

1920    Government of Ireland Act set up six northeastern counties as Northern Ireland.

1922    Irish Free State Act. Dissatisfaction of many with certain provisions brought Civil War.

1938    New Irish Constitution enacted by Referendum.

1949    Republic of Ireland Act ended special relationship with the Crown.

1973    Eire joined the European Economic Community.

# The St. Louis Irish

# Creating a French Colonial Community

S t. Louis was the last settlement of the French in North America in the second half of the eighteenth century, and it became the favorite city of the Irish in the first half of the nineteenth. Both the French and the Irish came as refugees from British harassment, one group across a great river, the other across the Atlantic and half a continent.

By the 1760s the French had lived for several generations in the rich bottomland on the east bank of the Mississippi between the mouth of the Illinois River and the confluence of the Kaskaskia, eighty miles to the south. In the Peace of Paris at the end of the French and Indian War (1763), King Louis XV gave up all of his territory east of the Mississippi to the British. The French commandant, Louis St. Ange de Bellerive, turned the French stronghold Fort Chartres over to the British in 1765 and set up his new headquarters across the river, fifty miles to the north.

There, one year before, Pierre Laclède, a merchant-trader from the Pyrenees, had set up a trading post and village and called it St. Louis in honor of the patron saint of the reigning monarch, Louis XV. An ideal place it was, solidly founded on a limestone terrace, safe from floods, backed by fertile prairie to the west, and joined to the outside world by the magnificent river. In the name of the French king, St. Ange approved what Laclède had done in staking out a village around his trading post.

The Illinois French were aware that British soldiers, abetted by Puritans from New England, had driven the French residents from Nova Scotia and scattered them along the Atlantic coast.

1

Many of these "Acadians" eventually found their way to southern Louisiana. Many French in the two Illinois settlements near Fort Chartres—Ste. Anne and St. Philippe—crossed the river to relocate in St. Louis.

The French had a strong desire to practice their religion freely, and they found the British occupation distasteful. The English looked upon the French residents as a worthless lot, even though their efforts had made the area the granary of the French Empire.[1] British officers sent to the Illinois country showed only disdain for, and treated shabbily, the French inhabitants of the area. As a result, many French followed Bellerive to the west bank of the river and settled in St. Louis, even though they learned that King Louis had secretly given the west bank of the Mississippi to King Charles III of Spain.

In 1798, in distant Ireland, courageous leaders planned to put an end to centuries of British oppression. They felt the time of the Shamrock had come and rose in revolt. With the assistance of a small French army, they gained minor victories. Britain sent overwhelming forces under Lord Cornwallis. While the British leader accepted the surrender of the French troops, and let them return to France intact, he smashed the Irish with ferocity. Many Irish fled to the New World. When they reached the eastern seaboard, distant St. Louis beckoned.

Almost a century had to elapse before the cities along the Atlantic gave the welcome to Irish newcomers that awaited them on the banks of the Mississippi. St. Louis had several outstanding advantages. First, the Catholic Church was established by law, as the Congregationalist Church was in the New England colonies and the Anglican Church in the South. In St. Louis, all residents— white, black, and red—were Catholic. The priest recorded all baptisms. Secondly, Native Americans felt at home in St. Louis. While English frontier settlements lived in constant fear of Indian raids and the people built stockades for defense, no wall surrounded the village of St. Louis. Only once did any tribesmen threaten it. That occurred during the American Revolution, when the British provoked upriver tribes to attack. Thirdly, the residents enjoyed a great deal of political liberty, functioning under the most liberal of all French laws, those of the city of Paris itself. This concern for liberty showed itself dramatically later on when St. Louis became part of the United States.

The French in St. Louis were a happy, easygoing lot. Except for a few rich traders, the townsfolk were generally non-acquisitive. They believed in enjoying life. They celebrated an amazing number of traditional feast days with enthusiasm. A future mayor of St. Louis, John Darby, described them as "the most happy and contented people that ever lived. There was a fiddle in every house and a dance somewhere every night. They were honest, hospitable, confiding, and generous."[2] No one locked their doors, yet all lived with a sense of security.

The trading post that quickly became a village stood at a strategic site. Twelve miles to the north, the turbulent Missouri River flowed into the

Mississippi and gave access to the tribes of the interior. Farther north, the Illinois, the Des Moines, and the Wisconsin Rivers flowed into the Father of Waters. One hundred and twenty miles to the south, the Ohio River poured into the Mississippi.

St. Louis French, merchant-traders like Laclède, or *voyageurs* or *coureurs-de-bois* like Joseph and Auguste Hebert, moved up these rivers to trade at numerous Indian villages. The French who wished to farm settled in Carondelet, a few miles south of St. Louis, or in the fertile Florissant Valley twenty miles northwest. St. Louis soon became the commercial depot of the mid-continent. When Irish immigrants began to cross the sea and half a continent, many entered the field of merchandising.

St. Louis was a small French-speaking village deep in the heartland of America. How did the Irish find out about it? Residents of Maryland, many of them of Irish background, knew of the religious freedom that Catholics enjoyed in the former French settlements. The hatred of Catholicism that had marked the English colonies from their earliest days peaked during the French and Indian War (1756–1763). The expulsion of the Acadians reflected this widespread hostility. Anti-Catholic feeling grew so strong that the father of Charles Carroll, a signer of the Declaration of Independence, seriously thought of moving to Louisiana Territory. At the end of the war with France, that intense hatred waned.

By the Treaty of Paris in 1763, King Louis XV ceded Canada and the lands between the Alleghenies and the Mississippi River to the English, and gave the area west of the river to his ally, King Charles III of Spain. A short time after the British took charge of Fort Chartres, they garrisoned the stone fortification with a Celtic infantry unit, the Irish Fusiliers. A majority of these soldiers were Catholics and their names began to appear in the local church records.

*The first Celts in the area were Irish Fusiliers, members of a unit of the British Army assigned in 1768 to garrison the English Territory on the east bank of the Mississippi, including Cahokia, in 1768. The Cahokia Courthouse was typical of French structures of the time.*

Creating a French Colonial Community    3

It may come as a surprise that young men from Ireland entered the British service at a time when the English government so mistreated the Irish people, and patriots were talking of revolting against the Crown. These young men wanted to get out of Ireland and, for many, British service was the only way of escape. As a result, Irish served at Fort Chartres and Cahokia when French in the neighboring Illinois villages were crossing the river to St. Louis.

Even before the end of the American Revolution, other Irish had found their way to Illinois. In 1780, for instance, a year and a half before Cornwallis surrendered, Henry O'Hara and his wife Bridget Bolton brought their five children to Father Pierre Gibault in Kaskaskia for baptism. When the Revolution ended in the fall of 1781, many of the neighbors of the Carrolls in Maryland moved into Kentucky and even farther west.

In the early 1790s a progressive lieutenant governor of Upper Louisiana Territory, Zenon Trudeau, a Louisiana native who had risen in the Spanish service, invited Kentucky families to settle on the west bank of the Mississippi. The largest group chose the area ten miles south of Ste. Genevieve, while several families pushed on to the rich Florissant Valley twenty miles northwest of St. Louis.

A second group of English-speaking residents of Upper Louisiana were Spanish soldiers of Irish birth. Even the commanding general in New Orleans, Alessandro O'Reilly, was Irish. To take care of the newly arrived English-speaking settlers from Kentucky and the soldiers in his army, King Charles IV of Spain decided to send a "priest of the Irish nation" to the area.

Restricted in educational opportunities by English law, Irishmen who felt a call to the priesthood, such as James Maxwell of Dublin, had to go to France or Spain for their education. Maxwell attended the "Irish College" at the University of Salamanca and was ordained there. In 1794 the Spanish King sent him to the New World to serve under Territorial Bishop Luis Penalver y

*Father François LeDru, pioneer missionary, witnessed the wedding of Patrick Lee, first Irish landowner in St. Louis, and Constance Conde, in the old log church on July 18, 1797.*

Cardenas. Two years later the bishop assigned Father Maxwell to Upper Louisiana where he took up residence near Ste. Genevieve, the oldest settlement on the west bank. Bishop Penalver urged Father Maxwell to visit St. Louis and to report on religious conditions.[3]

The Irish priest found the condition of the log church built in 1776 appalling. It was too small and its timbers had decayed. Bishop Penalver asked Lieutenant Governor Zenon Trudeau to cover a third of the cost of repairs. Trudeau must have acted on this request. A few years later a visiting priest described the church as in fair condition.

When Kentucky families took up residence in Florissant, Trudeau asked for another priest "of the Irish nation," but no other was available. Father Maxwell occasionally visited the area. Parish records in Florissant show several Irish newcomers: John Gates married Genevieve Morin, June 19, 1797, and Patrick Lee married Constance Conde, July 18, 1797.[4]

Father Maxwell moved far beyond the scope of the usual frontier missionary. A mini-empire builder, he had expansive plans for his fellow Irish. In 1797 he sought and won from the King an extensive land grant, totaling slightly over one hundred thousand acres. He intended to colonize the region with immigrants from his native land. The tracts lay ninety to one hundred miles west of Ste. Genevieve, one hundred and fifty miles southwest of St. Louis.

Father Maxwell built a general store on his "plantation." The area lacked the fertility of the Florissant Valley, of the bottomlands along the Mississippi River, or of the wide acres north of the Missouri River. Further, the disturbed conditions in Ireland, the long war of the revolutionary French against the British, and the Spanish King's secret treaty that gave the territory to Napoleon hindered Father Maxwell's plans.

While the "Irish Settlement" never came to be, the news of Upper Louisiana had reached Father Maxwell's relatives in Dublin. His nephew, Hugh Maxwell, came early in the new century, and prospered in business. Eventually he married Marie Odile Menard,[5] daughter of Lieutenant Governor Pierre Menard, a prominent Illinois merchant-trader and frontier statesman.

Records of St. Ferdinand's Parish in Florissant show the names of English Catholic Maryland families. In several instances, one partner was of Irish background. The Miles family was among the first of these English-speaking Marylanders to arrive. Thomas James Miles had married Mary Ann Hogan, a member of an old Maryland family. Vincent Carrico married Susan Quick. Their first child, Marie Elizabeth, was baptized at St. Ferdinand's in 1798, and three others were baptized before the area became American.[6]

In short, the area of St. Louis was a symbol of freedom, a mecca of opportunity, and many Irish knew of its advantages as a place of residence.

# Gauls Welcome Gaels

According to the reconstructed 1776 Census of St. Louis, only one resident, John Bodoin, claimed to have been born in Ireland and one of Irish ancestry, Henry O'Hara, was born in America. The wives of both were Native Americans. Bodoin's son, Jean Baptiste, had been born in Illinois before the family moved to St. Louis.[1] One-year-old Bryson, a son of Henry O'Hara, was born in St. Louis. During Spanish days, few Irish followed them to the village. At the time of the Louisiana Purchase (1804 in St. Louis), the name of only one Irish property holder, Patrick Lee, appears on historian Frederick Billon's plat of St. Louis. Son of Thomas Lee and Catherine Longlais of Quebec, Lee had married Constance Conde on July 18, 1797.[2] In 1804, he owned the northwest section of Block 37, facing the *Rue de L'Eglise*, three blocks south and across the street from the church block.

When the Stars and Stripes went up in 1804 at the Government Building in St. Louis, the first woman of Irish ancestry to arrive was Eliza Lowry of County Monaghan. President Jefferson had named her uncle, James Lowry Donaldson, attorney general of the Territory of Louisiana. Donaldson urged his niece to move to St. Louis. In 1806 she married Robert Morrison, a successful merchant of Kaskaskia. Father Maxwell witnessed the wedding.

A surprising number of Irish immigrants prospered in a short time. Among the first newcomers were Lieutenant Alexander McNair, a native Pennsylvanian of Irish parentage; William Sullivan, the first constable and coroner, who later opened a livery stable; James Rankin, who became sheriff later that same year; Major William Christy, whose Scottish ancestor had moved from Dundee to County Down in Ireland and married into the Moyallan family; and John Mullanphy, a native of County Fermanagh, who had spent time in France and learned the French language. In 1805 Mullanphy purchased for $160 two tracts from François Dunegant, Canadian-born commandant at Florissant during the Spanish regime. One plot ran west from the river almost a mile and a half, near the north end of Laclède's original village. This purchase put Mullanphy on the path to eventual riches. In 1808 he bought the government house in Florissant and moved his family there.

In 1805 another newcomer, Jeremiah Connor, an auctioneer, became sheriff and later collector and treasurer. He served from 1806 to 1810. Like Mullanphy and others, he gained valuable property in the area, especially a strip approximately 450 feet wide, between French-born Judge James Lucas' property on the south and Major Christy's on the north. It extended two miles west of Third Street, six blocks north of Market. A public-spirited citizen, Connor took a lead in civic and church activities.

In the early American years the martello fort, or circular tower of Spanish days, served as the city jail. James Sullivan, the jailer, walked lightly on his feet, even though he weighed over 350 pounds. He raised hogs that roamed widely but always answered his stentorian summons.

Off and on during these years, various French priests served in St. Louis for short periods of time, among them Donatien Olivier, pastor of Prairie du Rocher. Other French priests, stationed at Florissant, occasionally came into town. In 1806, Father Maxwell made one of his longer visits. In three months he baptized forty-five whites, sixteen blacks, and one Indian. He also solemnized three marriages.

In November a wandering Capuchin Franciscan, Father Thomas Flynn, arrived in St. Louis. He made an agreement with the church wardens to serve the parish for one year, offering Mass on the first three Sundays of the month. On the fourth he would serve the parishioners of St. Ferdinand and St. Charles. He offered Mass at 9:00 A.M. in the summer and 10:00 A.M. in the winter. He agreed to teach the children after Vespers every Sunday, to prepare them during Lent to receive the Sacraments, and to visit the sick when requested. In turn, the citizens agreed to pay him a salary of 360 Spanish dollars, or the equivalent in pelts or bushels of wheat. He would also receive fees for weddings and funerals.

Shortly after his arrival in St. Louis, Father Flynn wrote a letter to a friend, William McCordell, in Bardstown, Kentucky: "The Church is pretty decent. . . . Has a tolerably good bell, high altar and commodious pews. The house for the priest is convenient, but rather out of repair. There is annexed to it a large garden, well stocked with fruit trees, barn, stables and other out-offices."[3] The distance between priests in the area caused his only anxiety.[4]

In fourteen months in St. Louis Father Flynn baptized eighty-eight whites, eleven blacks, and one Indian; solemnized eleven marriages of whites; and buried thirty whites and nine blacks. The Irish among Father Flynn's list of baptisms include Catherine Lee, daughter of Patrick Lee and Constance Conde, baptized on November 9, 1806; Daniel Sullivan, son of William and Sarah McElhaney Sullivan, on February 3, 1807; and James Burke, son of John and Elizabeth Murphy Burke, on September 4, 1807.[5] Early the following year, on January 8, 1808, he resigned his post in St. Louis and wandered out of historical records.

Bachelors and an occasional married man of Irish descent continued to come to St. Louis. Most arriving Irishmen engaged in merchandising, among them Matthew Kerr,[6] Patrick Lee,[7] and William Shannon who added medicines and drugs to his general merchandise.[8] Two arrived in 1808 with distinct and needed skills—tailor Thomas Hickey and editor Joseph Charless.

Implicated in the Irish rebellion of 1795, Charless, a native of West Meath of Welsh ancestry, reached the United States the following year. He added an "s" to the end of his surname to ensure an Irish pronunciation. He married widow Sarah Jordan McCloud in 1798. After a time in the East, he reached St. Louis and edited the city's first newspaper, the *Missouri Gazette*. On July 12, 1808, he published the initial issue at his shop on the east side of South Main. The subscription price was three dollars a year. An advertisement cost a dollar. Often the clients paid in the goods they advertised. Commerce moved slowly at that time due to the struggle between England and France on the high seas and America's retaliatory Embargo Acts. St. Louis had as yet no postal service.

In spite of the bad times and an occasional challenge for a given stand, even by some of his fellow Irish, Charless succeeded with his paper. An acquaintance described him as a "noble specimen of the Irish gentleman, . . . warm-heartedness being his most characteristic trait."[9] Even in difficult times, his tenacity and sense of humor carried him through. Occasionally he called on his talent for humorous verse to win a point. However, his support of

Joseph Charless began St. Louis's first newspaper in 1808.

Presidents Thomas Jefferson and James Madison brought him political enemies. One challenged him to a duel. Unarmed in the face of a threatening pistol, he like David reached down for a small stone and with an accurate throw chased the pistol-packing Goliath from the field.

In 1809 John McKnight and Thomas Brady and their families broke the pattern of individual Irish arriving in St. Louis. They had formed a business partnership in Pennsylvania, floated down the Ohio River, and then rowed up the Mississippi River in their own boat. The colonial French welcomed the energetic boatload of people and dubbed them "the Irish Crowd." Thomas Brady, a Catholic, had with him his mother, Catherine Brady, a sister Patrice, a brother John, and a relative Uriah. John McKnight, son of Timothy McKnight, a Presbyterian, came with his five brothers and six sisters.

John McKnight and Thomas Brady set up the mercantile firm of McKnight and Brady on the southeast corner of Main and Pine Streets. On the south side of *Rue Orleans*, between *Rue Royale* (Second Street) and *Rue L'Eglise* (Church Street), Uriah Brady and Thomas McKnight set up the firm of Brady and McKnight. The energetic partners opened branches in Ste. Genevieve and St. Charles, and soon outdistanced all rivals. While most of the other residents owned property valued under $1,000, and some under $100, Brady and McKnight owned property assessed at $8,300 by 1811. Only merchant-trader Auguste Chouteau owned more property, which reached $15,664 in value.[10]

Robert McKnight went on a trading expedition to the Southwest in 1812. He timed his move poorly. The spirit of independence had stirred the country, but Spain still swung a stout sword. McKnight and his associates landed in jail in Chihuahua and languished there for some years. In the meantime, Thomas Brady went to Ste. Genevieve to marry Harriet Jones, the daughter of John Rice Jones, a Welsh judge who later became chief justice of the Missouri Supreme Court. Thomas and Harriet eventually built a home three miles north of town. John Brady married Mary Fitzpatrick.

In 1812, when Louisiana became a state, President Madison named Father Maxwell a member of the new Missouri Territorial Council. The priest came to St. Louis to take part in the organizational meeting of the legislative assembly. The members elected him president. Unfortunately, he died of injuries when thrown from his horse a short time later.

The only other priest in good standing to hold elective office in the early Republic was a fellow frontiersman, Father Gabriel Richard, a native of France, sent by Bishop John Carroll of Baltimore as a missionary to the Northwest Territory. Father Richard settled in Detroit, promoted education, and published a periodical. Elected as territorial delegate to the Eighteenth U.S. Congress (1823–25), he served with such distinguished Americans as Henry Clay, John Randolph, and Daniel Webster. A century and a half went by before another active priest entered Congress.

# The "Chief Irish Settlement in the U.S."

**E**ven such leading historians of Irish-America as Lawrence McCaffrey[1] of Loyola University and Kerby A. Miller[2] of the University of Missouri have ignored the record of the Irish in St. Louis. The Celtic experience in the Missouri metropolis stood in striking contrast to the widespread view of the Irish as "despised aliens,"[3] "an unassimiable menace,"[4] "agents of . . . ignorance and superstition,"[5] and "refugees . . . from destitution and oppression,"[6] who "pioneered the American ghetto."[7]

Miller saw the Irish not as immigrants, but as "involuntary, non-responsible 'exiles' compelled to leave home by forces beyond their control,"[8] constantly dreaming of home, wishing to return, and refusing to come to terms with their new situation. McCaffrey rightly questions this "social misfit" explanation.[9]

The Irish that McCaffrey and Miller wrote about formed "the first large group of non-Anglo Protestants to arrive in *American* cities."[10] It was not an American city that John Mullanphy and John O'Fallon, the Bradys and McKnights, and other St. Louis Irish reached early in the nineteenth-century. They arrived in a *French Catholic* city at the time it was becoming American, with Scots, Scotch-Irish, and Anglo-Americans arriving at the same time. The Irish intended to stay, had no regrets on leaving Cork or Kildare, and set out to establish themselves in the region.

A historian of Missouri, David March, saw this. Rather than ignoring the unique story of the St. Louis Irish, or combining their story with that of Irish immigrants in other cities, March gave the local Celts a careful study and came to a distinct and different conclusion. He called St. Louis "the chief Irish Settlement in the United States."[11] Similarly, in his book, *To the Golden Door*, George Potter rightly stated that "the Catholic Irish enjoyed a status of equality in . . . early St. Louis, denied them in the East."[12] Unfortunately, he missed the reason: the welcome the French residents gave their co-religionists from Ireland. Further, the word "early" misleads. This equality of status continued beyond the "early" years.

Potter attributed this fine reception to the spirit of the "raw frontier" in contrast to the "settledness" of the East.[13] His conclusion was sound, but one might question Potter on the whys of his analysis. If it was the lack of "settledness" rather than the French factor, why didn't the Irish meet a similar warm welcome in Memphis or Nashville, two not yet "settled" communities. If it was the "frontier" factor that brought about the welcome, why didn't the Irish find a similar welcome at a later but still frontier time in Topeka or Des Moines? In those frontier cities the Irish more readily found an entrenched and inhospitable Ku Klux Klan or an equally unreceptive American Protective Society.

The Irish were at home in St. Louis from the earliest days as in no other city in the country. They would profit both by their identity of faith with the original French inhabitants and the fact that some of them either had served in the French army or lived in France. The short-lived dispute over the language to be used in the cathedral sermons did not substantially disturb the rapport. The Irish also profited from the splendid cooperative spirit existing between the Anglo-American newcomers and the established French residents.

As a result, the Irish readily intermarried with both groups. Harriet, the daughter of Thomas Brady, married Ferdinand Rozier II, of Ste. Genevieve. The son of a French-Irish marriage, Jesuit Father John Verdin was the first native St. Louisan to become president of Saint Louis University. Several of the Mullanphy girls married Anglo-American officers of the United States Army assigned to the frontier country. Mary married William S. Harney, who gained fame as a general on the frontier. Catherine, the second daughter, married Richard Graham of Virginia, a staff officer under General William Henry Harrison. One of their daughters, in turn, married General Daniel M. Frost, a conspicuous name in St. Louis during the Civil War. Jane, the third Mullanphy daughter, was the only one to marry a native of Ireland, Charles Chambers, the son of an associate of Robert Emmett in the Freedom Movement of 1798. The fourth daughter, Ann, married Major Thomas Biddle, brother of the president of the Bank of the United States, Nicholas Biddle. After her husband's death in a duel, Ann never remarried. Instead, she gave generously of her fortune to Catholic and secular enterprises. These marriages took place at St. Ferdinand's Church in Florissant, a parish where the Mullanphys had lived since 1820. John

Mullanphy had given twelve hundred dollars toward the construction of the church in 1822.[14]

Other Irish pew-holders at the time were Hugh O'Neil, Patrick McDonald, Michael Castello, and John Kincaid. Several Irish young men had already married at St. Ferdinand's. The first were the Burke brothers: John married Celeste James in 1815 and David married Mary James the following year. Other Irish names appear in the parish record of marriages during the next ten years: Michael Castello and Anne McDonald; Owen Collins and Bridget McGovern; Michael Connel and Deborah Whitington; Arthur Fleming and Mary Dougherty; Patrick McDonald and Bridget Monday; and Dennis Murphy and Elizabeth Brotherton.[15] After that, the number of Irish names soared for several decades.

While some Irish settled in Florissant, many of their compatriots—the O'Haras, Sheas, McDonoughs, Fahertys, and others, along with Anglo-American Catholics from Maryland—found homes at a settlement in Illinois called O'Harasburg, near the old French village of Prairie du Rocher, forty-five miles south of St. Louis. This community, later called Ruma, would, like Florissant, send many of its sons and daughters to St. Louis over the years.

By that time, enterprising Irish immigrants had founded the Hibernian Relief Society and "outnumbered all other Europeans except the French," according to a contemporary witness, Professor Elihu Shepard of St. Louis College.[16]

In his reminiscences, *Persimmon Hill*, William Clark Kennerly, the son of merchant James Kennerly and Elise Saugrain Kennerly, tells of gatherings of young people that reflected the easy association of individuals of various national ancestry in early St. Louis. The grandchildren of Irish-born John Mullanphy, of French-born judge John B. C. Lucas, and of Kennerly's Anglo-American cousins, gathered regularly at the Kennerly home in the summer months and at the home of relative Lieutenant Governor Pierre Menard in Kaskaskia, Illinois, during the Christmas holidays. At that time the girls attended Menard Academy, the Visitation Sisters' Academy in Kaskaskia, and the boys went to St. Mary's College, the Vincentian school at Perryville, Missouri.[17]

In his *Autobiography*, Professor Elihu Shepard of St. Louis College gave another example of the friendly relationships of people of various nationalities in early St. Louis. He recalled the gracious hospitality of Mrs. McNair, the wife of the governor, when he began teaching at St. Louis in 1823. She offered the young couple living quarters at the governor's mansion and introduced Mrs. Shepard to all the prominent women of the city. Four McNair boys became Shepard's students at the college.[18]

In 1818 Joseph Charless published the first *Missouri Gazette*. That important landmark in St. Louis history was not the top story of the year. A remarkable prelate of the Catholic Church, the Very Reverend Louis W. V. Du Bourg, Bishop of Louisiana Territory, decided to settle in St. Louis.

A descendant of plantation owners in the French West Indies, Bishop Du Bourg had directed a seminary near Paris before the Revolution, escaped to America, founded St. Mary's Seminary in Baltimore, and served a term as President of Georgetown University. He dined with president George Washington at Mount Vernon at that time. One might have expected to meet such a talented prelate at the Cathedral of Rheims or Chartres, rather than at the log church of St. Louis.[19]

Du Bourg would leave St. Louis indebted to him, less for what he did himself than for the great individuals he recruited for educational and missionary work in the Midwest: Vincentian missionaries, among them Felix de Andreis and Joseph Rosati; Mother Philippine Duchesne and other members of the Religious of the Sacred Heart; and Jesuits, the most noted among them, Peter De Smet and Peter Verhaegen. Du Bourg decided immediately to build a fitting cathedral and called on St. Louisans to support his plans. All of the colonial French and the recent arrivals from the French West Indies supported the project. So did the Irish and many Anglo-Americans.

Only Auguste Chouteau among the older French residents contributed more than Irishmen Thomas Brady and Jeremiah Connor. Besides these two, the list Bishop Du Bourg carefully kept carries the following Irish names: Thomas McGuyre, John Mullanphy, William Sullivan, John McKnight, Michael Dolan, William Daley, P. B. Walsh, Pat Riley, John Hartnett, M. P. Dillon, John O'Hara, L. Ryan, James Dougherty, Alexander McNair, J. McGunnegle, Joseph Charless, John Brady, John Little, J. Cummings, B. Gilhuly, Thomas English, James Timon, Matthew Maher, Sam Wiggins, P. Daly, Patrick McDonald, Hugh O'Neil, James Nagle, M. Murphy, J. Handlan, P. Dolan, John Kennedy, Pat McKay, Matthew Dougherty, and Moses Cosgrove.[20]

*The Cathedral on the Waterfront was a wonder of the West in the days before the Civil War.*

It proved a truly ecumenic endeavor. Noted members of various denominations and ancestries contributed, among them, General William Clark, Thomas Hart Benton (later a U.S. senator), Manuel Lisa, Henry Von Phul, Charles Hempstead, Theodore Hunt, James Clemens, and Frederick Bates. A Jewish-American, J. Philipson, made a gift that rivaled all but the half-dozen largest pledges.

Consistent with his long-standing interest in education, Bishop Du Bourg planned St. Louis Academy for boys to open in the fall of 1818, directed by Father François Niel. Diocesan and Vincentian priests taught at the academy, as did layman Patrick Sullivan, professor of ancient languages. John Martin was prefect of studies. Shortly thereafter, public accountant Patrick Walsh became fiscal officer of the school. With the aid of Du Bourg's eight-thousand-volume library, by 1820 the school—with the name adjusted to St. Louis College— enrolled sixty-five students.[21]

In late May of that same year, Anthony Doyle, an enterprising young man, wrote to his brother of the advantages of the St. Louis area. He had a half interest in a grocery store with Francis Rochford and had invested seven hundred dollars in a limestone quarry. A mutual friend, Roche by name, had purchased a thousand acres of good land along the Missouri River west of St. Louis. Land was available for two dollars an acre. He planned to purchase 320 acres and offered half of it to his brother. Doyle admitted that some of his countrymen were failing, but that was not the country's fault.

Doyle praised the work and vision of Bishop Du Bourg. The bishop, Doyle alleged, said that the Irish were destined by God to bring the Catholic faith to the region. Doyle listed people from Wexford who had settled in St. Louis: Francis Rochford and his wife, Moses Coser and wife, and three unmarried men: John Conner, James Cosker, and James Kavanaugh. Doyle promised to travel east and meet his brother at Baltimore in late spring. They'd travel across Pennsylvania by stagecoach and come down the Ohio and up the Mississippi by boat.[22]

# Irish Business After the War of 1812

After the War of 1812, most exiles of Erin continued to arrive at St. Louis individually. Lured to the Mississippi Valley by prospects of mercantile trade, the new arrivals, unwelcome in established Anglo-American eastern seaboard communities, were met cordially both by the existent organizing St. Louis Irish and the city's larger predominantly French population. The young Irishmen quickly melded into the community through partnerships in business and marriage.

John Little of County Down came in 1815, and a year later, he married Marie Antoinette Labadie, a granddaughter of Pierre Laclède and Madame Chouteau.[1] Over those early years the church records of St. Louis, St. Ferdinand (Florissant), and Carondelet show many marriages of colonial French and new-coming Irish, among them those of Alex McClaude and Catherine Guitard, Thomas J. McGuire and Therese Grimault, Louis McMurry and Eleanor Dumoulin, Joseph Collins and Josette Salois, and Henry McKee and Brigette Roy.[2]

Thomas Hanly, another merchant, arrived in 1816 and opened a store next to McKnight and Brady. Steven Wiggins came that same year, followed by his brothers Sam and Will. The name Wiggins eventually became synonymous with ferry-boating, especially under Sam's direction. Patrick McMasters Dillon of Derry, who had taken part in an Irish rebellion in 1807 and escaped, led the way in 1817. He arrived in January before the first steamboat, the *Zebulon M. Pike*, reached St. Louis. Dillon sold dry goods and groceries, wines, and liquors. Later, after Missouri became a state, he bought land from Frederick Dent, U.S. Grant's future father-in-law, and eventually developed four subdivisions.

By 1818, individuals and families of Irish ancestry came to St. Louis in steady numbers. In that year, lawyer Arthur L. Magenis, came from Antrim. John Finney, a Methodist, brought his three sons and four daughters, born in Ireland. The sons followed their father in business and remained prominent in local affairs. Saddle maker William Higgins came with his wife and family. Thomas McGuire, Bernard Gillhuly, and John Thornton of County Louth found places in merchandising. Nicholas Thornton came with his brother John and made barrels.

"Our Irish citizens of that day (1817–1820) in St. Louis," historian Frederic L. Billon wrote, "included in their number a very liberal proportion of gentlemen of education and acquirements, some of whom held important positions in our then recently acquired territory. . . . James Ruskin, our first, and Jeremiah Connor, our second sheriff, Thomas McGuire, Moses Scott, William Sullivan, Patrick Walsh, justices of the peace; Luke E. Lawless, attorney, afterwards judge; Joseph Charless and James Cummins, first and second proprietors of the *Missouri Gazette*; John and Thomas McKnight, John and Thomas Brady, John Mullanphy, Thomas Hanly, Patrick M. Dillon, James Arnold, John Crawford, Hugh Rankin, Andrew Elliott, Robert H. Catherwood, James Timon Sr., Michael Daly and others, all merchants; Major Thomas Forsythe, United States Indian agent; Maj. James Gunnegle, quartermaster United States Army; James Nagle, Arthur L. Magenis, lawyers; Patrick Sullivan, Professor at the College; Francis Rochford, teacher; Matthew Murphy and others . . . were here in the territorial days of St. Louis."[3] Incidentally, Matt Murphy was a brewer employed by John Mullanphy[4] when he secured the building where Joseph Philipson had opened the first brewery back in 1816.[5]

The large number of Irishmen going into merchandising provokes two questions: first, among the many possible occupations on the frontier, why did so many choose this one, and second, to whom were they selling their products? The answer to the first is this: merchandising was one of the few occupations the Penal Laws in Ireland allowed an Irishman, Catholic or Protestant, to hold in the previous century. The Irish could not till the soil. Britain had taken all but 5 percent of the lands of Irish Catholics, who could not run for Parliament or even take part in the government of their own towns. Catholics could enter the medical profession, but no others, and seeking a medical education was far beyond the possibility of the average person. Laws limited their teaching in schools and their opportunities in education.

"In practice, they were rigorously excluded from manufacturing," Ireland's leading church historian, Patrick Corish, wrote recently, "but not from trade, in particular the important provisions trade, where many of them prospered."[6] As a result, before they came to America, many Catholic Irishmen had honed their skills as merchants. So had even more Protestant Irish.

Markets for products of the St. Louis merchants abounded. While the town itself had grown slowly, the rich lands on both sides of the river lured countless farmers. Many others moved through St. Louis to find land farther west, and others already had settled in towns along the Mississippi and the lower Missouri Rivers. Fur traders long had outfitted in St. Louis for trading in the Northern Rockies. The trade soared to new heights.

St. Louis merchants, first Alexander McNair then John O'Fallon, supplied the soldiers at the military installations—among them Fort Bellefontaine on the Missouri River, twelve miles north of St. Louis; Fort Anthony (later Snelling) on the Mississippi, near the mouth of the Minnesota River; Fort Crawford at Prairie du Chien, near the point where the Wisconsin River flowed into the Father of Waters; Fort Armstrong at Rock Island; and Fort Smith on the Arkansas River—all accessible by water from St. Louis. A short time later, Fort Atkinson on the Missouri, near the mouth of the Platte, quartered a thousand infantrymen. Most of its supplies came from St. Louis.

In the five years after the War of 1812, the Bradys and McKnights had

*John McKnight came to St. Louis with his brothers and their partners, the Bradys, before the War of 1812 and won the sobriquet "the Irish Crowd." Among other successful ventures, they traded with Santa Fe and opened the Missouri Hotel.*

continued to expand their enterprises: they had opened a two-story inn, the Missouri Hotel, in 1816; they laid out "Illinois-town," a real estate venture on the east side of the river, a forerunner of the town of East St. Louis; and they invested in a ferry boat operation. Finally, in 1820, they ended their partnership. When Thomas Brady died in October 1821, Bishop Du Bourg conducted his funeral service. John McKnight never married. A nephew of the same name made his fortune in northern Mexico and eventually returned to St. Louis. In partnership with his brothers and brothers-in-law, he continued the family business.

In 1821, Missouri merchant-trader William Becknell had reached Santa Fe with trade goods on pack animals. The following year he returned with wagons. The Santa Fe trade had begun. At first, the trail went directly from St. Louis, later from Westport, near Kansas City. Over the years, commerce with the Southwest brought silver and gold from the mines of Mexico to St. Louis, while other cities of the mid-continent dealt in unreliable paper money. "Averaging $50,000 annually in the next five years," historian Glen Holt wrote, "by 1828 the Santa Fe expeditions were bringing $100,000 in profits annually in to Missouri."[7] At that time, Thomas McKnight traveled to Santa Fe with a trading venture and then went on to Chihuahua to release his

Wagon-maker Joseph Murphy built the mighty Murphy wagons that brought prosperity to the Santa Fe traders and the entire town.

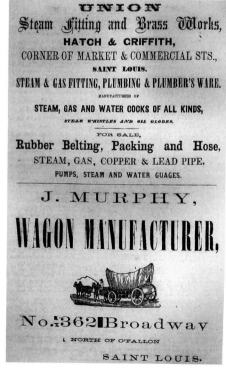

brother and his partners.

Irishman Joseph Murphy took a unique part in enlarging this trade. While Conestoga wagons moved through the Old Northwest Territory, Murphy wagons went to the Southwest, California, and Oregon. Born near Drogheda in County Louth in 1805 and the son of James and Mary (Holland) Murphy, Joseph came to Missouri at the age of thirteen to work a three hundred–acre farm his grandfather had purchased near Creve Coeur Lake. By the time he reached the area, a heavy mortgage clouded the ownership of the place. He worked for two years on a farm at Florissant. In 1820, he left the Florissant Valley and apprenticed himself to Daniel Caster, a St. Louis wagonmaker. Under Caster, young Murphy learned the trade well. He studied each piece and its workings, and he put the parts together patiently. When he was ready to start his own business, Murphy had gained a reputation as a judge of wood, especially Ozark oak. He rented a tiny shop in a small store in 1825. While repairing old wagons, he built new ones, at first making only one wagon at a time. A strong, hearty man, he went up the Missouri River to get good timber and rafted the lumber down. He split the logs by hand.

Murphy purchased a spacious lot on Broadway between Cass and O'Fallon and put up a large shop. Here he built the bulk of the wagons moving west. Quartermasters for the army heard of Murphy's skill and sent a representative to examine his work. The appraiser took an entire wagon apart and studied its making carefully. Large orders for supply wagons followed in the 1830s.

One historic factor affected his work dramatically. Mexican Governor Armijo in Santa Fe put a tax on wagons, irrespective of size. Large and small wagons paid the same tax. An ordinary wagon carried about one thousand pounds of merchandise. Murphy designed a teamster wagon, drawn by a team of four oxen, capable of carrying close to five thousand pounds of merchandise. These wagons could move steadily through Indian country since the Kiowa and Comanche were not inclined to rustle the ponderous beasts. As a result, many traders who might have gone bankrupt carried on a profitable business. Murphy stated that he decided the wheels should be as tall as he was: six feet in height. His venture grew gradually from a small concern to a million-dollar business. By his retirement at the age of eighty, he had built more than two hundred thousand wagons. Over the years, he married three times, and he had ten children by his third wife.[8]

Another highly successful arrival from Ireland, Robert Campbell, had suffered lung trouble in his home in Ulster. When the illness recurred in St. Louis in 1824, he accepted the doctor's advice to "go west." Life as a merchant-trader in the thin air of the high Rockies built up his strength. A popular painting depicts him with partner William Sublette riding out of Jackson Hole. Campbell prospered in the fur business and became a partner in the Rocky Mountain Fur Company. He was highly successful later in other enterprises. He owned many residences in St. Louis as well as the Southern Hotel. In 1837, he married Virginia Kyle, a young woman from North Carolina. They built a fine home at Number 20 Lucas Place. During the Mexican War, Colonel Campbell was inspector general of Missouri troops. Although of Scottish ancestry, Campbell always had warm feelings for his birthplace, Aughlane, in County Tyrone. In the aftermath of the Famine, he assisted the poor of Ireland. On his visit there, the Irish showed their appreciation by greeting him with their warmest welcome.

Edward Walsh, one of eleven children of a Tipperary family, had settled in Ste. Genevieve in 1818. Six years later, he moved to St. Louis, opened a general store, and purchased a flour mill. Then he gained an interest in steamboats and other river craft, and he began to ship lead from Galena, Illinois, prospering in all of these enterprises. In 1840, he married Isabelle De Mun, daughter of Viscount Jules De Mun and Isabelle Gratoit, a relative of all members of the Creole "ruling elite."

While Walsh built barge lines, he still saw the ultimate future with railroads and promoted the Missouri Pacific, the Ohio and Mississippi, and the North Missouri. His vision always looked beyond the horizons. He involved himself, too, in banking and insurance. Politically, he strongly supported Missouri's flamboyant legislator, Senator Thomas Hart Benton.

In the meantime, the Congress of the United States had welcomed Missouri into the Union as a state that allowed slavery. Judge David Barton, of Irish descent on the side of his mother, Hezekiah Murphy, presided at the convention that drew up Missouri's constitution on July 19, 1820. The general assembly chose him unanimously as Missouri's first senator at its first session under the new constitution. During his ten years in the Senate, he did not hesitate to oppose the popular president, Andrew Jackson. Barton's greatest senatorial speech, in fact, called into question some of Jackson's policies.

At the incorporation of St. Louis in 1822, Dr. William Carr Lane was elected mayor. He had served as surgeon for U.S. troops in Indiana during the War of 1812. After the conflict, he married Mary Ewing of Vincennes and began medical practice in St. Louis. Combining medical practice with public service as assistant to Governor Alexander McNair, he held the post of quartermaster of the state in 1822; then he became mayor.

In his book, *The Urban Frontier: Pioneer Life in Early Pittsburg, Cincinnati, Lexington, Louisville and St. Louis*, historian Richard C. Wade called William Carr Lane "the West's best student of urban affairs."[9] He began each year with a state-of-the-city address that outlined the needs of the city and offered a legislative program to meet those needs. He attacked immediate problems but always recommended long-range solutions. Convinced of the great future of St. Louis, he gave it stability. "Elected five consecutive times to the City's highest office," Wade wrote, "Carr Lane (as his constituents knew him) was not only a genial, warmhearted politician but also the shrewdest observer of urban problems in the West. . . .[10] Interested in beauty as well as utility, he fought the constant attrition of St. Louis's foliage, becoming a champion of shade trees and parks."[11] Later, Lane served as territorial governor of New Mexico. One recent sketch lists him of Irish ancestry.[12] Nineteenth-century documents, however, made no indication of his ancestry.

There was no question, however, of the ancestry of several other public figures. Lawyer Luke Lawless, brother of a noted Irish revolutionary leader, became a judge, along with others of Irish ancestry: Patrick Walsh, Thomas M. Dougherty, Alexander Hamilton, the first judge on the Dred Scot case, and Mathias McGirk, eventually a member of the Missouri Supreme Court.

An early St. Louis teacher of the classics, Professor Elihu Shepard, wrote that Joseph W. Walsh, clerk of the County Court of Common Pleas, ". . . from the organization of the court until his death in 1842, was a most able man and a fine scholar, having received his education in St. Louis, [incidentally under Professor Shepard's tutelage at St. Louis College][13] and was known to almost every individual in the county who always placed the most implicit confidence in his integrity and honor and favored him with any office he desired."[14]

# Three Scintillating Celts

**O**f all the great Irish personalities in St. Louis between 1810 and 1850, Mayor John Fletcher Darby, in his *Personal Recollections*, selected three for special mention: John Mullanphy in the 1820s, John O'Fallon in the succeeding decades, and Peter Richard Kenrick from the forties through the seventies. Darby's praise is so high that the reader concludes that these three superior citizens left St. Louis much better for their having chosen it as their home. They deserve a special chapter.

"Among the distinguished men engaged in laying the foundation of the City, and building up the same, no one was more prominent than John Mullanphy," Darby wrote. "He was among the earliest settlers in St. Louis after the acquisition of the country by the government of the United States, arriving here as early as about the year 1804. Except when occasionally absent, he lived here up to the time of his death in July 1833."[1]

After a time in France, John Mullanphy returned to Ireland and married Elizabeth Brown. They came to the United States in 1795 and lived in Kentucky. Mullanphy was a man of great

*John Mullanphy, a native of Ireland who had spent time in France before coming to America, prospered in merchandising and real estate, and he helped the Religious of the Sacred Heart in education and the Daughters of Charity in their dedication to the care of the sick.*

25

enterprise, foresight, and judgment. The fact that he spoke French gave him great opportunities in business dealings. He built many houses, frequently served as alderman, was a director of the Branch Bank of the United States, and was most liberal in his gifts for charitable purposes.

Besides major public gifts to the churches in St. Louis and Florissant, to the Daughters of Charity, and to the Religious of the Sacred Heart, Mullanphy provided help to the poor in many ways. When Daniel D. Page operated the only baker's shop in town, Mullanphy left several hundred dollars with him to provide bread for poor and indigent families. He left five hundred dollars in his will to each American Catholic bishop to aid orphans in his diocese.

A man of strong prejudices, he was most tenacious of his rights. He told Mayor Darby frequently that he would spend one thousand dollars before he would be cheated or defrauded out of one dollar. So, because of the many buildings he erected and the immense amount of property he owned, mechanics, laborers, and others frequently sued him. On one occasion, he lost the suit with an employee, Victor Hab, who claimed that Mullanphy owed him seven dollars. In each instance, as the case proceeded through the courts, Mullanphy lost. Eventually, each case went to the circuit court, where Mullanphy with lawyer John Darby lost again.

"My client paid me twenty dollars," Darby wrote, "rather than pay the two dollars difference between himself and the plaintiff, besides losing time in attending court; for he was always present and sat by the counsel who tried his suits."[2]

"At the time of his death," Darby asserted, "John Mullanphy was said to be the wealthiest man in the Valley of the Mississippi, his estate being reckoned by millions. He was a worthy and good man. In charitable deeds he never had a superior in the city of St. Louis. . . ."[3]

Many writers over the years since have reflected the high esteem Mayor Darby had for John Mullanphy. Among them was another contemporary, William Clark Kennerly, who said of him, "Mullanphy was an important name in the annals of St. Louis and its environs, for John Mullanphy was the city's first great philanthropist. Acquiring his wealth by wise investments in the Louisianas soon after the purchase, he used it largely for educational and charitable purposes."[4] Early in this century, Jesuit historian Gilbert C. Garraghan quoted Darby's tribute and then concluded: "One might dispute John Mullanphy's claim to the recognition and especially the gratitude of posterity if he had amassed his millions for purely private and personal ends. But his great fortune or much of it went to the financing of benevolent and humanitarian enterprises of various kinds."[5]

In more recent times George Potter singled him out in his book, *To the Golden Door: The Story of the Irish in Ireland and America*, when discussing the advantages of St. Louis for immigrant Irish.[6] Local historian Alice L. Cochran did her doctoral dissertation at Saint Louis University on the Mullanphy family and later published it in book form.[7]

Another great St. Louisan, John O'Fallon, was equally successful and generous but more easygoing and carefree in his giving. Historian Thomas Scharf spoke of the universal respect and enthusiasm St. Louisans had for outstanding individuals. "O'Fallon," he insisted, "went further and gained love and affection."[8] Scharf praised "the manner, the grace, and single-hearted purpose of the donation in every instance."[9]

John's father, Dr. James O'Fallon of County Athlone, an educated Irish gentleman of ancient lineage and high social standing, served as a surgeon in Washington's army during the Revolutionary War. The senior O'Fallon then moved to Louisville, Kentucky, where he met and married Frances Clark, sister of Generals George Rogers Clark and William Clark, army officers already famous in the development of the Mississippi Valley. As a small child, John was educated by his mother, his Uncle William, and another uncle, George Croghan, also an army officer.

In youth John O'Fallon served in the Indian Wars and in the War of 1812. After his military career, he came to St. Louis, where his Uncle William was an Indian agent, and John prospered in partnership with Alexander McNair and James Kennerly as a supplier for various army posts in the West. O'Fallon invested his newly acquired wealth in many local lucrative enterprises. He was president of the Branch Bank of the United States, one of the promoters of the Pacific and other railroads, such as the Ohio and Mississippi and the North Missouri. He was the first president of each of the early banks in St. Louis.

*John O'Fallon was a successful merchant and banker, and he built medical buildings for Saint Louis University School of Medicine and the Polytechnic Institute at Washington University.*

O'Fallon helped his Episcopal church and built a Methodist church at the northwest corner of Fourth Street and Washington for his wife's congregation. He put up two Federal-style buildings on Spruce Street for the medical college of Saint Louis University, where his son-in-law Dr. Charles Alexander Pope was dean. Later he built the O'Fallon Technical Institute, the forerunner of the Engineering School of Washington University.

John Darby spoke of him in this vein. "He was, beyond all doubt, the most open-handed and liberal man the City of St. Louis has ever produced, a leader in every noble undertaking, and the foremost and largest contributor in every public enterprise. He sprang to every businessman's assistance without waiting to be called upon. He has done more to assist the merchants and businessmen of St. Louis than any man who ever lived in this town. . . . When any of his friends were appointed to public office, requiring bonds to be given, he did not wait to be asked. . . ."[10]

O'Fallon built a mansion on his estate called Athlone on the terrace above the Mississippi River at the north end of St. Louis. The city would purchase it years later and set up a public park named in honor of the family.

A third scintillating Celt, Father Peter Richard Kenrick, was a recruit of Bishop Rosati. Born in Dublin in 1806, Kenrick attended Maynooth Seminary and was ordained in March 1832. A year later he went to Philadelphia to work with his older brother, Bishop Francis Patrick Kenrick, in a three-fold capacity: as vicar-general, rector of the Cathedral, and president of the seminary. He accepted Bishop Rosati's invitation to work in St. Louis. On April 24, 1841, Pope Gregory XVI appointed him Coadjutor Bishop of St. Louis.[11]

*Archbishop Peter Richard Kenrick was the first bishop in America to guide a diocese for fifty years. He saw more dioceses cut off from his original territory than any bishop at any time in history.*

When Rosati died two years later, Kenrick succeeded him. Mayor John Darby described the new bishop as "a learned and finished scholar. . . . A man of great erudition, pious, modest and unobtrusive, meek and unostentatious in manner, he seems to have devoted himself to his sacred and holy calling with a singleness and steadiness of purpose that few men have ever surpassed."[12]

One might more readily have expected the reflective Kenrick to be professor of Dogma at Maynooth or abbot of the Trappist Monastery of New Mellary, than overseer of a frontier diocese. A formal man, he stood on first-name terms with no one, not even his own brother, the bishop. He soon showed himself an able financier and a zealous pastor. No one would as much influence as he on the Irish in St. Louis for the next half a century.

Kenrick captivated the audience in the Cathedral with his impressive presence and his fluency in English. He spoke with conviction to a congregation increasingly English-speaking. A fine controversalist, on many occasions Protestant guests outnumbered Catholic parishioners at his Sunday evening discourses to hear him speak on such topics as the mysteries of religion, doctrines of the Church, and evidences of Christianity.[13] Historians credit him with many religious conversions.[14] A scholar by inclination, the archbishop urged his priests to study dogmatic and moral theology, scripture, church history, and the lives of the saints.[15] He started a small newspaper, the *Western Banner*, and gave it a great deal of attention. He contributed articles and advised as to editorial policy. It would be distinctively Catholic and have a high literary character, through essays, reviews, and in well-chosen reprints.

In his early years in St. Louis, Kenrick did a lot of missionary work. He had a free black servant who accompanied him in his carriage.[16] They drove through the country without regard to seasons or weather. Once, while touring outstate Missouri, he spoke on the glories of the Christian faith to the miners at the iron works at Meramec Springs.

He wrote letters to the mission-helping societies in Lyons, France, and Vienna, Austria, outlining the development and needs of the diocese. He sought priests from Ireland and Germany more and more as Catholics from these two countries stepped off steamboats at the levee. He sent Father Joseph Melcher, later bishop of Green Bay, to Europe to recruit English- and German-speaking priests to work with them.

Immigrants from Europe came to recognize Kenrick as the father of immigrants. He understood their varied backgrounds and accepted their diverse languages. He always wanted bishops who spoke German in those areas where many German Catholics lived, such as Quincy, Illinois. He wanted a Polish priest, St. Louis pastor Father Joseph Patchowski, named a bishop, but a century passed before Rome designated a priest of Polish ancestry to the episcopate.

Bishop Kenrick showed his great concern for the poor in St. Louis—immigrant and native—by giving his encouragement to young Father Ambrose

Heim who started and successfully ran a "People's Bank." To increase the number of poor people using this forerunner of the modern credit union, the archbishop moved Father Heim to the Cathedral and opened membership to all the city's people. The list of members included every nationality and name from Brenero to Schulte. Kenrick himself later ran the day-to-day affairs of the highly successful bank.

The bishop avoided the political scene and remained silent on strictly political issues. No evidence exists that he ever met Generals Grant or Sherman, Governors Sterling Price or David Francis. His Latin motto was *"Noli Irritare Leononem"*—Don't Goad the Lion. Over the years people came to refer to him as "the Lion of the West."

St. Louis historian Thomas Scharf called him "one of the most distinguished prelates of the American Church, a learned theologian, an able administrator, and a man of greatest generosity and benevolence."[17]

# Irish Help Irish—And Others

I n nineteenth-century St. Louis, the surname Mullanphy was
synonymous with philanthropy. John, daughter Ann, and
son Bryan contributed greatly to institutions and individuals
intent on helping the needy. In addition to the Mullanphys, the
St. Louis Irish established many organizations that reached out
to Irish and non-Irish alike.

John Mullanphy invested heavily in real estate. Prior to the
War of 1812, John Mullanphy's landholdings comprised seven
scattered tracts of less than 750 acres. He soon added three
plantations totaling 2,900 acres, and three plots, two near
St. Louis and one near Florissant, to his holdings.[1] In 1827
Mullanphy gave the Religious of the Sacred Heart twenty-four
acres on Fourth Street near the old French Market on the
southside, a brick residence, and one thousand dollars to help
the nuns open an academy for girls. The gift had one condition:

*The Academy of the Sacred Heart was
originally located in St. Charles.
St. Charles Borromeo Church stands next to
the Sacred Heart Convent in the 1865
photograph.*

the nuns had to educate twenty orphan girls as well. He promised a slight subsidy for each orphan and a gift when she finished her schooling.

By this time, Mother Duchesne and her French associates had welcomed English-speaking students at their school and candidates in their community. Among the first, and destined for prominence in the congregation, Anna Shannon of County Wicklow had come with her family to Callaway County, Missouri, in 1820. Her father, James Shannon, prospered in Missouri and sent her to school at Florissant under Mother Duchesne's direction. She entered the novitiate in 1826. Fluent in French and English, she served as Mother Duchesne's interpreter and taught Potawatomi girls at Florissant.

While Mother Duchesne accepted John Mullanphy's offer and moved to St. Louis, Mother Anna Shannon's destiny was to serve God and His people with distinction in St. Michael's, Louisiana.[2] Mother Mary Anne O'Connor, who came from Ireland and joined Mother Duchesne's group, taught at St. Louis, then in St. Charles and Florissant. After that she spent her last quarter of a century educating Potawatomi girls in Kansas.

The most noted of the Jesuit missionaries among the Potawatomi, Father Maurice Gailland, penned a splendid tribute to Mother O'Connor:

> Mary Anne was distinguished for many virtues, . . . she was graced with humility, and with constant application to hard work no matter how lowly, and with a burning zeal for souls. Because of these extraordinary gifts, lay women constantly sought her advice, and they never left her presence without experiencing a deep benefit for their own souls. Because of her good common sense, whole families were converted to the Catholic Faith.[3]

Besides helping the Religious of the Sacred Heart move their school to St. Louis, John Mullanphy played a great part in the development of the first Catholic hospital in the United States. It was the first hospital under the auspices of dedicated women anywhere in the country. He invited the Daughters of Charity, founded in Maryland by Mother Elizabeth Seton, to begin the hospital and offered them "a piece of ground with two houses, another lot with houses that will bring a revenue of $600 per annum, $350 for traveling expenses, and $350 to furnish the house."[4]

The Council of the Sisters voted unanimously to accept the invitation and chose four sisters as the pioneer team, two of them of Irish ancestry, Frances Xavier Love and Frances Regis Berrett. They received their first patients on November 26 of that same year, 1828. They welcomed all the sick—black and white, slave and free. The charge for paying patients was $1.50 a week. The city paid $1.25 for indigents. In at least one instance that first year, a master paid the fee for his slave.[5]

The following day, in a letter to Mother Augustine at Emmitsburg, Bishop Rosati assured the provincial superior that John Mullanphy had turned the property over to him. The bishop gave full authority to the sisters in the use of the property in conformity to the rules and customs of their institute.[6] A few years later the mayor of the city, Dr. William Carr Lane, declared the sisters' hospital the "official city hospital."

When Bishop Rosati invited the Jesuits at Florissant to man St. Louis College in 1828, they planned a new building on Washington at Ninth Street, in the block that Jeremiah Connor had designated as a site for a college. Unfortunately, the seven-year time limit had passed for obtaining the property as a gift from Connor's estate. Eventually the Jesuits had to purchase the property. At this juncture, Major Thomas Biddle hosted a dinner meeting of prominent men in the city and invited the Jesuit Superior Father Charles Felix Van Quickenborne to talk of the new school. Among those present were Biddle's father-in-law, John Mullanphy, Pierre Chouteau, Bernard Pratte, and John O'Fallon. The contributions reached almost four thousand dollars. Among the donors were Biddle, Mullanphy, O'Fallon, and members of the French colonial gentry.[7] The student body likewise included French, Anglo-Americans, and Irish, among them Bryan Mullanphy, John Shannon, Howard Christy, Thomas Forsyth, and Julius Clark, as well as Edward Chouteau, Edward Paul, and Francis, Julius, and Du Thil Cabanne.

Father Peter Verhaegen, assisted by Father John Elet, came in from Florissant to teach and direct operations at the new building on Ninth and Washington in the fall of 1829. Father Peter Walsh, the first Irish priest to work with the previously all-Belgian Missouri Jesuit priests, came from Maryland to be prefect of studies and teach English, geography, and history.[8]

During the same year, John Mullanphy offered further help to the Jesuits, but his stipulation that they also conduct a trade school for poor boys went beyond the scope of the Jesuit ministries. The superior, Father Charles Felix Van Quickenborne, turned down Mullanphy's offer and centered the limited manpower on the academic area.

In 1832 the school won a university charter from the state. At this juncture, the Jesuit father general sent the best-known Irish Jesuit, Father Peter Kenney, as official visitor to the Missouri Jesuits. Kenney left wise guidelines.[9] He saw the value of a college on the frontier and urged the Belgians to continue. To finance the school, he suggested that Bishop Rosati ask the Pope to allow the school to take tuition, a change from a centuries-old Jesuit tradition. Father Kenney told the young priests to end the European practice of wearing the cassock in public and recommended a black suit.

Back in 1818, Jeremiah Connor had invited a group of his fellow Irishmen to his residence to discuss the formation of a benevolent society. Thomas Brady chaired the meeting and Thomas Hanly served as secretary. Brady appointed a committee to frame the scope and purposes of the organization. The members included John Mullanphy, James McGunnegle, Alex Blackwell, and Arthur Magenis. Not until the fall of 1819 did the association planted firm roots under the title of the Erin Benevolent Society. On October 18, 1819, it met again at Connor's residence and chose the host as chairman. James Nagle, a businessman moving into law, acted as secretary.

The members adopted a constitution for the Erin Benevolent Society and set the date October 21 for election of officers. They met as promised and elected Jeremiah Connor president and Hugh Rankin secretary. Rankin must have been an impressive young man. He and his two brothers, Robert and David, had come that very year from Derry and opened a store. David amassed a fortune in the tea trade in the years to come.

Connor set up two committees for the society. Thomas English, Robert Catherwood, Joseph Charless, Hugh O'Neil, and merchandiser James Timon, who like the Rankin brothers had arrived that year with his brother John, formed the standing committee. Francis Rochford, who had opened the first English-language school in St. Louis, served with John Timon and Robert Rankin on the visiting committee. The Erin Benevolent Society looked to the interests of distressed Irish both in St. Louis and in the homeland.

The wealthy French had no similar societies to assist their fellows coming into the town from the Old Settlements along the river, from Canada, or from the mother country. No wealthy Anglo-Americans made provisions to assist newcomers from eastern states, even though needy individuals and families were moving into the St. Louis area or going through town on their way west.

*Mayor and Judge Bryan Mullanphy found imaginative ways to give away his inheritance. Ultimately, most of it went to the Mullanphy Emigrant Fund that gave newcomers a chance to get started in the New World.*

On March 17, 1819, the members of the Erin Benevolent Society marched in a procession that ended with a banquet in honor of St. Patrick. A few years later, as steamboats became more palatial, the Irish arranged for a luxury steamer to moor at the levee on St. Patrick's Day to host the banquet. The toasts on one occasion honored heroes from St. Patrick to General Richard Montgomery, who died in the colonial attack on Canada during the American Revolution. By 1820, the Irish Americans numbered one out of every seven residents of St. Louis.

In 1840, second-generation Irish, under the leadership of Christopher Garvey, began a "Society for the Diffusion of Alms" that concentrated on helping the needy at home. The best known members were Bryan Mullanphy and James P. Barry, both later mayors of the city, and John Timon and John T. Mitchell. Garvey assigned at least one man to look after the needs of the poor in each ward of the city: John O'Rourke in the First Ward on the far southside; Joseph W. Walsh in the Second Ward on the near southside; Patrick Walsh in the Third Ward on the near nouthside; and Matthew Lyon, M. Hagan, and John Walsh in the more needy Fourth Ward farther north.

On November 8, 1841, Judge Luke Lawless presided at the first meeting of the "Friends of Ireland" at the courthouse. The group elected John O'Fallon president. The four vice presidents were Lawless, James Clemens, Jr., Edward Walsh, and John P. McNeal. Following the plan of Garvey's group, they chose representatives for the realigned wards: D. Carton and John Corcoran for the First; J. G. Barry and P. M. Dillon for the Second; William Tighe and Michael Kelly for the Third; John McDonald and John Pace for the Fourth; and Hugh O'Brien and Matthew Hogan for the new Fifth Ward.

Irish nuns more than matched the generosity of the laymen. In that same year, 1841, Mother Angela Hughes, sister of Coadjutor Archbishop John Hughes of New York, led Sisters Frances McEnnis, Prudentia Dorsey, Winifred Mullen, Mildred Doyle, and Bibiana O'Malley to begin the Catholic Orphans' Association. During the succeeding years, Catholic men of prominence gave support to the Orphan Asylum and Day School for boys. Later in the 1840s, the all-male board consisted of two well-known French-Americans, John Sarpy, president, and Amadee Valle, treasurer, as well as these Irishmen: John Haverty, vice president, Thomas Flaherty, secretary, and active members Edward Walsh, Bryan Mullanphy, Joseph Murphy, and Patrick Ryder. The association managed two diocesan orphan homes.

Also in 1840, American-born Jesuit Father George Carrell took offices, the first Saint Louis University president of Irish ancestry. He set out to enroll local students and made less effort to recruit Louisianans, as his predecessors had done. After he completed a successful term in St. Louis, Pope Gregory XVI named him bishop of Covington, Kentucky.

At the same time, missionaries from St. Louis, among them the Religious of the Sacred Heart under Mother Philippine Duchesne, left for the Potawatomi in Kansas. The Sacred Heart foursome included Mother Mary Anne O'Connor who had already taught Indian girls at Florissant. She spent more than twenty years teaching Potawatomi girls at Sugar Creek near Missouri's western boundary, and later at St. Marys, Kansas.

A few years later, Catholic men of St. Louis—Irish and others—started the first American unit of the St. Vincent de Paul Society, a new organization begun in France shortly before by a convert, Blessed Frederick Ozanam. The Vincentian superior, John Timon, an Irishman who had grown up in St. Louis and in 1836 had turned down Pope Gregory XVI's invitation to be auxiliary bishop of St. Louis, conferred with the top officials of his congregation in Paris in 1845. While there, he learned of the society. He saw the vision of Ozanam and the possibilities of the society in America. Determined to learn more about it, he visited the office of the society in Dublin and obtained a copy of its bylaws. He returned to America intent on making the society known. He soon found a splendid opportunity. Bishop Kenrick had agreed to consecrate the new St. Vincent de Paul Church on South Eighth Street in St. Louis on November 16, 1845, and invited Father Timon to preach. In his message he discussed at length the St. Vincent de Paul Society. Many in that crowded church answered his challenge by attending an organizational meeting four days later, November 20.[10]

Twenty names appear on the list of founding members and Bryan Mullanphy served as temporary chairman. The overwhelming vote was to organize. The group chose as president Dr. Moses Linton, professor of Medicine at Saint Louis University, a convert, controversialist, and editor of the first medical journal in the West; Bryan Mullanphy as vice president; Dennis Galvin as second vice president; James Maguire, Jr., as secretary; and Patrick Ryder as treasurer. The members were to survey the needs of the poor people in their respective parishes. The president designated a committee of Judge Mullanphy, John Everhart, and Thomas Anderson to visit the bishop and win his approval. Bishop Kenrick welcomed them without delay. The fledgling society met again a week later, November 27. Dr. Linton read the bishop's letter of approval. No one was surprised that Bishop Kenrick named as spiritual director Father Ambrose Heim, assistant at the Cathedral and well known for his concern for those in need.

The newly forming St. Vincent de Paul Society took up a collection to place money in the hands of the "visitors," the men in each parish who had the duty of locating needy families. To acquaint their pastors with the new society, Dr. Linton chose John Byrne, Jr., Dr. Thomas Anderson, George Ridener, John Ennis, James C. Bury, and M. O'Keefe. He assigned a committee to seek affiliation with the General Council in Paris. Bryan Mullanphy penned the letter in his best French. The president-general approved the new unit on

February 10, 1846, and within six years the number of active members reached eighty-nine. Sixty-three claimed Irish or Irish-American ancestry. Five were French-American. Ten were of German ancestry, one Slavic, and ten Anglo-Americans, either converts like Dr. Linton, or born Catholics from Maryland or Kentucky. As new parishes took root at the time, new units joined the original Cathedral conference, among them Annunciation, Immaculate Conception, and St. John's.[11]

Besides the highly influential members of the first unit noted earlier, other early members ranged widely in the business and cultural life of St. Louis. Among these were G. A. Manning, a judge; Martin E. Power and J. J. Donegan, businessmen; Joseph O'Neil, a lawyer who would serve in the state senate before becoming a judge; Robert Mitchell, a skilled architect whose promising career ended when a storm wrecked his ship in the Atlantic and he drowned; Henry Spaunhorst, another future member of the state senate who would head the most influential German-American Catholic Organization in America, the *Central-Verein*; John Haverty, director of the local office of the Superintendency of Indian Affairs; and Dr. Florence Cornyn, head of City Hospital, who during the Civil War cared for the wounded at the Battle of Shiloh and later captained a Union cavalry unit.

John F. O'Neil, a brother of Joseph O'Neil and a western outfitter, sold supplies to the Mormons for their trek westward and found them affable and responsible people. Yet, family lore recalls their puritanical neighbors in Illinois accused John O'Neil of overriding greed for dealing with "a mad and heretical people." These same critics said nothing when Forty-niners came by for equipment. O'Neil found them trigger-happy rounders and wastrels, as rude as the Mormons were gracious. A year later O'Neil entered the Jesuit seminary at Florissant.

A look at the spread of the St. Vincent de Paul Society to other parts of America will highlight the leadership of the men of St. Louis. With the approval of Bishop John Hughes, who learned of the society in Ireland and France, Father John Loughlin, assistant at St. Patrick's Cathedral in New York, applied to Paris a full year after the St. Louis chapter, on December 11, 1847. He won approval on March 27 of the following year.[12]

In the meantime, the new Holy Father, Pope Pius IX, named Father John Timon, C.M., bishop of Buffalo. This time the Vincentian superior accepted the call to the episcopacy. Two months after his consecration on October 17, 1847, he organized the third American unit of the St. Vincent de Paul Society.[13] A fourth unit was organized in Milwaukee in 1847, then one in New Orleans in 1852, and another in Louisville in 1853. Shortly after that, Father John Loughlin, who had headed the New York chapter at its inaugural in 1847, became the first bishop of Brooklyn and began a Vincentian unit there in 1855. Other cities followed.[14] But none could boast of a vice president to match Bryan Mullanphy.

The only son of John Mullanphy, Bryan cruised in a unique orbit. After studying under the Belgian Jesuits at Florissant, he attended a college in Paris. Before he came home, his father had boasted that he intended to give him a fortune, with an income equal to that of the president of the United States. After Bryan returned in 1827, the senior Mullanphy had second thoughts.

Bryan studied law, and he entered politics as a Democrat. He served as alderman, before winning a term as mayor. Later, a governor appointed him judge of the Circuit Court. As judge, his manner offended a Virginia lawyer, Ferdinand W. Risque, who had Mullanphy indicted for oppression in his office. The judge stood trial and was acquitted.[7]

In the meantime, his imaginative ways of giving away the money he inherited annoyed his extremely wealthy father, who was equally generous but cautious and controlled in his charitable giving. On one occasion, Bryan found a poor family squatting in Mullanphy-owned buildings. Instead of having the sheriff oust them for trespass, he listened to their needs, said they could remain, and hired them "to watch the family property." On another occasion, he saw a woman from Illinois trying to sell a cow. When she told him she was selling the cow to get needed money, he asked how much she hoped to get. He offered twice that amount. Since his stable was not yet ready, he wondered if she would pasture the cow for him. He paid her for that trouble and told her to give the milk to her children. He never bothered about the animal from then on.

As a result of such uses of the family money, the senior Mullanphy put his only son out of his will. When their father died in 1833, however, Bryan's six sisters gave him a sixth of their inheritance. He never married. Mayor John

*A large share of the Mullanphy Emigrant Fund went to the Mullanphy Emigrant Home.*

Darby wrote in his *Personal Recollections* that the one young lady Mullanphy loved, the daughter of a German immigrant, felt that she could not cope with the idiosyncratic Irishman.[16] In spite of his wealth, she hesitated to become Mrs. Mullanphy.

Attending daily Mass at the Cathedral, Bryan noticed that a young newcomer often worshipped in the same pew. After the last blessing one morning, he greeted the young man, John O'Hanlon. John had come from Stradbally, Ireland in 1842 and worked on a steamboat. He had studied for the priesthood at Carlow College before his family left for America, and he hoped to continue his studies. Mullanphy took O'Hanlon to the bishop's office. With Mullanphy's help, O'Hanlon completed his preparation for the priesthood in St. Louis.

Years later, O'Hanlon, by then a priest at St. Patrick's Parish on Sixth and Biddle, frequently went to the waterfront a few blocks to the east to help refugees of the Famine arriving by steamboat. Appalled at the severity of their illness, he went to see his patron. Mayor Mullanphy personally paid for the conveyances that took the destitute immigrants to the Sisters' Hospital, and he later made provisions for better health care on the arrival of newcomers.

That action typified the great generosity that he had for the relief of emigrants and travelers on their way to settle in the West. These sixteen words and thirty-three others he scribbled on a sheet of paper and handed to the city comptroller in 1849 did not die. When bachelor Bryan passed away in 1851, the "undivided one-third" of his estate that he left to the city for the relief of emigrants and travelers heading west amounted to two hundred thousand dollars.

By 1860, relatives who felt they could put the money to better use made an effort to break the will, but in vain. Shortly after the Civil War, the estate had increased to $571,832. The commissioners handling the fund decided to build the Bryan Mullanphy Emigrants' Home at Fourteenth and Howard Streets. Applicants for aid from the fund lived at the home while staff members studied their needs, and then provided equipment and transportation to help them settle in the West.

After a few years, the need for such a home lessened. The building became the Douglas School. The city fathers sought help from the fund in times of disaster, such as after tornadoes and floods. The suits continued, however, both from the Mullanphy heirs on one side and the city government on the other. The Mullanphy Fund survived this two-front attack and came to serve the general public permanently as "Traveler's Aid."

# Celts Teach, Learn, and Care

T he Irish and other St. Louis families had more opportunities for the education of their children than their counterparts in any cities of the country but New York and Baltimore.[1] They could send their sons to Saint Louis University and St. Mary's College in Perryville and their daughters to the Convent of the Sacred Heart in St. Louis, St. Joseph's Academy in Carondelet, and the Menard Academy in Kaskaskia, Illinois, accessible by steamboat.

The Sacred Heart Academy on Convent Street at Broadway, just south of Chouteau Avenue on the near southside, welcomed Irish as well as French-speaking girls. Nine, including two born

*Saint Philippine Duchesne moved her academy from Florissant to a site on Broadway near Convent Street on the near southside, with the encouragement of John Mullanphy.*

in Ireland, attended in the early 1830s. Twenty more studied at the academy in the late thirties, including Mary and Anna Martin, who were born in Ireland. Forty-six attended in the 1840s, and sixty-four in the 1850s. The list of names covered the counties, with five Kellys, four Walshes, and four Caseys leading the way. Seven girls had been born in Ireland, and one, Mary Moore, on a boat coming from Cork.[2]

The faculty at the convent on South Broadway and the one in St. Charles, where some girls from St. Louis County took classes, soon included twenty-two members of the Society of the Sacred Heart who were born in Ireland. Among them were Sisters Judith and Margaret Shannon, Joanna and Honora Callaghan, Ann Daly, Catherine Barry, Mariella McMahon, and Mary Ann Roche.[3]

In the early days of St. Louis College, French, Italian, and Anglo-American teachers taught boys of French or Anglo-American families. When the Jesuits from Florissant took over in 1829, two lay teachers and one priest from Ireland joined the otherwise Belgian faculty—Bartholomew McGowan and Benjamin Eaton, and Jesuit Peter Walsh. By way of contrast, no Catholic was welcome on the faculty of University College in Dublin, through much of the nineteenth century.

The student body remained predominantly French and Anglo-American, with a sprinkling of Irish names. The pattern changed in the forties and fifties; many Irish came. The first native of Ireland to enter the Jesuit seminary in Florissant, Francis O'Loghlen, became the second Irish-born Jesuit to teach on the faculty of Saint Louis University.

Many Saint Louis University graduates of Irish ancestry gained prominence in their chosen fields: Julius Walsh in business, Matthew Hastings in painting western scenes and people; Fathers Patrick Francis O'Reilly and Francis Fitzpatrick in church administration; and Jesuit Father James Hayes and his brother, Captain Michael Hayes, in the field of literature. The former wrote children's books, the latter stories of the sea.

The Visitation Sisters, who had developed an excellent school for girls in Georgetown, D.C., came to Kaskaskia, the first capital of Illinois, in 1834 with the support of wealthy merchant-traders, William Morrison and Lieutenant Governor Pierre Menard. The nuns named their spacious four-story school Menard Academy after the distinguished Creole merchant and statesman. Mother Agnes Brent, niece of Archbishop Leonard Neale of Baltimore, headed the team of eight Maryland-born nuns of English or Irish background. Sister Helena Flanigan was head mistress. Students came from St. Louis, Ste. Genevieve, and other towns along the Mississippi. The school flourished, and novices entered the convent.

Irish young people profited from the teaching of French and Anglo-American nuns and French, Italian, and Belgian priests. All the while, Ireland nurtured what Patrick Corish, one of Ireland's leading church historians, calls "a worldwide empire of the Catholic faith"[4] by sending priests, brothers, and nuns to America and other English-speaking countries of the world. This burst of missionary zeal rivaled that of St. Columbanus and his band of missionary monks in the sixth century, whose story Thomas Cahill told in his book *When the Irish Saved Civilization*.[5] A call to the life of religious service swept Ireland. As the Irish moved from their homeland to America, countless clergy accompanied them. A variety of factors—religious, economic, and sociological—worked together to send young men into seminaries all over Ireland. At the same time, Corish points out that "a real explosion in numbers took place in the Christian Brothers and with the nuns."[6] The number of Irish nuns rose from 120 at 1800 to almost 8,000 in 1880. A great percentage of these priest, nuns, and brothers came to America.

Thanks to the hospitality and concern of the people of St. Louis, the city was a beneficiary of this amazing growth in the numbers of individuals totally committed to educating the young, caring for the sick, and preaching the Word. The Irish had one advantage over other immigrants: they spoke English with their own unique but understandable flavor.

Irish, Anglo-Americans, and Germans continued to come to St. Louis in ever-growing numbers. The town census noted ten thousand new names in the 1830s. While established Anglo-Americans moved directly west as the movement of their churches indicated,[7] the prosperous Irish fanned out to the west from Park Avenue on the south to Franklin Avenue on the north. Some joined with old French and Maryland families in building St. Vincent's Church on South Tenth Street at Park Avenue in Soulard in 1844, and St. Francis Xavier on Ninth and Christy, one block north of Washington Avenue in the central west area.

The Irish and French in the two congregations welcomed nuns to teach their children. The predominantly French congregation of St. Vincent's invited the Sisters of St. Joseph, mostly of French ancestry at the time, to come in from Carondelet and open an elementary school. In 1845, at Third and Poplar Street, they also opened a school for one hundred free black girls. The nuns taught reading, writing, arithmetic, religion, needlework, and French. They also invited one hundred girls still in servitude for religious instruction after work hours. Most of the nuns at both schools were of French-American ancestry. In 1847, the state legislature outlawed education to African Americans, both free and enslaved. The sisters faced rioting but carried on. As few French immigrants came, and steadily more Irish ones, the Flanagans and McDonoughs joined the Fontbonnes and Pommerels on the faculties and in the classroom.

The Sisters of Charity already had sent a team to open the hospital and a second team to start St. Philomena's Free School at Fifth and Walnut. When St. Francis Xavier Church opened in 1844, the sisters followed with

St. Vincent's Free School for 150 girls. The nuns soon found better quarters in a new building on Tenth and St. Charles, on property given by Ann Lucas Hunt. Five nun-teachers taught 280 young girls. People came to call the school "Sister Olympia's School," in honor of the director, Sister Olympia McTaggert. Shortly after, the Sisters of Charity opened up a "select" or tuition school for daughters of well-off families. This school helped defray the cost of the "free" school. At the same time, Jesuit seminarians, half of them from Ireland, opened an "English Male Free School" in the basement of St. Francis Xavier Church. The attendance soon reached 350 boys.

Apparently, the Sisters of Charity had great regard for St. Philomena, who lived more in legend than in history. In 1846 they opened another school that bore her name, this one an Industrial and Technical School. Girls between twelve and eighteen learned domestic skills, including sewing, laundering, cooking, housekeeping, dress-making, and fancy needlework. The girls supported themselves by making trousseaus, layettes, shirts, and soldiers' uniforms. The sisters began the House of the Guardian Angel a few years later, and it combined features of an orphanage and an industrial school.

Back in 1834, when the Visitation nuns opened Menard Academy in southwestern Illinois, infant Chicago and the rest of northern Illinois regrouped after the sweep of Black Hawk and the Sauk Indians through the valley of the Rock River. Ten years later, thriving Chicago became the head of a diocese that covered all of Illinois, including Kaskaskia, which the bishops of St. Louis had shepherded. Wishing to have a Visitation school in his diocese, Bishop Kenrick appealed to Mother Agnes Brent, then in her second term as superior, to begin an academy in St. Louis. On April 14, 1844, Mother Agnes and six sisters boarded a steamboat for the six-hour, fifty-five mile trip up the river, already at high water from early heavy rains in the lower Missouri River valley.

*The Daughters of Charity opened this first hospital west of the Mississippi in 1830 at Fourth and Spruce Streets on land donated by John Mullanphy.*

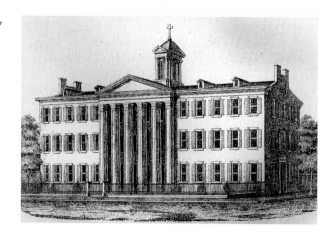

Ann Mullanphy Biddle offered her home on Broadway at Biddle Street as a temporary residence. Hardly had the nuns reached St. Louis, however, when "the Flood of the Century" sent waters to the third floor of Menard Academy. A steamboat churned up the main street of Kaskaskia to rescue the nuns and girls. These refugee nuns followed the earlier team to St. Louis. For a short time the two groups taught girls at different locales but finally found spacious quarters appropriately on Menard Avenue.

The student body at the time included several members of the old French families: the Papin, LaBeaume, and Bogy, daughters of prominent Anglo-Americans such as General Stephen Watts Kearney and Mayor Luther B. Kennett, and many Irish, among them Julia, Maria, Margaret, and Mary Walsh, Helen O'Fallon, and four granddaughters of John Mullanphy.[8]

In 1847 the newly elected pope, Pius IX, recognized the validity of historian Richard C. Wade's appraisal that St. Louis "remained the focus of Western Catholicism" and raised the diocese of St. Louis to the rank of archdiocese ahead of New York, Philadelphia, Boston, and New Orleans. Only Baltimore anticipated it in the organized states. A year later, Archbishop Kenrick called upon Irish priests in the area to open up a seminary in Carondelet to supplant the one the Vincentian fathers had conducted for a few years in Soulard. Father James Duggan, a native of County Kildare, who had taken his early studies at Kenrick's own *alma mater*, Maynooth, taught rhetoric and headed the new school. Father Anthony O'Reagan, former head of St. Jarlath's Seminary in Tuam, Ireland, and a classmate of Archbishop Kenrick at Maynooth, arrived two years later. He succeeded Duggan and taught moral theology.

*Ann Mullanphy Biddle never remarried after her husband, Captain Thomas Biddle, was killed in a duel. She helped many Catholic parishes and sisterhoods, such as the Visitation Sisters, who built their "Castle in the Patch" on property she gave them on Cass Avenue.*

The other members of the faculty were Father George Ortleib, a native of the Rhineland who lectured in dogmatic theology; Father Patrick Fleming, who drilled the seminarians in logic; and Archbishop Kenrick himself, who drove his buggy to Carondelet twice a week to teach scripture and dogma.

The directorship of this little seminary in Carondelet proved the sure-fire path to the episcopacy. Fathers Duggan and O'Reagan became successively bishops of Chicago. Father Patrick Feehan served as bishop of Nashville, then as first archbishop of Chicago, and Father John Hennessy headed the archdiocese of Dubuque.[9]

At that time, Father John O'Hanlon, an immigrant helped by Bryan Mullanphy who had served in outstate Missouri, resided at St. Patrick's. The archbishop began to invite O'Hanlon to accompany him twice a week to Carondelet. O'Hanlon lectured on English literature, rhetoric, and composition, and later he held the post of Prefect of Studies. O'Hanlon was to publish his first book, *The Irish Emigrant's Guide for the United States*, in 1851.[10] The book offered an assortment of sound suggestions from surviving sea-sickness to counteracting the bullies who charged exorbitant fees for simple services. Recurrent bouts of bronchitis cut short Father O'Hanlon's American career, and he returned to Ireland a few years later. In losing him, St. Louis lost a creative personality. He wrote about the seminary in Carondelet in his book, *Life and Scenery in Missouri*.[11] Eventually he published a monumental two-volume *Irish American History of the United States*,[12] which gives, among other assessments, an impressive picture of the Irish soldiers in the Civil War.

In February 1849, cholera began a fatal march across St. Louis. By the middle of the summer it had taken one out of every six residents. Two Irish Sisters of Charity at the St. Louis Hospital—Sisters Columba Long and Patricia Butler—and two at St. Vincent's Convent—Sisters Frances Nally and Justine Mulhall—gave their lives caring for the sick. Three other nuns of Irish background succumbed: Sister Antoinette Kinkaid at St. Joseph's Orphanage; Sister Veronica Corcoran at Visitation Academy; and Sister Louise Griffin at the Convent of the Sacred Heart. In the midst of the epidemic, a fire swept through the boats and businesses at the riverfront and threatened the Cathedral. This disaster had *one* good result. The City Fathers decided to drain Chouteau Pond, the once lovely picnic spot that had fallen victim to industrial waste. City growth now looked west.

In early fall 1849, three Christian Brothers accepted the invitation of Archbishop Kenrick to teach in St. Louis. They lodged in the building on Walnut Street just west of the Cathedral and soon welcomed two hundred boys. The brothers opened a novitiate there, and by May of the follow year, twelve brothers and six candidates made up the community, most of Irish birth or ancestry. The tuition fee at the school was fifty cents a month for those who could afford it, according to the testimony of Father David B. Doherty, a priest of the archdiocese. He had attended the school and years later wrote about

Catholic education in St. Louis.[13] Abram J. Ryan, who became famous later as the "Poet Priest of the South," also attended the school.[14]

Brother Facile, assistant general for the United States, founded a more ample residence for the brother-teachers at the Rider Mansion on Eighth and Cerre Streets on the near southside. The brothers easily could walk to their three schools at the time; but new brothers were coming—and new challenges. In 1850, a year after the first brothers arrived, they replaced lay teachers at the boys' school in St. Vincent's Parish and Jesuit seminarians at St. Francis Xavier Parish. In opening a school at St. Patrick's that same year, they established themselves in the four original parishes of the city. Eventually they staffed ten elementary schools, two academies, and a college.

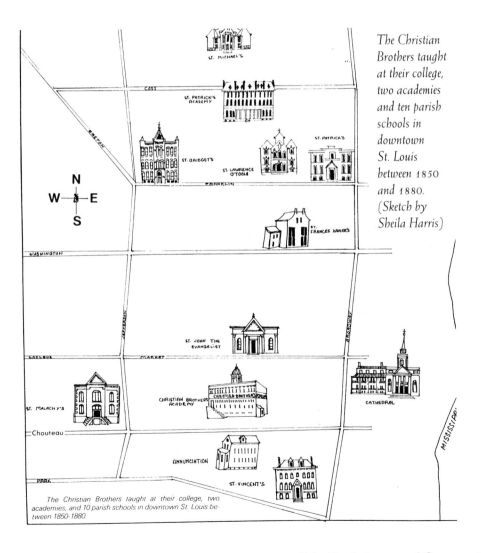

*The Christian Brothers taught at their college, two academies and ten parish schools in downtown St. Louis between 1850 and 1880. (Sketch by Sheila Harris)*

The Christian Brothers taught at their college, two academies, and 10 parish schools in downtown St. Louis between 1850-1880.

All the while, the increase in population called for more parishes in the city. One hundred Irish Catholic families settled northwest of St. Patrick's Church and opened St. Michael's Parish at Eleventh and Clinton in 1849. Dublin-born Father John Higginbotham came from Potosi, Missouri, to be pastor. After a short time, Father Michael Prendergast succeeded him and then Father William Wheeler, another native of Dublin, a theologian, the son of a converted English father and Irish Catholic mother.

With the draining of Chouteau Pond, a number of Irish and a few French families formed a new congregation thirteen blocks west of the Cathedral on Fifteenth at Chestnut Street. Father Patrick O'Brien, the son of Dan O'Brien, a surveyor and engineer from Cork, who had settled in Potosi, became pastor and soon gained great popularity among his people. Farther west and to the north another group of Irish families scattered beyond the old "Kerry Patch." Father Christopher Fitnam, another native of Cork, began St. Bridget's Church on Jefferson Avenue at Carr. It would have a significant place in the history of the St. Louis Irish.

Some rural areas near St. Louis, such as Randolph County, Illinois, continued to welcome immigrants from Ireland. Many newcomers from

*In his first year as a priest, Father James Henry marshalled the men of his congregation to protect St. Patrick's Church from Know-Nothing rioters during the off-year election of 1854, an action that brought him national fame among Irish-Americans.*

Tipperary found rich acres near the already mentioned settlement of O'Harasburg in the 1840s. Led by Patrick Lynch, David Donoghue, and Tim Duggan, the Murphys, Maddens, Cullens, Finnertys, and O'Learys found their way there. By 1853 they had built a prosperous community named Tipton after their home county of Tipperary. Eventually many second-generation Irish from Tipton, Ruma, and other Irish villages in the area came to Christian Brothers College in St. Louis and stayed.

A large group of Irish moved into the Ninth Ward on the nouthside, between Carr and Mullanphy Streets, west of Twelfth Street. The ward included the old Kerry Patch district, where good housing had supplanted the hutches of the squatters. This move directly west of St. Patrick's Parish pointed the way many working-class Irish would move in succeeding decades. The well-to-do Irish families moved to the Central West End, along with Anglo-Americans.

In 1855, Jane Graham, daughter of Major Richard Graham and Catherine Mullanphy, gave property on Fourteenth and O'Fallon Streets for a new church to be named for St. Lawrence O'Toole, archbishop of Dublin in the twelfth century. The parish built a church of Gothic style. Father James Henry, a young priest who had won national acclaim a year earlier by facing up to rioters in defense of St. Patrick's Church, guided the people.

One might have presumed from the courageous action that Father Henry matched John Wayne with a stentorian voice that cowed the mob. Actually, he rivaled the "Quiet Man" of the story, not of the movie, with his moderate build and soft voice. He gave no stirring sermons; instead, he explained Catholic beliefs clearly. A scholar and a linguist, he spoke fluent French and Latin and cherished the Greek classics. He labored all his life among poor, recently arrived immigrants and helped them find their way in America. Few contemporary pastors received esteem equaling that of Father Henry's parishioners for him.

By the 1850s, efforts in places such as Lowell, Massachusetts, to coordinate parochial religious and religiously neutral schools to meet the needs of all citizens had run into logjams. Clearly, the newly developing public school system had become an institution with a generally Protestant ethos, sometimes openly hostile to Catholicism.[15] As a result, newcoming Catholics decided to open their own schools. At St. Lawrence O'Toole they built classrooms on the lot adjoining the church given by Jane Chambers, another granddaughter of John Mullanphy. On one occasion, Father Henry marched his school children in procession by the neighborhood public school to dramatize its limited and generally Protestant focus.

In the same year that St. Lawrence O'Toole opened, the rapidly expanding Christian Brothers moved from elementary to secondary and collegiate education, with the support of Archbishop Kenrick. Brother Patrick Murphy applied for a state charter for the Academy of the Christian Brothers at Ninth and Cerre. His co-incorporators were Brothers Paulian Fanning, Dorotheus Poinchaud, Barbas Finigan, and Noah Maloney. Within a few years, the enrollment at Christian Brothers College reached five hundred. Forty brothers including novices and postulants resided at the college. The brothers asked no tuition at the elementary schools. The college supported the lower schools.

Since the Rule of the Brothers restricted them to elementary subjects, Archbishop Kenrick had to seek permission from Pope Pius IX for the school to teach Latin. The pope granted this request. Over the years, Kenrick came to look upon Christian Brothers College as his preparatory seminary and urged pastors to enroll young men who aspired to serve God as priests. One hundred and sixty-three future priests, several bishops among them, began to study Latin under the brothers' direction, either at the college or in parish schools. The brothers already had taught boys in three parish schools. Eventually they were to teach at eleven parish schools and had tremendous influence, especially in the Irish parishes.

Catholic girls, too, long had enjoyed greater opportunities for education than Catholic girls in other cities and local girls of other religious denominations. The Convent of the Sacred Heart continued in its near-southside location. The Visitation nuns moved from temporary quarters in the Soulard area to a stately new building that faced south on Cass Avenue at Eighteenth on property donated by John Mullanphy's daughter, Ann Mullanphy Biddle. Sisters of St. Joseph saw Carondelet Academy, or "Mother Celestine's School" as it was locally known, continue to grow. By 1850 the community had forty-four members, 36 percent of them American-born. During the next decade, ninety-two young women entered the congregation. Most of them were of Irish or German ancestry and had been born in America. The Ursulines opened an academy for girls on Twelfth Street at Russell. Lorretines, under the leadership of Mother Mary Elizabeth Hayden, a native of

*By 1870, fifty-seven Christian Brothers taught at ten parish schools, two academies and their college on Cerre Street. In this photograph, Brother Alnoth, on the left, and Brother Augustine on the right, sit with their third and fourth graders and a Passionist priest, Father Gaudentius, P.P.*

Kilkenny who grew up in Perryville, Missouri, replaced the Religious of the Sacred Heart at the academy in Florissant.

While St. Louis had four flourishing academies for girls and one new one underway in 1855, Baltimore, Boston, Chicago, Cleveland, Dubuque, and Philadelphia had one academy each; Detroit, Louisville, New Orleans, and New York had two; and Cincinnati had three.[16] No other denomination opened schools to match. Mary Institute belonged to a later decade.

Historian Wade on two distinct occasions singled out St. Louis among midwestern cities for special praise in the area of education. In discussing the improvement of life on the frontier, he wrote: "St. Louis's large Catholic population provided a broad and expanding base for a college of that faith."[17] A short time later he added: "St. Louis remained the focus of Western Catholicism . . . partially realizing the hope of its first bishop that it would become 'the center of all religious and literary instruction of the extensive country' around it."[18]

While so many religious sisters taught school, others entered new areas of health care at home. Mother Seton's congregation had affiliated with the Daughters of St. Vincent de Paul in France in 1850. Three years later four nuns of the new affiliation came to St. Louis from Emmitsburg, Maryland, to open the first foundlings' home in the country. At a residence in the Soulard District, they combined it with a maternity hospital and St. Ann's Widows' Home. Support came from the estate of John Mullanphy. Five years later, the daughters moved to a new building at Tenth and O'Fallon Streets, erected on a lot given by the ever-generous Ann Mullanphy Biddle.

The Daughters of Charity continued their work in schools and orphanages, and they advanced a step in healthcare. At first the daughters accepted psychiatric patients at their general hospital. By 1858 the number of such patients suggested the opening of a special hospital for them. The answer was a four-story building in Soulard. Dr. John Leavy, an early member of the St. Vincent de Paul Society, held the post of house doctor. He later served as physician with the First Missouri Confederate Brigade.

Almost every area of education and health care found nuns active. Only one area of concern for the marginalized called for help. An apostolate of ready response to the poor, the sick in their homes, and the prisoners in jails called for dedicated Christian women. Father Arnold Damen, the Jesuit pastor at St. Francis Xavier Church in St. Louis, learned of a congregation that responded to these needs: the Sisters of Mercy founded in Ireland by Catherine McAuley in 1827. She had planned an entirely new way of life, close in scope and spirit to the secular institutes approved by Pope Pius XII more than a century later. Unfortunately, church law tended to hamstring innovative individuals. She had to modify her free-wheeling plans but carried her spirit forward within the limitations of church law of the time.

With the support of Archbishop Kenrick, Father Damen appealed to the Mercy superior in New York in 1856. When she agreed to send six sisters under the leadership of Sister Mary De Pazzi Bentley, a native of Dublin, Archbishop Kenrick authorized fellow immigrant Father Patrick Ryan to meet them in Manhattan. Ryan escorted them to the mission center at Tenth and Morgan Streets, four blocks from St. Francis Xavier Church at Ninth and Christy.

On arriving to St. Louis, the sisters immediately divided the city into districts and went two by two to visit the sick in their homes and care for the poor. They visited the City Hospital, especially the tuberculosis ward. They notified priests of those whom they thought needed the last sacraments. On July 16, 1856, they visited the jail. Sister Mary of Mercy Brennan and Sister Mary Louis Farrell looked to the material and spiritual needs of the prisoners with gratifying success. They sought the help of wealthy businessmen to find jobs for those liberated. They worked to have a chaplain appointed and helped prepare others for death.

Many prominent women of St. Louis of various national backgrounds became aware of the work of the Mercies and assisted. Among them were Mrs. Julia Maffitt, Mrs. Charles Bates, Mrs. Edward Walsh, Mrs. Sarpy Peugnet, Mrs. Ann Hunt, and Mrs. James Chambers. Among the men who helped were James Lucas, John Withnell, W. Sarpy, and A. V. Reyburn. Several Jesuits at Saint Louis University gave benefit lectures at the Mercantile Library to promote the work of the Mercy Sisters. With such backing, the Mercies opened a Home for Orphans. In its first five years, it provided bed and board for 448 children.

In 1860 the archbishop prevailed upon the sisters to build St. Joseph's Convent of Mercy on property he gave them at Twenty-Second and Morgan Streets. The Jesuits provided a chaplain. Several wealthy families—French, Anglo-American, and Irish—enlisted as patrons of the institution. To help defray the cost of the free school the sisters operated, Archbishop Kenrick encouraged them to open a "select" or tuition school to help pay for the free school, as the Christian Brothers were doing. Sister Mercy Brennan, already praised for her work at the jails, opened the school with twenty-six pupils, mostly of Irish background, in September 1861. It soon matched strides with the older academies.

Some years later, the sisters opened a place where poor women could lodge overnight, the Night Refuge, or Night Hospitality as it later was called. During the thirty-five years of its existence, it offered temporary shelter to an average of 2,632 women every year. Sisters Angela Molloy and Martha Kettler assisted Sister Magdalen Dowling in conducting the refuge.[9]

# Expanding Neighborhoods
# Welcome a Windfall

S teamboats had crowded the levee to discharge close to thirty thousand newcomers in the early 1840s. During the decade the population grew by 372.8 percent, and by 1850 the city had a population of 77,860. It stood eighth in the nation, and second to Cincinnati in the Midwest.[1] By 1860 the count reached 160,773. Immigrants from Ireland numbered 29,926, far more than from any other country except the still disunited German states. Including Switzerland, the count from German-speaking provinces reached 50,510.[2]

The early Irish had come from towns and counties all over the island. They had experience in merchandising, and many prospered, some dramatically. Numerous others established themselves in a wide variety of fields. With the potato blight hitting Ireland in the mid- and late-forties, a wave of less-skilled Irish from the rugged rural counties of the west reached American shores in the early 1850s. Many of these found their way to the busy local levee.

Unaccustomed to city living, and with few urban skills, they brought energy, resourcefulness, a willingness to learn, and— unique among immigrants—they spoke English. Further, they could call upon benevolent societies set up by earlier arrivals.

Newly arriving Irish young women readily found employment in domestic service. When young Father John Hogan, later bishop of St. Joseph, Missouri, assisted at St. John the Evangelist Parish in 1854, he found that many colleens attended Mass at 5:00 A.M. every Sunday. "The five o'clock

Mass," he wrote, "was celebrated for them at that early hour so that they could return in time to prepare breakfast for their non-Catholic employers who'd not yet risen from their beds. And the number of Catholic girls attending several other Catholic churches in St. Louis was even greater than at St. John's."[3]

Young Irishmen came in far greater numbers. The St. Louis economy beckoned. "By 1854," labor historian Russell M. Nolen wrote, "the city harbored twenty-four flour mills, twenty or more saw mills, twenty-five foundries, numerous machine shops, a large sugar refinery, several cotton and woolen manufacturing concerns, railroad works, two car shops, several harness and saddle makers, several tobacco and cigar concerns, several metal, rope and baggage concerns, several wagon and carriage makers, and several furniture manufacturers."[4]

In many of these enterprises, a newcomer, even without previous experience, could find work. Many hoisted cotton bales on the levee, where 3,307 boats already had docked in the first six months of 1854.[5] A dozen Irish gardeners planted Osage oranges and trimmed hedges on Henry Shaw's estate that became the Missouri Botanical Garden a few years later. The list of hired men includes Thomas Meehan, Patrick Costan, Oliver Dalton, Robert Dempsey, James O'Bryan, and Dan Daly.[6] All the while, the men who built Shaw's country residence were Anglo-Americans.[7] A few decades later, Irish built homes and Bohemians planted the ginko trees.

Soon the Irish worked in a wide variety of occupations. Patrick Burns of Leitrim and Patrick Caniff, who later distinguished himself for bravery as a captain with the Missouri First Confederate Brigade, worked as saddle makers. Edward Dowling came from Roscommon and constructed railroad lines. Redmond Cleary of Tipperary sold grain. James Fitzgibbon of Cork worked for an uncle, Morris H. Fitzgibbon, a general contractor who built many important buildings in the city. Porter White of County Tyrone plastered most of those famous structures, such as the Planters' Hotel and the Wainwright Building. John Donovan of Galway ran a hotel. Dublin native Thomas Furlong studied architecture under George I. Barnett and designed the St. Louis High School in 1858. Dr. Edward Montgomery of County Antrim developed a fine general practice and wrote for medical journals; he was elected president of the Missouri State Medical Association. Irish-born Lawrence Harrigan began his career as a shoemaker and then joined the police force, becoming sergeant in 1857, lieutenant in 1866, chief of detectives in 1868, and chief of police in 1874.

Meanwhile, another big opportunity for the newly arriving Irishmen seeking employment took them out of town. Back in February 1849, Senator Thomas Hart Benton had urged the building of a Pacific Railroad west from St. Louis. A month later the general assembly chartered the Pacific Railroad Company. Mayor James Barry called successfully for widespread support of the project.

John O'Fallon, Thomas O'Flaherty, and William Walsh, among others, served on the board of directors. Thomas O'Sullivan, the chief construction engineer, drew up plans. By September 1851, a thousand men worked on the railbed. The rails came from London the next year, followed by the first locomotive. In December 1852, the first cars rolled out toward Cheltenham, the clay-mining area two miles west of the city limits. As the rails moved west, so did the workers.[8]

Where did these new-coming Irish find homes? Some of the track workers settled on the hill to the north of the railroad in Cheltenham, an area famous for its rich deposits of clay. There they formed St. James Parish, the first west of Kingshighway. This area kept its Irish character long after other Irish locales ceased to be Celtic.

The largest group of Irish settled around St. Patrick's Church at Sixth and Biddle Streets on the near northside. Small shopkeepers and workers, skilled and unskilled, made up this group. They were to take the brunt of the Know-Nothing hostility during the election years of 1853 and 1854. Gradually, the Irish area spread westward between Carr and Cass Avenues. Central to the new

*With the approval of Archbishop Kenrick, Father (later Bishop) John Hogan chose as his flock the Irish railroad workers pushing the lines west.*

section, St. Lawrence O'Toole Church rose at Fourteenth and O'Fallon Streets. By 1860 others had spread beyond the old "Kerry Patch" to St. Bridget of Erin parish, slightly more than a dozen blocks to the west.

Visitation students, daughters of wealthy St. Louisans, proudly called their school on the north side of Cass Avenue "the Castle of the Patch." The hutches and lean-tos of the early famine refugees gave way to family dwellings of brick. Some few Irish families had moved north toward St. Michael's parish, but the northside Irish tended to move almost straight west.

The well-to-do Irish lived in various sections of the central corridor of the city and attended the Cathedral or St. Francis Xavier Church, then on Ninth and Christy, one block north of Washington Avenue. As the 1850s moved on, more and more of them found homes to the west in new St. John the Evangelist Church on Sixteenth and Chestnut Streets.[9] A few had settled on the near southside in Assumption and Annunciation parishes.

The energetic St. Louis Catholics of all national backgrounds had opened churches, schools, orphanages, and health-care centers to an extent matched by few dioceses in the country.

These institutions and the churches and schools being built for an expanding populace demanded great sacrifices of the Catholics of the city. In 1858 unexpected help "fell from heaven." John Thornton, a little known St. Louis merchant, had died the year before. He had taken part in no religious or civic organizations, such as the St. Vincent de Paul Society, the "Friends of Ireland," or the Erin Benevolent Society. A researcher looked in vain for his name on the list of donors or pew-holders at Bishop Du Bourg's Cathedral.[10] even though Thornton's brother Nicholas had rented a pew in the church at its opening.[11] Perhaps John shared his brother's family pew. John Thornton held no public office, and authors of histories of the city saw no reason to mention his name. But the financial records of the archdiocese show his great influence on the development of parishes and the strengthening of Catholic institutions. A grand-nephew searched out his story.[12]

Born in 1795 in a small village in County Louth, on the east coast of Ireland not far north of Dublin, John Thornton came to the states in July 1816 with his brother Nicholas, a cooper, and settled in St. Louis. A few years later, Nicholas married at the Cathedral, but John never married. John started life as a grocer and expanded into other areas of merchandising. Shortly, he had money to loan. He distrusted banks, loaned to rich and poor alike, and picked up mortgages. He purchased land in the lead and farming areas near Dubuque, Iowa. When his younger brother Patrick settled there in 1845, John gave him six forty-acre sections of rich northern Iowa land. John soon amassed a fortune.

A man of impressive appearance, Thornton greatly resembled President Grover Cleveland of the succeeding generation. When he died in 1857,

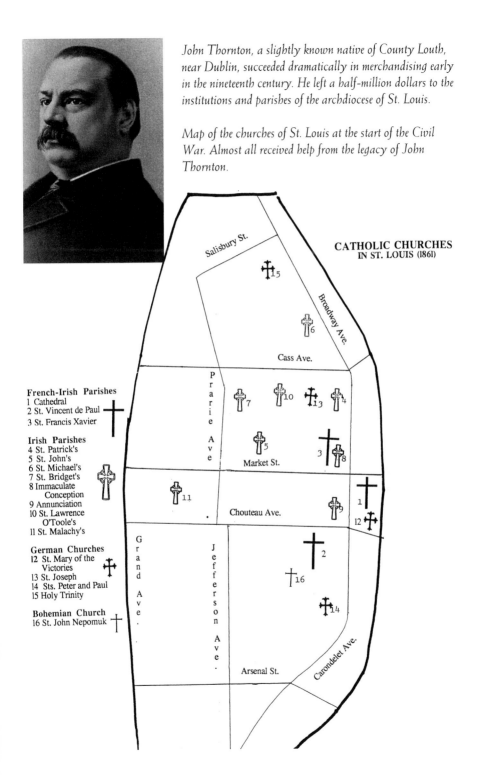

*John Thornton, a slightly known native of County Louth, near Dublin, succeeded dramatically in merchandising early in the nineteenth century. He left a half-million dollars to the institutions and parishes of the archdiocese of St. Louis.*

*Map of the churches of St. Louis at the start of the Civil War. Almost all received help from the legacy of John Thornton.*

**CATHOLIC CHURCHES**
IN ST. LOUIS (1861)

**French-Irish Parishes**
1 Cathedral
2 St. Vincent de Paul
3 St. Francis Xavier

**Irish Parishes**
4 St. Patrick's
5 St. John's
6 St. Michael's
7 St. Bridget's
8 Immaculate Conception
9 Annunciation
10 St. Lawrence O'Toole's
11 St. Malachy's

**German Churches**
12 St. Mary of the Victories
13 St. Joseph
14 Sts. Peter and Paul
15 Holy Trinity

**Bohemian Church**
16 St. John Nepomuk

John left ten thousand dollars to each of his five nephews and nieces. The remainder, amounting to $461,488.41, went to the archdiocese of St. Louis for various uses at the discretion of the archbishop. Kenrick, in turn, designated close to a quarter of a million for hospitals, asylums, schools, convents, homes for the poor, and other religious institutions.[13] Even though this gift went through archdiocesan offices, the uses had interdenominational consequences. The hospital and schools run by nuns offered their services without reference to religious affiliation.

The other half of the Thornton bequest went exclusively to Catholic parishes as loans for building purposes. Archbishop Kenrick presumably put one norm for these interest-free loans. The parishes paid back their debts *if* and *when* they could. Some acted promptly; others moved slowly. Eventually all these immigrant parishes could build without the worry of having to pay back within narrow time frames.

The Thornton bequest spurred church building during the decade of the 1860s when the population of St. Louis jumped from 160,773 to 310,825 to make it the fourth largest city in the country. When one considers that the 1849 church of Saints Peter and Paul cost eighteen thousand dollars and the first St. Francis de Sales Church went up for ten thousand dollars in 1867, the significance of the Thornton bequest awes one.

*Several well-known Irish—among them John Byrne, Thomas Green, Michael Hartnett, and Judge John O'Neill—joined with Catholics of other national backgrounds in the first unit of the Third Order of St. Francis in the West. Father Servatius Altmicks, O.F.M., served as their spiritual director.*

In the next twelve years, Thornton monies helped twenty parishes: one multinational, eight German-speaking, and eleven Irish. The first church to locate west of Jefferson, St. Malachy's, opened at Ewing and Clark. It received $15,855.05 of Thornton money. Father Patrick Ryan built Annunciation, a church of classic beauty, on the near southside at Sixth and Chouteau in 1859. It eventually received $34,950.85, the largest of the Thornton parish legacies. Among the lowest of the grantees, Assumption at Ninth and Sidney Streets needed only $1,742.56.[14] Father J. B. O'Brien soon boasted more than 250 families in attendance there.

To understand and put into focus this tremendous growth of Irish Catholic parishes in St. Louis, a look at the statistics in *The Catholic Almanac* for 1859 throws light. At this time, Detroit had one parish for the Irish, the Cathedral; Cleveland had two, St. Patrick's and St. John the Evangelist; Cincinnati and Chicago had four; and New Orleans had one listed as an Irish parish and three others with Irish-named pastors.[15] At this time, St. Louis Irish formed a large percentage of three of the four original general parishes—the Cathedral, St. Francis Xavier, and St. Vincent de Paul—and all of St. Patrick's congregation. St. John's had several old French families among the many Irish. Six other parishes were almost exclusively Irish: St. Michael's, St. Bridget's, St. Lawrence O'Toole's, Immaculate Conception, Annunciation, and St. Malachy's.

During these years of growth, the first Bohemian parish in America opened at Twelfth and Russell, and six churches welcomed German-speaking Catholics: St. Liborius and Holy Trinity on the nouthside, Sts. Peter and Paul and St. Francis de Sales on the southside, and St. Boniface in Carondelet. All received Thornton money. The Franciscans opened St. Anthony Friary and Church on Meramec Avenue in Carondelet. The pastor, Father Servatius Altmicks, began the first local unit of the Third Order of St. Francis, a society of laymen who pledged to live according to the spirit of that holy man. Several prominent Irishmen, among them John Byrne and Judge Joseph O'Neil, joined the initial unit.

# Bigotry and Blunders Break the Bond

Hostility to immigrants, mainly Irish and German Catholics, swept the country in the mid-nineteenth century. Historians, such as Professor Ray Allen Billington, an expert on Protestant-Catholic tensions, documented this fact. In his definitive book, *The Protestant Crusade, 1800–1860: A Study of the Origins of American Nativism*, he wrote: "Hatred of Catholics and foreigners had been steadily growing in the United States for more than two centuries, before it took political form with the Native American outburst in the 1840s and the Know-Nothingism of the 1850s."[1]

Catholics had faced hostility throughout most of colonial English America. Even in Maryland, a colony founded by Catholics, life had turned sour. The founders of the colony had welcomed Protestants. These soon became the majority and deprived Catholics of equal justice under the law.[2] Only Rhode Island offered Catholics full civil and religious rights by 1700, and even there, Billington writes, it is unknown what the interpretation of the liberal statutes might have been.[3] Hostility grew during the French and Indian Wars (1756–1763) when Protestant Britain and its colonies fought Catholic France and Spain. This hostility had been muted during the American Revolution, when France and Spain declared war on England, and their help made it possible for the colonies to win independence.

The Protestant majority had lived in peace with the few Catholics in the eastern seaboard states during the first quarter of the nineteenth century. Heavy Catholic immigration from Ireland and Germany in the 1830s and 1840s, however, caused dismay to some Anglo-Americans. Militant Protestants took their long rifles from the racks. They began a three-point attack on Catholics, both the established and the newcomers. First, these militants set out to control the "public school" system and gave it a Protestant orientation. Second, they filled all available print with bitter denunciations of "popery." Third, they stirred hotheads all over the country to assault Catholics and Catholic institutions.

The first drive affected St. Louis slightly. The Catholics had started their own academies and colleges before the public system opened schools. Lutherans began parochial schools in 1838. Mainline Protestants had been sending their children to Visitation and Saint Louis University. Only after the Civil War did wealthy Protestants open Smith Academy for boys and Mary Institute for girls. Public schools started slowly in St. Louis, but when they got underway they met Protestant requirements.

The second thrust hit St. Louis. Preachers in the East, such as the Reverend Lyman Beecher, brother of Harriet Beecher Stowe, began to see the activity of the Jesuits in St. Louis, and later in Cincinnati, as a danger to the freedom of the republic. The man who spearheaded this anti-Catholic activity in St. Louis later became a hero as an abolitionist martyr. In St. Louis, Elijah P. Lovejoy denigrated Catholics and Catholic activities at least as much as he denounced the slaveholders. Establishing the *St. Louis Observer* as a Presbyterian publication in November 1833, he attacked the Catholic Church with a series of "Letters from Rome," three or four columns in length. Lovejoy claimed that foreign money and foreign influence spread Catholicism.[4]

Alongside his own outpourings, Lovejoy printed letters highly critical of the Catholic Church. One of these stated: "The Mississippi Valley was in danger of falling into the hands of strangers, the well-known oppressors and persecutors of mankind."[5] The Holy Alliance planned to use Roman Catholics as a political organization to overturn American political institutions. The secret agents of this European scheme were the Jesuits.[6]

Had Lovejoy merely walked a few blocks to Saint Louis University and talked to the priests there, he would have found that the Jesuits once had to flee to escape the evil plans of the Quadruple Alliance, which Lovejoy mistakenly called the "Holy Alliance." The Quadruple Alliance was an agreement between Russia, Austria, Prussia, and Great Britain in 1815 to suppress revolutionary outbreaks wherever they occurred. To compensate Holland for the loss of the Cape Colony, the alliance put Belgium under oppressive Dutch rule. These European powers had given Belgium, the native country of the St. Louis Jesuits, to Holland. The King of Holland had set up a rule so rigid that future Jesuits seeking freedom had to leave Belgium surreptitiously. But Lovejoy made no effort to see the Jesuits.

When Judge Luke Lawless refused to prosecute any individuals of a mob that had lynched a steamboat steward by the name of McIntosh in March 1836, Lovejoy denounced the judge. Lawless had blamed the crime on abolitionists. In his criticism of Lawless's questionable position, Lovejoy alluded strongly to Lawless's religion and ultimately blamed Pope Gregory XVI himself.

Lovejoy met opposition chiefly from proslavery men. A mob threatened the Observer's office, threw Lovejoy's type in the street, and upset the press. Alderman Bryan Mullanphy made a valiant effort to stop the mob and was determined to prosecute its leaders. Mullanphy criticized the dangerous precedent of mob action. Lovejoy never attacked the slave owners with the bitterness he reserved for the Jesuits.

Even in his last issue before leaving for Alton, Lovejoy wrote that "he had been made the victim of popular violence . . . especially for honestly endeavoring to open the eyes of my countrymen to the danger which threatens their civil and religious rights, from the workings of a foreign despotic influence, carried forward here by its appropriate instruments, the Jesuits. . . ."[7]

In 1839, Dr. Joseph Nash McDowell, of uncertain Celtic ancestry who had taught medicine for three years in Cincinnati, moved to St. Louis. A self-assured young man, he sought a partnership with the illustrious surgeon, Dr. William Beaumont. The only advantage to the veteran physician in the partnership was this: with the young doctor at hand, no one could complain that Dr. Beaumont had more patients than he could properly treat or that they had to wait a long time in his office. St. Louisans soon found out that Dr. McDowell had a brilliant mind, but an extremely erratic manner.

The young physician began a small medical school in 1840 in association with Kemper College, an affiliate of the Protestant Episcopal Church that opened in the southwest section of St. Louis County. Dr. John S. Moore, a physician of Irish-English ancestry, joined him that same year. He would teach medicine in St. Louis for thirty years at "McDowell's College."

In 1842, the Medical College of Saint Louis University, chartered earlier than McDowell's College, got underway. The school soon enrolled a distinguished faculty and student body that included men destined for prominence in medicine. None of the faculty and only one early alumnus, Dr. Edmund O'Callaghan, was Irish. O'Callaghan's fame would come not from medicine but his editing of *New York State History*.

In that same year, 1842, the citizens of St. Louis elected their first immigrant mayor, George Maguire of Omagh, in County Tyrone. Mayor Maguire appointed Dr. James Prather, dean of the Saint Louis University Faculty of Medicine, as head physician at the City Hospital in place of Dr. McDowell. Presumably irked by the opening of the College of Medicine at Saint Louis University, and his ousting from the City Hospital—staffed by the

Dr. Joseph Nash McDowell, a skilled physician but eccentric personality, owned and operated the first medical school in the West in this octagonal building at Eighth and Gratiot. When the Civil War came, the entire faculty served the Confederacy, but federal authorities eventually turned the building into a prison for Confederate officers.

Daughters of Charity—McDowell launched a series of lectures against "Jesuitism." A fluent orator with an entertaining approach, he called upon a great store of anecdotes in his presentation. To his dismay, he found that he had misread the audience. People disliked his tactics.

As a result, McDowell "ran scared." He wore a breastplate and carried a weapon at all times. He planned an octagonal college building that resembled a fortress. He purchased 1,400 muskets the army was discarding and cast six cannon. He stored this great armament in the basement of his college. Rumor had it that he intended to launch an attack on the Mexican Territory of Alta California. Later, when the Christian Brothers built their college directly across from the "fortress," McDowell permanently mounted two cannons aimed at the brothers' school. During graduation exercises he marched his new physicians by the CBC campus and ordered them to spit on the lawn. Intended to demean CBC, it contributed instead to the community's growing conviction that

McDowell was an "odd-ball."

The controversy over McDowell grew when a writer in the *Native American Bulletin* saw a foreign plot in the action of Mayor Maguire in appointing Dr. Prather of Saint Louis University as head physician at the hospital.[8] Another writer in the same paper stated that a change of doctors at the City Hospital was a normal procedure and that Dr. McDowell was just as "Irish" as Mayor Maguire. In fact, he had been one of the "big guns" at a recent meeting of the Irish Repeal Association. The roiled waters along the Mississippi quieted for a time.[9]

The first outbreak of anti-Catholic violence in St. Louis occurred at Saint Louis University on George Washington's birthday in 1844. Inflamed by unsound rumors, a mob threatened the university's School of Medicine. Mayor Bernard Pratte called out the militia. The leaders of the mob agreed to disperse and did, and the militia went home to supper. Elements of the mob, however, regrouped that evening, smashed into the medical school, and destroyed all the equipment. After this outburst, local nativists kept quiet for several years.

This interdenominational hostility failed to split the Irish community. Protestant John O'Fallon gave two buildings of Greek Revival style to the Saint Louis University School of Medicine at a new location eight blocks south of the main campus of the Jesuit school. Citizens of all nationalities and various faiths elected a Catholic, Judge Bryan Mullanphy, mayor of the city that same year, 1847. When the potato blight hit their homeland, the "Friends of Ireland" met in the hope of relieving the sufferings of their countrymen. More Protestant Irish attended the meeting than Catholic.

The United States was a predominantly white Protestant country of people whose ancestors came from the British Isles or Calvinist districts of Germany. In the late 1840s and early 1850s large boatloads of immigrants came from Ireland and the still disunited German states. The Irish were mostly Catholics. These Germans were anti-clerical Free-Thinkers for the most part and had worked in vain for unity in Germany.

While America offered religious freedom, and its government never confiscated church property or exiled clergymen for preaching the Gospel, most European countries—Catholic, Protestant, or Orthodox—harassed those who did not adhere to the established church. Catholics had no legal rights in Sweden or Norway, Lutherans in Spain or Italy. Instead of recognizing the splendid situation in the United States, as American church leaders like Bishop John B. Purcell of Cincinnati urged, Pope Pius IX (1846–1878) condemned in successive documents freedom of speech and press, representative government, and the separation of Church and State, freedoms all cherished by Americans.

As a result, Protestants had justifiable fears as Catholic immigrants poured down the gangplanks. Protestants had to prevent Catholics from becoming a majority and taking control of the country. In turn, Catholic apologists Robert Bakewell, editor of the *Shepherd of the Valley* did intellectual flip-flops to justify this strange concession to kings in the sixteenth century that became church dogma in the nineteenth.[10]

The influx of these newcomers from Ireland and Germany brought a reaction from nativists—white, Anglo-Saxon, and Protestant. Taking it for granted that they were God's chosen people, and that America was the land God chose for them, they set out to harass the Canaanites, in this instance, the Catholic immigrants. When asked about their organization and goals, the nativists declined to answer. As a result, they won the nickname "Know-Nothings." A local pack stirred up mob violence during the election year of 1852, when a Democrat, Governor Franklin Pierce of New Hampshire, challenged the Whig candidate, the Mexican War hero General Winfield Scott, for the presidency.

The "Know-Nothings" ignored the recently arrived "Kerry-Patchers," destitute refugees of the famine who had squatted beyond the Eighteenth Street city limits, and smashed homes, small stores, and shops of established Irish residents on the near northside—Giligan's on Cherry Street, Brady's on Fifth and Morgan Streets, and Murphy's on the levee not far from St. Patrick's Church on the near northside. Young Father James Henry gained national acclaim among Irish for facing up to rioters in defense of his church. The Belgian-born president of Saint Louis University, Father John Baptist Druyts, S.J., imitated Father Henry. He walked up and down in front of St. Francis Xavier Church at Ninth and Christy, reading his Psalms with such a calm mien that the mob presumed the basement hid several platoons of armed Irishmen. It didn't. But they dispersed. It was McDowell's College, not Saint Louis University, that had an arsenal in the basement.

The physicians at Saint Louis University College of Medicine, even though located well away from a heavily Irish district, asked to separate from the university. Father Druyts showed his usual calm. He told the physicians that the school had the medical charter. If they left, he would enlist other physicians. They remained.

From the outset of the Republic, American Catholics cherished the liberties that their country gave them. Many of them were to give their lives a decade later that "a nation so dedicated might live" for their children to enjoy. Unfortunately, Roman authorities had no experience in, or love for, the ways of freedom. To make the situation more tense, Pope Pius IX decided to send a special representative to the United States in 1853. Instead of commissioning an American or an Irish or Canadian prelate who spoke English, the pope chose Archbishop Gaetano Bedini, who had ruled the Papal States in central Italy with severity. Many immigrants from Central Europe then living in America strongly disliked the new delegate of the pope.

When Bedini came, he met a cordial reception from President Franklin Pierce. This visit stirred up ill feelings in certain areas. Had he come to establish diplomatic relations? Numerous Americans thought so. As a result, they questioned all dealings with Bedini. Demonstrators threatened him as he moved west from Pittsburgh to Cincinnati, and then to Louisville. An Italian revoluntary society allegedly intended to assassinate him. He returned directly to New York and then back to Italy. Archbishop Kenrick thought the entire visit was "a collection of blunders."[11] No apparent good came from it.

Another election, this one off-year, was at hand. Two years before, in 1852, Senator Thomas Hart Benton, who had served for thirty years in the Senate but lost in 1850, a hero to the majority of Irish, ran for a local congressional seat and won. In 1854, he was challenged by Luther Kennett, a Whig who numbered a few wealthy Irish among his supporters. Behind these local and personal races lurked the great issues of slavery, states rights, extension of slavery into the territories, and ultimately secession. Firebrands outnumbered fire extinguishers.

On election day, August 7, at a polling place in the heavily Irish Fifth Ward, a judge slowed the election process by minutely scrutinizing naturalization papers. The lines lengthened. The day grew hot. Poll-watchers grew edgy. Many bared their tough knuckles. In the words of historian James Neal Primm, "a flashy Irish knife found a target."[12] The knife-wielder fled the scene with an angry crowd in pursuit. Soon the Fifth Ward outdid the best of donnybrooks. Mayor John Howe called eight platoons of volunteer soldiers into service to restore and preserve order. The more sensible citizens, surfeited with violence, supported the mayor. Calm came. The medical professors, seeking to disaffiliate, came again to the university president, now Father John Verdin, S.J., and a native of St. Louis of Irish-French extraction. A conciliatory man, he acquiesced in the separation. It was unfortunate that he had done so. Within a few years, the Nativist Movement quieted.

John O'Fallon and other former friends of Saint Louis University turned their support to a new school, the Eliot Seminary, founded that same year (1854) by a fellow Irish Protestant, Wayman Crowe. He named the institute for the Reverend William Greenleaf Eliot, a former member of the board of Saint Louis University's College of Medicine and grandfather of poet T. S. Eliot. A few years later the new institution took the name of Washington University. John O'Fallon set up the O'Fallon Technical Institute in conjunction with the young school.

Gradually other Protestant Irish besides John O'Fallon, such as Robert and Hugh Campbell, joined with Anglo-Americans in their organizational, religious, and cultural life. John E. Liggett, son of an immigrant from Derry, entered the tobacco business and went into partnership with George S. Myers. Liggett & Myers became one of the largest tobacco manufacturers in the nation. Liggett also prospered in real estate. Socially, he moved in Anglo-American circles. He was at home with the Skinkers and Bridges, not the

Walshes and Chambers. Gradually other Protestant Irish came. Taking no part in Irish societies were such men as Gerald B. Allen of Cork, who prospered in railroading and bridge-building, and David Ranken, Jr., of Boystown, County Derry, who amassed over a million dollars in real estate and stock transactions. Early in the next century, incidentally, Ranken would leave his entire fortune to a School of Mechanical Trades that bore his name.[11] No local parishes of the Church of Ireland took root in St. Louis, and no Methodist, Presbyterian, or Episcopalian congregation identified itself as Irish.

All the while, Catholic Irish opened new parishes and began new organizations. The first one, the Shamrock Society, arose in 1854 in response to the Know-Nothing riot. In September a group of Irish men, not active in earlier Irish groups, met at the home of Patrick Moran on Eighth at Biddle Streets in St. Patrick's Parish to relieve the distress of those who had suffered at the hands of the Know-Nothings. All who took part were Catholics, among them M. J. Dolan, William Delehunt, Marty Keary, William Hughes, Patrick Monaghan, and the first president, Edward Lester. Within six years it numbered three hundred members.[13]

The later Irish organizations differed drastically from the earlier societies in personnel and purpose. The earlier groups had been associations of established Irish offering help to people in the homeland or to less fortunate, unestablished newcomers to America. The new societies were fraternal organizations of small businessmen or workers concerned with personal and group advancement.

The "Know-Nothings" went the way of the "Loco-Focos," an Equal Rights Party of the previous decade. Unlike the "Loco-Focos," however, who flashed a moment on the political scene and then, like heat lightning on the horizon, vanished, the "Know-Nothings" left a sad legacy that marked a watershed in the history of the Irish in St. Louis. They split the Irish community, Protestant from Catholic.[14] From 1854 forward, to be Irish in St. Louis meant to be Catholic.

Necessarily then, over the succeeding decades, the story of the Irish in St. Louis will intertwine with the annals of the Catholic Church. The Irish identified themselves more and more with their parishes and their pastors. Further, archbishops of Irish ancestry would shepherd them religiously for a century. The first already has appeared in these pages. The other two left memorable records. Their public careers are part of this great story.

# The Camp Jackson "Affair": Blessing or Bane?

W hen the Kansas-Nebraska Bill of 1854 opened the territories west and northwest of Missouri to the possible extension of slavery, Kansas became a battleground between abolitionist newcomers from free states and proslavery raiders from the western counties of Missouri. Free-Soilers and other opponents of slavery coalesced in the newly forming Republican Party.

*This night view shows the area of Camp Jackson east of Grand between Lindell and Laclede where the state militia under General Daniel Frost held its annual encampment in May 1861. A regular army officer, Captain Nathaniel Lyons, mustered four thousand recruits, mostly recent immigrants from Germany, and took Frost and his men prisoners as secessionists.*

When the Republicans accepted the Know-Nothings, the Catholic Irish even more firmly clung to the Democratic Party.

Many Irish immigrants enlisted in the various units of state militia when it reorganized in 1858. Captain Daniel Morgan Frost, a veteran of the Mexican War, led the "Washington Guards," assisted by Lieutenants Patrick Gorman, Robert Tucker, and Patrick O'Connor. Captain J. C. Smith commanded the "Emmet Guards," assisted by Lieutenants Edward Byrne, Philip Coyne, and Edward Mulholland. Captain Joseph Kelly headed the "Washington Blues," a secession-inclined unit, assisted by Lieutenants P. E. Burke, John R. Drew, and C. W. Hogan. On reading these predominantly Celtic surnames, an observer might be inclined to ask if these were Sarsfield's Men, defending the town of Limerick against "Dutch William," or the green-clad units with King James II at the Battle of the Boyne.

The chaplain of the state guard was John B. Bannon, a graduate of Maynooth who had volunteered for work in the archdiocese in 1853, the year of his ordination in Dublin. After he had assisted for several years at the Cathedral, Archbishop Kenrick sent him to build a large church at the new parish of St. John, Apostle and Evangelist, north of the former area of Chouteau Pond. Architect Robert Mitchell drew up the final plan, modifying Patrick Walsh's original effort. Timothy Cavanagh signed a contract for the masonry, James George for the brickwork, and T. Dowd and Company for the ironcasting. St. John's opened for Mass at Fifteenth and Chestnut Streets in 1858.

*General Daniel Frost went south after his parole in late 1861 and served for several years with the Missouri Confederate forces before joining his exiled family in Canada. Granted amnesty by President Andrew Johnson after the conflict, he returned to St. Louis and took an active part in civic affairs.*

Father Bannon, the pastor, also chaplained the Temperance Society. Six-foot-four in height, with a stout physique, an impressive presence, and a pleasing voice, Father Bannon stood out in any group. He had served as secretary to the archbishop and was known by all bishops of the Midwest. Many saw advancement in the Church for the young pastor, but that was not to be. His dedication to his men in uniform led him in another direction.

Shortly after the election of Abraham Lincoln in November 1860, Kansas abolitionist raiders, called "Jayhawkers," threatened the Missouri border in the area south of Kansas City. Governor Robert M. Stewart wisely called out the St. Louis units of the state guard under Generals Frost and John B. Bowen, rather than those from the embattled western counties who had taken part in the earlier border wars. Father Bannon took the train with Frost's men to the railhead at Sedalia in western Missouri. This show of force quieted the area for a time. In December, South Carolina seceded from the Union.

All the while, local secessionists, who called themselves Minute Men, organized under the leadership of three young men, Basil Duke, Colton Greene, and Brock Champion, described as "a bold, enthusiastic young Irishman."[1] Many other Irishmen belonged to the Minute Men. They presumably had their eyes on the arsenal that held sixty thousand muskets, more than half the number in the entire South.[2]

On January 11, 1861, forty regulars arrived from Newport Barracks, North Carolina, under the leadership of Lieutenant Thomas W. Sweeny, who had lost an arm in the Mexican War. Sweeny marched his men to the courthouse on Third and Olive Streets where the government held four hundred thousand dollars in gold. Many local citizens looked upon this military venture as an unwarranted federal intrusion in a sovereign state. Tempers flared. General William Harney wisely advised Sweeny to move his forty soldiers to the arsenal thirty-three blocks to the south, which he did.

On the day after Sweeny arrived, Archbishop Kenrick advised the Catholics of St. Louis to avoid situations where a spark could set off an explosion. He stated:

> Beloved Brethren: In the present disturbed state of the public mind, we feel it is our duty to recommend to you to avoid all occasions of public excitement, to obey the laws, to respect the rights of all citizens, to keep away as much as possible from all assemblages where the indiscretion of a word, or the impetuosity of the momentary passion might endanger the public tranquility. Obey the injunction of the Apostle Peter: "Follow peace with all men."[3]

Pro-Confederate officer Lieutenant St. George Croghan confronted Lieutenant Sweeny with the warning that the Minute Men would try to take the arsenal. Sweeny said to Croghan: "I'll blow it to hell first, and you know I'm the man to do it." [4]

In early February, Captain Nathaniel Lyon, an unconditional Union man, brought his company of regulars in from the West. By that time, six gulf states had followed South Carolina out of the Union. On February 19, the newly elected president of the Confederacy, Jefferson Davis, gave his inaugural address. Lyon moved federal supplies to a safer place across the river.

In April 1861, with the election of Daniel G. Taylor as mayor of St. Louis, Governor Clairborne Jackson approved the police board. In turn, that body elected James McDonough chief of police. While so many noted Irish in St. Louis were either merchants or clergymen, James McDonough had pursued a career that would challenge many Irish after him. A man of powerful physique and commanding voice, he had come to the city in 1839 and took work as a city guard. He held this post under Mayors Bernard Pratte and Peter G. Camden. He retired in 1846 and started a detective agency. Named county treasurer in 1856, he drafted an authorization bill for the police force and helped to organize it. In 1861, he took control of a tense city.

Hardly had Chief McDonough gotten his new task in hand when the Confederate President Jefferson Davis ordered General Gustav Beauregard to fire on the flag at Fort Sumter in Charleston Harbor. President Lincoln called for four thousand volunteers from Missouri to defend the Union. In May, General Daniel Morgan Frost called the nine hundred militiamen for their annual encampment, held in Lindell Grove at the western limits of St. Louis. Three hundred Minute Men joined them. Streets in the encampment bore the

*James McDonough, a man of fine presence and superb tenor voice, was chosen chief of police in St. Louis at the outset of the Civil War and served in the more friendly years after the conflict.*

names of Jefferson Davis and General Beauregard. A few individuals wore Confederate insignia. Further, the encampment had received supplies stolen from the federal arsenal at Baton Rouge, Louisiana.

A historical evaluation of the pros and cons of the succeeding events belongs to the pages of state histories or political analyses, not to a history of the Irish in St. Louis. What pertains is this: Captain Nathanial Lyon mustered four thousand Union volunteers and surrounded the encampment on May 10. He forced Frost to surrender to the overwhelming numbers of federals. A perusal of lists of Lyon's men shows an overwhelming number of German names with a few Slavic, Anglo-American, and very few Irish names, among them Alex Hart, Thomas Garner, and Phil Carrol.

Lyon moved the captured militia north to Olive Street and down through crowds of relatives and friends of the militia men back toward the arsenal. Someone fired a shot that killed one of Lyon's officers, a Pole, Captain Constantin Blankowski. The Germans fired back. The majority of those killed had Anglo-American names, and six were clearly Irish: three children, John English, Rebecca Ann McAuliffe, and James McDonald; and three adults, Francis Whelan, a quarryman, Thomas Ahearn, a tinman, and Benjamin J. Dunn, a carpenter.[7] Father David Lillis, pastor of St. Bridget's, the nearest church to the scene, came quickly to provide the last sacraments to wounded and dying Catholics and offered spiritual consolation to others.

The Camp Jackson affair left a tense atmosphere, much like that after a tornado warning. Police Chief McDonough asked for regular troops to help keep peace in the city, as fights broke out between pro-North and pro-South militants. On May 16, Archbishop Kenrick published an appeal to the Catholics of the city in the daily paper. He called for a spirit of brotherhood, a rejection of vindictiveness, and a recognition that unauthorized killing was murder.[8]

German immigrants on the southside and in Baden on the northside answered Lincoln's call for volunteers. The Second, Third, and Fourth Missouri Infantry Regiments were almost entirely German. The First Missouri under Colonel Frank P. Blair was the only regiment of the four not predominantly German. Forty-four percent were Anglo-Americans and 8 percent Irish. Most of these Irish served in Company K, under Captain Patrick E. Burke or Company I, under Captain Madison Miller and First Lieutenant David Murphy.

David Murphy had taught school in Union, Missouri, until the firing on Fort Sumter. A day later he cancelled classes and packed his gear. Since Governor Clairborne Jackson of Missouri refused to heed Lincoln's call for volunteers, Murphy headed for Illinois to fight for the Union. On his way, he met former Congressman Francis Blair in St. Louis. Blair then was organizing the First Regiment of Missouri Volunteers to defend the Union. Blair urged him to return to his area, gather similarly inclined Union men in that otherwise secessionist section, and join the First Regiment. Murphy and his recruits had to face up to Captain John A. Kelly and the taunts of other secessionists who threatened to block the passage of their railroad train at Gray Summit.

An Irishman, Colonel John McNeil, who had come from Nova Scotia in 1840 and served in the state legislature, led the Third Regiment, U.S. Reserve Corps, although few serving under him were Irish or Scotch-Irish. One of those few, William Knox Patrick, son of James Patrick, a previously mentioned businessman of St. Louis, served with Company K of the Third and rose to the rank of major. Seventy-five percent of its 1,028 men were Germans with 20 percent Anglo-Americans and 5 percent of other nationalities. They had taken part in surrounding Camp Jackson and won a small engagement at Fulton, Missouri, in July before their ninety-day enlistments expired.

Secessionists began to speak of the German volunteers who had surrounded Camp Jackson as "Hessians," the name of the soldiers King George III hired to win back or kill his former American subjects. Alerted to the potential danger of this situation, General William Harney asked the War Department for a special appeal from President Lincoln to the St. Louis Irish. No call came from the White House, but the federal authorities in St. Louis renewed efforts to enlist Irish St. Louisans.

Captain Morgan L. Smith, a Mississippi River boatman from upstate New York who had recently located in St. Louis, accepted the challenge by organizing a Union regiment out of his fellow rivermen and dockhands. He enlisted six hundred men, chiefly Irish immigrants, for the Eighth Missouri Infantry. The regiment wore colorful uniforms, similar to those of the French Zouaves. The apparel was suitable for parades on Lafayette Avenue and less

*Morgan Smith organized the Missouri Eighth Union Regiment, the "Irish Zouaves," from his crew of Irish workers on the riverfront when the war department called for Irish volunteers in the summer of 1861. Smith rose to the rank of general during the conflict.*

appropriate for chasing "Rebs" out of Missouri.

Captain Smith sent word of his effort to his brother Giles, a hotel manager in Bloomington, Illinois. Since Northern Illinois units had filled rapidly, while Missouri units still had openings, Giles Smith came to St. Louis with recruits from Bloomington, Pekin, and Peoria. The men of the Eighth drilled in Lafayette Park. Then they fought guerillas along the North Missouri Railroad. A few more Missourians joined later when they moved south under Grant's command toward Cape Girardeau, Missouri.

Other Irish St. Louisans served the Union in various ways. Dan Dillon, born in St. Louis of Irish parentage, went to CBC and shortly before graduation joined Company A of the Thirteenth Missouri Infantry. He fought at Vicksburg, marched to the sea with Sherman, and was mustered out as captain. Thomas Lee Carnahan rose to the rank of major in the Second Brigade, Third Division, Twenty-First Army Corps of the Army of the Tennessee. Pat Gorman, born in Kilkenny and educated at St. Vincent's College in Cape Girardeau, worked for his uncles, Julius and Edward Walsh, in various enterprises. He served as president of the old Union Fire Company, of the Hibernian Society, and other organizations. He was killed while in command of his vessel, *Henry Von Phul*, during the Civil War.

Captain Henry J. Moore built boats, among them the famous *Sultana*, which went down in a storm north of Memphis at the end of the war. The boat carried several thousand released prisoners, weakened and ill from their long imprisonment at Andersonville, Georgia. Political pressures to get them home once the war ended led to the overloading of the vessel and resulted in one of the greatest maritime disasters of all times when the boiler exploded during a driving, cold rain. Two thousand veterans drowned.

John Coleman was first lieutenant of Company H of the Fifth Missouri Infantry that numbered many Irishmen in an otherwise heavily German (655) regiment. Many of the Irish later transferred to the Seventh Regiment. Among the officers of the Seventh Missouri Infantry under Colonel John D. Stevenson were Lieutenant Colonel Thomas Curley, Captain James Sullivan, and Lieutenants James Coffee, Frank O'Mara, Dan McBride, and William B. Collins. The great number of Irish officers in the Seventh suggests that many of the rank and file were Celts as well.

# St. Louis Irish in Blue and Gray

The Confederate victory at Wilson's Creek near Springfield, in southwest Missouri, on August 10, 1861, and the capture of Colonel James Mulligan's three thousand Chicago Irish at Lexington on the Missouri River by General Sterling Price shook the supporters of the Union in St. Louis. Uncertain in his actions and severely criticized for his failure to aid Mulligan, the Union Commander in St. Louis, General John C. Fremont, declared martial law. He put Provost-Marshall Justus McKinstry in charge of the city. In October, Police Chief McDonough submitted his resignation.

Federal troops garrisoned six forts just inside the western limits of the city, generally along Jefferson Avenue. The city came to rival a police state with continual surveillance, impeded travel, excessive fines imposed on those suspected of Confederate sympathy, and forced removal of individuals to other areas. The federal authorities sent several women into exile in Mississippi. General Frost's wife took her family to Canada.

When the outbreak of the war threatened the work of the Sisters of St. Joseph in Mississippi, the Mother Superior recalled the nuns to St. Louis. They had trouble getting through the Union lines. "We were looked upon as spies . . . ," Sister Mary Louise Lynch recalled. "Soldiers in uniform came hurriedly through the car, opened our trunks and our baggage, and even examined our lunch basket."[1]

The tensions that prevailed in the city did not stop at the convent walls. The Academy of the Sisters of St. Joseph in

Carondelet numbered Northern and Southern sympathizers among the students. Irish-born Sister Winifrid Sullivan gained deserved praise for her deft handling of the situation.[2]

All the while, the Missouri militiamen, captured at Camp Jackson and paroled, slipped through the Union lines and going South. Captain Emmet McDonald declined parole and won his case in court. He then joined his fellow militiamen. Father Bannon followed, leaving a letter for the archbishop that Kenrick never opened. The Union command exchanged General Frost for Colonel Mulligan. Frost, too, left for southwestern Missouri. Frost and Bannon joined many Irish Catholics who served with the First Missouri Confederate Brigade under General Sterling Price, former state governor.

Father Bannon estimated that a thousand Catholics belonged to General Price's command. The vast majority of them were Irish. The few notable exceptions included the two young men who had gone south with Father Bannon, Bauduy Garesche, of French ancestry, and Robert Bakewell, an Anglo-American; General Daniel M. Frost; and two graduates of Saint Louis University, battery commander Captain Henry Guibor, of Alsatian ancestry, and Captain Samuel Churchill Clark, a teenaged grandson of the explorer and general William Clark.

*Father John B. Bannon was pastor of St. John's Church, chaplain of the militia captured at Camp Jackson, unofficial chaplain of the First Missouri Confederate Brigade, special agent of the Confederacy in Ireland (1863–64), and leading Irish pulpit orator of the 1880s.*

Scattered throughout the First Missouri Brigade, Catholics did not form a majority in any one regiment. By the time Father Bannon arrived, all regiments had elected chaplains. Since the Confederate High Command authorized no brigade chaplains, Father Bannon retained his civilian status as "unofficial" chaplain to be available to all soldiers of the First Brigade. He was granted a special commission a year later, retroactive to February 1, 1862.

Father Bannon was the only chaplain in either army to give up a major city parish to serve the men in the field. He was one of the few full-time diocesan priests in either army. Most of the chaplains were members of religious orders. The majority were Holy Cross Fathers from Notre Dame University or Jesuits from Louisiana in the South or New York and New England in the North.

The best known Confederate officers among the St. Louis Irish were Colonel Joseph Kelly, Lieutenant Colonel John Kelly, and Captains Joseph Boyce, Patrick Canniff, and the previously mentioned Emmet McDonald. Captain Boyce would recall many years later: "Most of the captured [at Camp Jackson] entered the Confederate service."[3] The above-mentioned Kelly joined the Confederate forces in Carondelet, fought in Southeast Missouri, and fought with General Henry Little in northern Mississippi until Little was killed. Captured at Smithville, North Carolina, Lieutenant Colonel Kelly remained in prison for thirteen months and endured severe punishment.

The quartermaster of the First Missouri Confederate Brigade, Albert C. Danner, stated: "There came South with General Sterling Price's army from Missouri, a company of infantry, also a fine battery, fully equipped, of Irishmen,

*The gun-boat St. Louis, built by James B. Eads in Carondelet, led Grant's attack on Fort Henry in Tennessee and ran into heavy fire from the Confederate artillerymen from St. Louis under Captains Wade and Guilbor in defense of Vicksburg.*

fine fighters, and all members of the Catholic Church. Accompanying them from St. Louis, as their chaplain, was a young priest, Father John Bannon. Father Bannon was brave, courageous, energetic, and liked by all in the Missouri army, Protestants as well as Catholics."[4]

Dr. Joseph McDowell and the entire staff of the McDowell Missouri Medical College at Eighth and Gratiot Streets left to serve with the Confederate Medical Corps. The federal authorities turned McDowell's college into a prison for Confederate officers. Regularly wives and sweethearts of the imprisoned men, arrayed in bright red dresses, picketed the Gratiot Street Prison, as it came to be called.

Looking back from the vantage of a century and a half, one might well ask how so many Irish in good faith could fight in the interests of disunion and slavery. The answer is simple: the issues were not clear-cut. Their spiritiual leader, Archbishop Peter Richard Kenrick, who towered over the Church in the Midwest, had condemned wanton killing in the city immediately after the attack on Camp Jackson, but he made no pronouncement on the issues between the states. Even Pope Pius IX, who wrote the archbishops of New York and of New Orleans, urging them to work for peace, hesitated to pronounce on the causes of the war. Lending strength to this position, the issues in the struggle were as uncertain as March weather. President Lincoln said that he fought the war to save the Union and would deal with slavery only in relation to that overriding issue. When General John Fremont issued an emancipation proclamation as a war measure in Missouri in August 1861, the president revoked it the next day.

Many people in the Southern states, the Old Northwest, and border states looked on the struggle as a matter of states' rights. If the states freely came in, they could freely leave. It was not until after the conflict, incidentally, that the Supreme Court ruled that the Constitution looked to an indestructible Union of indestructible states.

In recent times, as the issue of racism has taken central stage in public consciousness, many social observers simplify the struggle as over slavery. Slavery made the states of the Deep South stand together. It was a significant issue, but not the sole concern. Many historians see the war as a struggle for economic domination of the sections. To support this position, they point out that the Republicans in Congress would forget the blacks, once they had pushed through their "Big Business" agenda. Irishmen, like General Patrick Cleburne of the First Arkansas Regiment and Father Bannon, looked on the South as an agricultural nation seeking freedom from the materialistic Northeast, as Ireland was seeking freedom from England.

Several well-known members of Frost's command at Camp Jackson joined the Union Army. J. K. Cummings, who had come from Coleraine in County Derry in 1854 and had taken part in the Southwest expedition in the fall of

1860, broke with Frost and joined the Seventh Regiment Union volunteers. He rose to the rank of Lieutenant Colonel.

When someone raised a separatist flag at the encampment, Dr. Florence Cornyn, head of the City Hospital and reserve surgeon for the state guard, also resigned. He became surgeon of the First Mission Union Regiment under Colonel Francis Preston Blair. The carnage at Shiloh so appalled him that he made a strange decision. Believing that the war had to end as soon as possible, he organized the Tenth Missouri Union cavalry unit to strive for that goal. Unjustly accused of misconduct by a fellow officer a year later, he won his case before the military court in Tennessee. His overwrought adversary pulled a pistol in the courtroom and shot him. Friends brought his body back to St. Louis. His military funeral at St. Francis Xavier drew the largest congregation in St. Louis history up to that time.

Other notable Irish physicians served the Union, among them Dr. Charles H. J. Hughes, a native of St. Louis of Tipperary ancestry, who graduated from St. Louis Medical College in 1859. He joined the first Missouri Union Volunteers as a surgeon in 1862 and served at many hospitals in the region. Under the tutelage of his brother, Dr. Thomas O'Reilly, Patrick Sarsfield O'Reilly had attended Saint Louis University and studied medicine in Dublin and London. He volunteered as a foot soldier at the outbreak of the war. Since the Union forces needed physicians, he soon headed a medical department. He suffered a leg wound in battle.

Even before the First Battle of Bull Run, soldiers had come to the Daughters of Charity Hospital with dysentery, typhoid, and other fevers. The government paid the Daughters of Charity $2.50 a week per patient. Catholic

*Dr. Thomas O'Reilly combined medical practice with a wide interest in the development of the city. Legend has it that he suggested to his friend Henry Shaw the gift of Tower Grove Park to the people of St. Louis.*

nuns were the only trained nurses in the country at the start of the Civil War. In puritanical America, no woman cared for the sick outside her own family.

On December 22, 1861, thirty-six railroad cars brought thirteen hundred Confederate prisoners to what had been Lynch's Slave Pen at Myrtle and Broadway. Three Daughters of Charity nursed the sick and wounded among them. Federal authorities soon closed that miserable place and sent the prisoners to the Gratiot Street Prison. When transports began to bring the casualties from the mutual massacre at Shiloh in southern Tennessee in 1862, Daughters of Charity served on the transports that brought survivors to St. Louis. General Fremont asked them to care for the wounded at the St. Louis Military Hospital, formerly the House of Refuge for Wayward Boys.

Father Patrick Ryan, the pastor of Annunciation parish in the area, worked closely with the sisters. Eventually they instructed and baptized more than five hundred patients. Offered the position of paid chaplain with the Union forces by General Francis Blair, Father Ryan declined so that he could continue to minister with equal zeal to Union wounded and Confederate prisoners at the Gratiot Street Prison.

During those sad days, the Sisters of Mercy shared with the Daughters of Charity a concern for unfortunates in both Blue and Gray. They visited wounded soldiers at the Good Samaritan Hospital and the Confederate officers at the Gratiot Street Prison. On one occasion, the sisters brought along two children to see their fathers in prison.

All the while in the camp of the First Missouri Confederates, Father Bannon preached to a growing congregation of Irish. He matched stride with his infantrymen at the Battles of Pea Ridge in Arkansas and Corinth in Mississippi, where the Confederates had concentrated after the Battle of Shiloh. Captured with the fifteen thousand survivors of the siege of Vicksburg and paroled, he went to Richmond to report to Bishop John McGill.

*The Missouri Monument at Vicksburg stands as a sign of contradiction. St. Louisan fought against St. Louisan. John O'Dea was one of ten members of Missouri's Irish Eighth Infantry Regiment who won the Congressional Medal of Honor for the assault on the ridge near where this monument stands.*

Confederate President Jefferson Davis asked him to run the blockade and go to Ireland to explain the cause of the Confederacy, which he did effectively.

Facing the Irish in the First Missouri Confederate Brigade during that long siege of Vicksburg, ten Irish in the Eighth Missouri Union Regiment won the Congressional Medal of Honor. Among them were James Cunningham and John O'Dea of Limerick.[5] The Eighth already had fought at Fort Donelson, Shiloh, and Corinth and went on to take part in all of the battles in Tennessee and Georgia and the march with Sherman to the sea. Moving north, they were in at the surrender of Joseph E. Johnston's Confederate forces in North Carolina. After Lee's surrender, they paraded in the Grand Review in Washington.

In spite of this memorable record, they never received the recognition that went to the St. Louis Germans who "fought mit Sigel" or the Irish gunners who served with Henry Guibor's Confederate battery. A historical sketch of the Union cause in St. Louis, published while many veterans of the Eighth still lived, totally ignored them.[6]

During the last year of the Civil War and the first postwar year, as many as twenty thousand St. Louisans got their news from the *Daily Press*, a paper owned and operated by its printers and other trade unionists.[7] The paper spearheaded the development of a labor party that won more than 35 percent of the votes in the 1864 mayoral elections. At that time, St. Louis was the third largest manufacturing city in the country. Iron molding, wire and machine tool production, metalworking, needle trades, shipping, boots and shoes, and sugar refining were leading industries. Most of the workers in St. Louis were Irish or German. German workers tended to dominate the most skilled positions in manufacturing. The Irish moved strongly into the building trades. A few years later Karl Marx told two American socialist organizers "a coalition of the German workers with the Irish . . . is the most important job you could start at this time."[8]

While most of the early leaders at the *Daily Press* were Anglo-Americans, Nat Griffin and Tom Fleming had their part in its founding. The paper obviously sought support in the Irish community by continued and positive coverage of the Fenians, a revolutionary group discussed at length in the next chapter.

# Reunited St. Louis Irish

After the fall of the Confederacy, many veterans came back to St. Louis. Men in Blue came first. Dr. Patrick Sarsfield O'Reilly returned to St. Louis and became Coroner in 1865. He opposed the "Radical Republicans" and supported the Fenians, two groups that will surface later in this chapter. Dr. O'Reilly became vice president of the newly forming Missouri Historical Society and of the Knights of St. Patrick.

Captain Dan Dillon attended St. Louis Law School, was admitted to the bar in 1868, and was elected Judge of the Circuit Court. Major Thomas Lee Carnahan took a position with the Plano Manufacturing Company, a firm that made agricultural implements, and managed the concern for seventeen years. All the while, he took an active part in the activities of the Frank Blair Post of the Grand Army of the Republic. Major William Knox Patrick won the race for the post of Alderman of the Eleventh Ward in 1869, and worked for better streets during his four-year term.

As tensions in the city lessened, General Sterling Price, leader of the Missouri Confederates, moved to St. Louis, where he died a short time later. Most of the Irish who had worn gray resisted the call to Mexico that many Confederates heard and found their way back to the city. Captain Joseph Boyce was one. When Union veterans of Germanic ancestry sought donations to erect a statue to General Franz Sigel in Forest Park a few years later, Captain Boyce responded with a donation.[1] Father John B. Bannon remained in Ireland, where he had gone to plead the

Confederate cause. He joined the Jesuits and became Ireland's greatest preacher in the1880s. He still rated among St. Louis's fifty most influential citizens at that time.

Dublin-born Lieutenant Colonel John Kelly, a veteran of Camp Jackson, returned from a federal prison to St. Louis after the war and worked on the Iron Mountain Railroad. In 1879 he succumbed to mining fever and went to the Rocky Mountains. He invested in the Mary Murphy Mine and later managed the operation. He remained in Colorado six years and even represented Chaffee County in the state legislature. When he returned to St. Louis, he refused regular invitations to run for office.

Other veterans chose to move to St. Louis after the conflict. Among those who fought on the Southern side were a Virginia planter, John Boland of the Army of Northern Virginia, and William E. Hughes of the First Texas Artillery. Victorious Union veterans came too, among them Dr. Alexander Mullen of the 35th Indiana, who had served on the staff of General William Rosecrans, and Owen Cowan, who had marched to the sea with the 90th Illinois Volunteers under Sherman. Cowan joined the Christian Brothers, taught in St. Louis, and eventually became head of the congregation. James Connolly of Dublin served on the gunboat *Denton* during the Civil War. He came to St. Louis in 1868 and became general superintendent of the Missouri Car and Foundry Company.

Richard Kerens, of County Meath, Ireland, served in the Civil War with the Transportation Department of the Army in the East, then in southwest Missouri and northwest Arkansas. There, he engaged in the transportation of mails, express, and passengers by stagecoaches to points on the frontier beyond the advance of the railroads. After the war, he prospered in mining and railroading, served on the central committee of the Republican Party, and became Ambassador to the Austro-Hungarian Empire.

Back in 1861, when Illinois units filled rapidly, eighteen-year-old James E. Flynn came from Pittsfield, Illinois, to St. Louis to join the Sixth Missouri Union Regiment. At Vicksburg, he volunteered for special duty that brought death to 85 percent of the participants. His bravery brought him the Medal of Honor.[2] After the conflict, he resided in St. Louis into the next century. After his death, on January 1, 1913, he was buried in Calvary Cemetery.[3]

Another Medal of Honor recipient, Lieutenant Henry D. O'Brien of St. Anthony Falls, was among the few members of the First Minnesota to survive the battle of Gettysburg. Wounded the following year at St. Petersburg, he returned to his native town and served as postmaster until he became government pension agent in St. Louis, where he lived the rest of his life.[4]

John O'Neil, who had been colonel of the Third Missouri Regiment at the outbreak of hostilities, headed the Second Missouri Union Cavalry with the rank of Brigadier General in November 1862. On different occasions, he faced General John S. Marmaduke in southeast Missouri and General Joe Shelby in the southwestern corner of the state. But for most of the conflict, he chased guerillas and bushwackers in north-central Missouri. Neither side observed the standard rules of war. O'Neil reacted drastically at times, with arbitrary executions. In spite of this and his hesitancy to attack in the Battle of Westport in 1864, he won the honorary title of Major General before the end of the War. He returned to St. Louis and served twice as clerk of the criminal court of St. Louis County and as county sheriff. He held a series of Federal offices, including superintendent of the St. Louis branch post office.

One older newcomer had served in the Mexican War. James L. D. Morrison, a native of Kaskaskia, whose mother, Eliza Lowrey, was one of St. Louis's first residents, had served in the U.S. Congress and ran unsuccessfully for Governor of Illinois as a Democrat in the election of 1860. Then he moved to St. Louis. Some time after the death of his first wife, he married Adelaide Sarpy, a member of a prominent St. Louis family who gained recognition for her acts of concern for others.

Before the end of the war, President Lincoln had called upon all to bind up the nation's wounds, but a group of "Radical Republicans," led by lawyer Charles Drake caused the wounds to fester. They passed a law that required all teachers, lawyers, and clergymen to swear that they had not aided the Confederacy in almost one hundred specific ways. Archbishop Kenrick told his priests to refuse the oath and promised his support. State authorities arrested no priests in St. Louis.

But Father John Cummings of Louisiana, Missouri, who had served earlier in St. Louis, refused to take the oath and was tried and convicted. No outstate supporters came to Father Cummings's assistance. But Archbishop Kenrick and Major General Frank Blair gave him strong support. The details of the case in the Missouri courts and in the Supreme Court, fascinating as they are in themselves, are beyond the scope of this book. Father Cummings won a five to four decision. The case became a landmark in American civil liberties. Justices Fred Vinson and Byron White cited it in the post–World War II period. Father Cummings died of illness in St. Louis a short time after the trial and remains an anonymous hero in American legal history.[5]

While Drake provoked external problems, the Irish community faced an internal problem: the Fenian Movement. "While most Irish-American nationalist plans had a fantasy-land quality," Professor Leo McCaffrey wrote, "Fenianism was something more; it was a tough, hard-nosed commitment to revolution."[6] The Fenians preserved maximum secrecy and security by organizing into "circles" commanded by a "Centre." Each circle had smaller cells. Recruits took oaths of secrecy, obedience to officers, and loyalty to the Irish republic. They planned to launch an attack on Canada from American soil.

The Brotherhood was strong in St. Louis. Doran Killian, who before the war had edited the Catholic paper, *The Western Banner*, strongly advocated

Fenianism. Shortly after the conclusion of the conflict in August 1865, the highest official of the St. Louis Fenian Brotherhood, Centre Henry Clarence McCarthy, died in St. Paul. His friends made plans for his funeral at St. Patrick's Church in St. Louis.

In a letter of August 30, 1865, Archbishop Kenrick forbade the pastor of St. Patrick's Church to allow any funeral service or other religious ceremony to take place on that occasion. He further directed the superintendent of Calvary Cemetery to exclude any procession of men or women bearing the insignia of Fenianism from entering the gates.[7] As mentioned earlier, the *Daily Press* supported the Fenians. The editors carried the entire text of the oration at McCarthy's funeral and estimated the crowd at ten thousand. They printed a letter from Fenian State Centre that challenged the archbishop's position. The letter brought several resignations, among them of long-time *Daily Press* staff member J. L. Clements. In reality, the Centre's main message was that Fenians were good Catholics.[8]

Since the printers and other trade unionists owned and edited the *Daily Press*, it could have had great influence among the Irish workers in St. Louis. However, the left-leaning editors looked upon the labor movement as a vehicle "to free Irishmen from the Church's dominance."[9] They totally misread the mind of the average American Irish worker. He had few complaints about Church dominance, but he might readily grumble in the decades ahead that the archbishop refused to support organized labor when the majority of union workers were Catholic. Many factors—the paper's radicalism, ethnic rivalries, anti-union attitudes of many powerfully placed people, and the status of the recently freed black worker—forced the paper to cease publication shortly after the war. That was unfortunate, because it had served a needed purpose.

In spite of the sectional hostility that found Irish Catholics fighting on both sides, the St. Louis Irish community "got its second wind," and moved ahead. Archbishop Kenrick consecrated as bishops two former presidents of the Seminary in Carondelet: Father Patrick Feehan, a native of County Tipperary, as bishop of Nashville, Tennessee, on July 7, 1865, and Father John Hennessy, born in County Limerick, as bishop of Dubuque, Iowa, on September 30 of the following year. Father Feehan, as pastor of St. Michael's, had looked to the spiritual welfare of Union soldiers stationed in St. Louis. Now he shepherded ex-Confederates. Father John Hennessy had attended All Hallows' College, Dublin, and came to St. Louis in 1847. After a term as Seminary Rector, he served as pastor in northern Missouri until his consecration as bishop.

A significant event in the history of the Church, the Plenary Council of Baltimore, took place in 1866. The coming together of bishops for a peaceful discussion of the needs of the Church so soon after the conflict amazed many. The Catholic Church throughout America reflected Lincoln's spirit of "binding up the nation's wounds," as the Irish in St. Louis had done in those postwar years. Father Patrick Ryan of St. Louis gave a brilliant sermon at the Plenary Council, which alerted the American bishops to his superior talents.

Back home in St. Louis, German Catholics planned a torchlight procession for November 30, 1866, the 25th anniversary of the archbishop's episcopal consecration. Kenrick looked on torchlight processions as belonging to the political arena. But the people had gone to great expense in preparation, so he accepted their regard. Two years later, Kenrick visited Ireland and Rome. When he returned, a procession three miles long welcomed him.

A long-time observer of the local scene, former Mayor John Darby, wrote in amazement: "When the venerable and distinguished archbishop returned from a visit to Europe . . . he received (unsought for) from the good people of the city of St. Louis a spontaneous and welcome reception, such as had never been awarded to any private individual in an unofficial government position in the country."[10]

# Irish Carry On in a Changed Community

B efore the Civil War, St. Louis had been an Anglo-American, French, and Irish community. A few French had come from the West Indies during the first half of the century, but almost none from France itself. While few English came, Germans had been arriving in great numbers, and by the Census of 1870 they were numerically the largest immigrant group, with 59,040 living in St. Louis. Irish-born St. Louisans numbered 32,239.[1] Those individuals identifying themselves as Irish were now almost entirely Catholic, since, after the Know-Nothing riots, the Protestant Irish coalesced with the Anglo-American community.

The St. Louis Irish had been immediately involved in many significant institutions of pre–Civil War St. Louis—the St. Louis Cathedral, the City Hospital, and the schools Saint Louis University, Sacred Heart Academy, Visitation, and Christian Brothers' College. After the Civil War, many institutions grew up beyond the Irish perview: Washington University at Seventeenth and Washington, Smith Academy for boys, Mary Institute for girls, and the O'Fallon Technical Institute. St. Luke's Hospital opened at Tenth and St. Charles, and four churches of significance grew: the Episcopal Christ Church Cathedral at Thirteenth and Locust Streets, Centenary Methodist on Sixteenth Street at Pine, First Presbyterian on the northwest corner of Fourteenth and Locust Streets, and the Church of the Messiah on Garrison Avenue at Locust. Henry Shaw gave to St. Louisans the Missouri Botanical Garden and the city's first large park, Tower Grove, adjacent to the garden. One Irishman allegedly had a part in this last venture. Dr. Thomas O'Reilly, Shaw's friend and personal physician, reportedly suggested that he donate the park area to the city.[2]

The Anglo-Americans, abetted by the prosperous Protestant Irish, dominated the scene economically and politically. The citizens elected only one Irish Catholic, Edward Noonan, and one German, Henry Obverstolz, to the office of mayor in the last half of the century. However, the Germans made steady advances in music, science, and philosophy. They joined with Anglo-American thinkers in the St. Louis Movement in philosophy that concentrated on Kant and Hegel. Saint Louis University philosophers, led by Walter Hill, a Kentuckian who wrote philosophical textbooks widely used in Catholic circles, favored the medieval philosophers over those of modern Germany.

When Chancellor Otto Von Bismarck united the German states under Prussia in 1870, the Free-Thinkers rejoiced that unity had come to Germany. German Catholics had only misgivings about the autocratic policies of the "Iron Chancellor." Bismarck set out to mold all German people according to a Prussian Protestant pattern. Many fled from oppression. Hundreds came to St. Louis from the diocese of Paderborn in Westphalia, the home province of most Catholic Germans in the Missouri metropolis. The Catholics now outnumbered each of the other three German groups: Lutherans, Evangelicals, and Free-Thinkers.

Prewar Irish had dealt successfully with French and Anglo-Americans. The postwar Celts had to relate more closely with their fellow Catholics from Westphalia. The presence of two strong and distinct ethnic groups strengthened religion in St. Louis in a way unknown in eastern seaboard cities, where the attitudes of one nationality dominated. Both groups had good leadership. The leading German pastors, like Francis Goller and William Faerber, were scholarly men who wrote regularly for priestly journals of national circulation in German. The better-known Irish pastors, like James Henry and William Walsh, were locally significant public figures. Two Irish priests became widely known in the ensuing years: Patrick Ryan for his oratory and David Phelan for unique editing.

The St. Louis archdiocese always had one vicar for the English-speaking parishes and one for the German. The Thornton legacy, a gift of an Irish immigrant, helped Irish, German, and other congregations. They celebrated their Catholic faith together in other ways and on various occasions. When thousands of St. Louis Catholics gathered to witness the laying of the cornerstone of St. Francis de Sales Church in South St. Louis in September 1867, the Hibernians, the United Sons of Erin, and members of St. Bridget's Total Abstinence Society and the Shamrock Society, marched from St. Lawrence O'Toole's Church on the near northside to Lafayette Park. Adorned with badges, banners, and flags, these Irish joined with their fellow

Catholics of German ancestry and paraded up Gravois to the site of the new church, destined shortly to be the central German Catholic parish in the city.[3] The Germans and Irish filled the pews at the dedication of Sts. Peter and Paul Church, another German parish, twenty years later. Bishop Patrick Ryan held a place of honor. Bishop Michael Heiss of Milwaukee offered the Pontifical Mass. Bishop Edward Fitzgerald of Little Rock preached in English, and Bishop Francis Xavier Krautbauer preached in German. Irish and Germans adored in the beautiful Gothic church built by German immigrants with great devotion and little wealth.

The average Irish pastor thought of his parish as receptive of other nationalities, yet history shows that the later-arriving groups, such as the Bohemians and the Italians, used the German parish buildings until able to build their own. Many German pastors had been educated in Rome and were facile with a number of languages. Belgian-born priests had established even wider rapport with immigrant groups as well as with English-speaking Catholics.

Since he spoke English, an Irishman could get off the steamboat at the levee and consider himself an American the next day. On one occasion, recent arrivals from Cork complained to Archbishop Kenrick that their assistant pastor, Father Charles Ziegler, was a "foreigner." As a matter of fact, he was one of only two American-born priests in the area. A native of Ste. Genevieve, he spoke English with a Kentucky twang.

Many newcoming Irish tended to call the southside Germans "Dutch." Was it because they identified the Germans with the real Hollanders who had come with their king, William of Orange, and defeated King James II and his Irish allies at the Battle of the Boyne? Or was it because the Germans called themselves Deutsch? Industrious Germans, in turn, sometimes questioned the capacity of the Irish to stay on the job and get it done.

Only one incident of unpleasantness occurred between a German priest and Irish members of his congregation. When Napoleon III, Emperor of the French, declared war on Prussia in 1870, Father Peter Wigger at Holy Cross Parish in Baden asked prayers for the success of the Prussian Army. In response to this questionable request, a group of Irish, led by parishioner Edward Dowling, rose and left the church. When they complained to Archbishop Kenrick, he decided to start a new parish nearby, Our Lady of Mount Carmel, and summoned Father David Phelan of Edina in northeastern Missouri to be pastor.

Father Phelan, a Nova Scotian by birth and of Irish ancestry, had shown his skill as a writer by defending nuns against bigots in his weekly, the *Edina Watchman*. He brought his sharp pen and acute intelligence to the metropolitan area, changed the title of his paper to the *Western Watchman*, and assumed the responsibility of defending the people. Father Phelan made his newspaper available to all in the St. Louis area. It was his personal press. His brother Michael a state legislator, assisted him as business manager.

A well educated and widely read man, Phelan knew several languages, among them German. As time went on, Father Phelan saw himself as defender of the people, not only against bigots, but also against arbitrary bishops.[3] As a result of some of these writings, Bishop Baltes of Alton published a pamphlet a few years later condemning Phelan for attempting to weaken and undermine the authority of certain bishops by criticizing their public policies. Phelan relished opposition and continued to write in the hope of keeping bishops from unwise policies. He objected to parochial schools when they trained young people to be ethnic Catholics, rather than to be simply Catholics.[4]

Father Francis M. Kielty, a popular priest and able writer born in Ireland— and pastor of Holy Angels Church on the near southside—went beyond Father Phelan's position. He opposed the development of a separate parochial school system. In this he took the view of Bishop Ireland of St. Paul and a nationally prominent New York clergyman, Father Edward McGlynn.

*No Catholic editor before or after Father David Phelan, publisher of the* Western Watchman, *matched his distinctive editorial policies. Archbishop Kenrick recognized his verve in fighting bigotry in outstate Missouri and offered him an urban parish, Mt. Carmel in Baden.*

# Women of Distinction in Post–Civil War St. Louis

**M**ary Felicite Christy was the daughter of Samuel C. Christy, of Scotch-Irish background, and Melanie Jarrot, the daughter of a French merchant of Cahokia who had built the first brick residence in the St. Louis region. Mary was born in the Jarrot mansion and baptized at historic Holy Family Church nearby. She attended Visitation Academy in 1849, shortly after the school had moved to St. Louis from its original location in Kaskaskia.

In 1858 she married a Southerner, Lieutenant John R. Church, a recent graduate of West Point. The two lived at Fort Washita in Indian Territory until the Civil War broke out. Whereupon, Church resigned his commission in the U.S. Army and became a colonel of Confederate volunteers. In the second year of the war, he met death in battle. In spite of the difficulties of travel between hostile lines, Mrs. Church brought her two infant sons back to the ancestral estate in St. Louis.

She rejoined the Sodality of Our Lady at Visitation in 1864 and became president in 1865. She continued membership for many years. During this time, the school moved from Cass Avenue, east of Jefferson, to a large property on Cabanne Place west of Union. After the war she participated in many charitable activities, especially in helping distressed people of the South. She took part in a drive to pay the debt on one of the city's most beautiful churches, the Annunciation at Sixth and Chestnut Streets. One of the organizers of the Daughters of the Confederacy, she remained a staunch member.

After seven years of widowhood, she married James J. Scanlan of Philadelphia, who had engaged successfully in business in St. Louis. They had five children. She lived with her family for five years in Europe then returned to St. Louis and resumed leadership in various activities. On December 12, 1881, she hosted a group of French officers at the Scanlan mansion at Grand and Lucas. Many of the visitors were descendants of veterans of the Battle of Yorktown and had come to America to commemorate the centennial of the defeat of Cornwallis. Several years later, when President Grover Cleveland visited St. Louis, his wife was a guest at the Scanlan mansion. Still later, Mrs. Scanlan helped in the drive for the new cathedral on Lindell. The lawyer Alonzo Christy Church, a son by her first husband, served in the state legislature.

While Mary Christy Scanlan and other prominent women of St. Louis were born in the city and spent most of their lives there, Ellen Ewing Sherman, wife of the great Civil War hero General William Tecumseh Sherman resided in St. Louis only for short periods from 1850–90s. But she and the General cherished their home in the city and insisted on being buried in Calvary Cemetery.

Ellen Sherman was the daughter of Senator Thomas Ewing of Ohio, whose wife, Maria Boyle Ewing, was of Irish Catholic ancestry. The senator followed his wife into the Catholic Church. He urged William Tecumseh Sherman, a neighbor's son who lived with the Ewings, to apply at West Point in 1836. Sherman and Ellen Ewing corresponded during those cadet years.

Thomas Ewing was the first American to be a member of two presidential cabinets. President William Henry Harrison named him Secretary of the Treasury, and President Zachary Taylor asked him to serve as Secretary of the Interior. President Taylor, members of the cabinet, and the great senators of the

*On the Sherman family plot in Calvary Cemetery, Ellen Boyle Ewing Sherman, the wife of the general whose grave is on the right of this photograph, was Irish. One of their sons, Thomas, became a priest and the greatest priest-orator in 1900.*

West, Stephen Douglas of Illinois and Thomas Hart Benton of Missouri, attended Ellen Ewing's wedding on May 1, 1850, to the young army officer, "Cump" Sherman.

As hostility between North and South moved from shouting in the Senate to shooting in the South, Sherman found few others who foresaw a long and deadly struggle between the sections. He met only ridicule. When he judged that the North needed two hundred thousand men in Blue to win in the Midwest and open the Mississippi, commentators called him deranged. That he eventually proved correct brought no apologies. Only his wife Ellen kept up her great confidence in his judgment.

Sherman, too, was one of the first generals who saw that modern war was as much a matter of transport and supplies as tactics and gallantry. His destruction of property on his march through Georgia and South Carolina brought him opprobrium.

Ellen Ewing Sherman gave her husband strong support in those years of criticism. After the war, she never begrudged her husband's refusal to run for the presidency, even though it prevented her from becoming First Lady of America. When General Sherman's position in the army brought him to St. Louis as head of the Department of the West, a grateful citizenry gave the Shermans a fine home on Garrison Avenue a few blocks north of Washington.

Mrs. Sherman devoted time to charitable activities, especially with the U.S. Sanitary Commission, a body organized to give material and spiritual help to soldiers during and immediately after the Civil War. She also supported the great missionary among the Native Americans, Father Peter J. De Smet, a family friend. A historian, A. McAllister, published an account of her life in 1836.[1] *The New Catholic Encyclopedia* also carries her life story.[2]

A son, Thomas, a lawyer, became a Jesuit priest, a teacher at Saint Louis Universitiy High School, and later a famous orator. In his public addresses, he early advocated women's higher education, and he opposed Marxist Socialism long before people thought it a danger to civilization.

While Mary Christy Scanlan and Ellen Ewing Sherman stayed in the limelight of St. Louis Society, many nuns of Irish ancestry quietly achieved in education and health care. The Religious of the Sacred Heart, originally a French order, enlisted many Irish members. So did another French-based congregation, the Sisters of St. Joseph of Carondelet. Under the leadership of Mother Agatha Guthrie, a convert to the faith, the Josephites expanded widely in parochial education. By the end of the century, eighty-nine sisters taught at fourteen parishes—ten Irish, three multinational, and one German, St. Anthony's. Instead of residing in groups of only threes or fours at parishes, the sisters resided at regional convents, such as Our Lady of Good Counsel at 1849 Cass Avenue and later at a convent on Cabanne Place in St. Teresa's Parish.

Although the Daughters of Charity continued to grow in St. Louis, they boasted few members who made the headlines. All were inconspicuous heroines. Sister Genevieve Kuesenkothen, Archivist of the Province, summarized the spirit of her congregation in these words: "Stores of worldly greatness do not seem to be in our holdings."[3] Of the 268 Daughters of Charity who taught in St. Louis during the nineteenth century, thirty-seven were born in Ireland, and one hundred and fifty-nine had at least one parent with an Irish surname. Since by community custom the superiors missioned sisters in other than their hometown, only five born in St. Louis of Irish ancestry served in the city.

The Visitation Sisters, originally daughters of either Maryland Catholic planters or converts from Protestantism, gained Irish-American members at their academy on Cass Avenue. The Sparkhill Dominicans and Sisters of Charity of the Blessed Virgin Mary, predominantly Irish, opened schools. In the mid-1870s, the Carmelites sent four sisters to open a new convent in New Orleans and moved to a new location at Eighteenth and Victor. Other sisterhoods, such as the Ursulines, Franciscans, and School Sisters of Notre Dame, who developed in German environments, welcomed individual Irish novices.

When the Sisters of Mercy school reached an enrollment of 600 pupils shortly after the Civil War, the sisters built a new one. In 1871, they turned the old school into an infirmary, the forerunner of St. John's Hospital that opened on March 1, 1871. In the seventies and eighties, Mercy sisters staffed three parish schools. Sisters Veronica Fitzpatrick and Xavier Kinsella taught at St. Ann's in Normandy; Sisters Regis Fitzpatrick and Borgia Gallagher at St. Peter's in Kirkwood; and Sisters Mercy Brennan and Stanislaus Tennelly at St. Cronan's on South Boyle. Sisters Teresa Barbaroux and Euphrasia Hanker taught a predominatly Irish group of boys for a short time at the Old Cathedral School in 1878, while Sisters Michael Funnell and Bernard Dunne, invited by Father Caesar Spigardi, prepared Italian boys and girls for First Communion at Our Lady Help of Christians.

One of the most quietly influential sisterhoods in the history of St. Louis, the Sisters of Loretto at the Foot of the Cross (also known as the Lorettines), began in pioneer Kentucky in 1812 and reflected the American way of life, unencumbered by European traditions. While the young men of Kentucky agitated for war with England, three young Kentucky women of Maryland Catholic background, led by Mary Rhodes, formed a sisterhood to teach the young.

They sought the advice of their pastor, Father Charles Nerinckx, who in turn won the approval of Bishop Benedict Joseph Flaget, first bishop of the American West. Their way of life had appeal, and the congregation grew rapidly. Eleven years later, in response to a request of Bishop Du Bourg, twelve sisters opened a school among former Marylanders in southeastern Missouri.

When the Religious of the Sacred Heart decided to move from Florissant, six Lorettines, under the direction of Sister Eleanor Clarke, staffed an academy for girls. Three of the sisters were Irish, two French. In 1882 Mother Ann Joseph Mattingly planned a more substantial building for the school.

In the meantime, between 1862 and 1864, the Lorettines taught at a school in the old College Parish at Tenth and Morgan Streets. They accepted their first parochial school in St. Michael's Parish at Eleventh and Clinton on the northside in 1869. At first they taught only girls, while the Christian Brothers taught boys. A few years later, the brothers withdrew and the Sisters of Loretto taught both girls and boys. Impressed by the work of the Lorettines at St. Michael's, Father James McCabe invited them to open a school at Sacred Heart. Sisters Matilda Barrett, Joachim Houlehan, and Robert Jarboe resided at St. Michael's and commuted to Sacred Heart. In 1875, the sisters accepted an invitation to teach at the Cathedral School at Third and Walnut Streets. They remained in the downtown area until 1934, long after the New Cathedral had opened on Lindell.

Lorettines also taught in many Irish parishes; at Visitation Parish School at Taylor and Evans, St. Rose's at 5808 Etzel, St. Ann's in Normandy, St. Cronan's at 1200 South Boyle, St. Pius V on South Grand, St. Paul the Apostle in Pine Lawn, Immaculate Conception in Maplewood, and Mary Queen of Peace in Glendale. A large percentage of the teaching sisters claimed Irish ancestry, as a casually chosen list of names indicates: Sisters Mary Magnan, Claudia McCauley, Paschalita Linehan, Leo Kenny, Corsina Callahan, Barbara Roche, Ursula Ryan, Rose Patrick Curren, Mary Margaret Kinnealy, and Ann Sullivan. On the secondary level, the Lorettines opened Loretto Acaemy on property owned by Anne Lucas Hunt at Jefferson and Pine in 1874. They later moved their school to a spacious building on the north side of Lafayette, facing Reservoir Park just east of Grand.

Parochial education continued to grow, with the School Sisters of Notre Dame and the Sisters of St. Joseph staffing a large percentage of the schools. The public school system, under the leadership of William Torrey Harris, strode ahead. Harris enlisted many young Irish women to teach in the public schools.

Sisters from St. Louis made numerous visits to Ireland for recruitment purposes. Thousands of young women came to the United States to enter the convent, and many others entered religious communities after emigration from Ireland. In her book, *Erin's Daughters in America*, historian Hasia Diner provides some insights. Female Irish immigrants outnumbered their male peers and often emigrated in groups. They left their homeland for America because of economic and social factors that made their future in Ireland a grim prospect, leaving no meaningful roles for them. The Irish married later in life, gender segregation lessened social life, and celibacy had a stronger place in Irish culture than in other European countries. Women religious were highly respected in Ireland. Irish congregations of nuns rarely were contemplative. Most chose the active ministries of teaching, healing, caring for destitute women and children, and administering all types of social services. Nineteenth-century Irish women were at the forefront in founding new orders in Ireland and in the United States.

Hasia Diner wrote:

> These young women, the daughters from the thousands of small farms that dotted the countryside, the daughters of the survivors of the great Famine, saw themselves not as passive pawns in life but as active, enterprising creatures who could take their destiny in their own hands. Although possessed of a profound religiosity that belittled what people could do for themselves to alter the course of human events, the Bridgets, Maureens, Norahs, and Marys decided to try just that.[4]

St. Louisans were the fortunate recipients of a disproportionate share of their generous efforts.

# And Still They Came!

**D**uring the immediate postwar years, St. Louis surpassed all American cities except New York and Philadelphia in the number and value of its manufacturing plants. Iron production in Missouri employed twenty-three hundred workers in the vicinity of the city. Brewing, clothing, brick- and furniture-making, and quarrying employed more than forty thousand persons. Jobs were available. In spite of this fact, most immigrants from Eastern and Southern Europe who originally had settled elsewhere in the United States overlooked St. Louis and swarmed into the cities of the Great Lakes. Chicago burst its boundaries. As St. Louis had been the focal point of the mid-continent in the heyday of the steamboat, so Chicago took the lead in the time of the trains.

Even with the growing popularity of Chicago among Irish immigrants, many still favored the Missouri metropolis. And, while other cities of the north and east gained large quotas from Eastern and Southern Europe, few came to the Mound City. St. Louis continued as an Anglo-American, German, and Irish community. The city had 28,536 residents born in Ireland and 36,309 born in Germany in the 1880 census.[1]

Historians William Hyde and Howard L. Conard carried sketches of more than eighty St. Louisans of Irish birth or ancestry in their four-volume *Encyclopedia of the History of St. Louis.*[2] Many of them arrived during the post–Civil War years. Second-generation Irish began to come from western Illinois towns such as Ruma and Tipton. Edmund Faherty, one of Ruma's founders, had arrived in Baltimore from Galway in 1793, married, moved to Kentucky in 1812, and to Illinois in 1818. Patrick, the oldest of his eight children, fought in the Black Hawk War. The youngest, Ned, represented Randolph County in the Illinois legislature of 1860. He later moved to St. Louis. Within one hundred years of Edmund's death, 109 of his descendants resided in St. Louis.[3] Many of the young Irish from Ruma originally came to St. Louis to attend Christian Brothers College or Saint Louis University and stayed.

Individuals continued to come to St. Louis from all counties of Ireland, especially Galway, Cork, Louth, Tyrone, Donegal, Mayo, Carlow, Kerry, and the city of Dublin itself. Even though the economic picture in St. Louis sparkled and her manufacturing plants could provide jobs, many newly arrived Irish chose merchandising, an area where a number of earlier Irish had prospered. William Kinsella of County Carlow developed a thriving coffee and spice business. Thomas C. Nolan, born in Canada of County Carlow ancestry, sold shoes. J. K. Cummings purchased the St. Louis Glass Works and distributed bottles and fruit jars. Peter O'Neil and Robert Noonan sold real estate. James Lyons of County Kerry ran a confectionary. Pat Little opened a hardware store. Joe Duffy, a commission merchant, expanded into real estate. William Dooley set out to wholesale groceries. Michael L. Kelly specialized in fancy dry goods. John F. Boland sold jewelry. William Henry Haggerty of Cork learned business in New Orleans and began a retail store on Seventh Street. After his education at CBC, SLU, and Notre Dame, Zach Mulhall followed his father in stock-raising on a large ranch in Oklahoma. John E. Hagerty of County Louth sold furs. He had come to St. Louis from New Orleans on the *White Cloud*, the boat that in 1849 carried fire from one boat to another on the riverfront, thanks to an unexpected strong wind.

Many Irish immigrants went into manufacturing and some into construction. John McCullagh of Dublin fashioned and retailed billiard tables. Stephen Moriarty manufactured lead. Peter Manion built boats and barges and opened an iron works. John Rohan of Kilkenny fabricated boilers. Henry O'Hara built railroad cars. Thomas J. Kelly became president of the Builders' Exchange. James O'Neil erected buildings. Patrick Grady of Tipperary made a comfortable fortune in the construction business with architect and builder L. D. Baker. Michael Hanick of Mayo constructed railroads and terminals. Peter Ferry, an iron-monger from Fermanagh and a business associate of Chouteaus and Valles, manufactured furnaces.

Charles Green of Galway ventured widely and wisely in real estate, street railways, and finance. He strongly supported the St. Louis Agricultural and Mechanical Fair Association and became president of that body in 1880. John Brady, a successful businessman, served many years on the school board, along with other Irish, M. J. Murphy, William Patrick, John E. Hagerty, and Jack Sheahan, son of Dennis Sheahan, whose strong personality had won him the title of "King of Kerry Patch." Brady's continued insistence year after year that the school system provide free textbooks for poor children finally brought victory and earned him the nickname "Text Books" Brady.[4]

John T. Manning, son of a Confederate veteran, entered the field of law. Attorney M. B. O'Reilly, brother of the pastor of the Cathedral, Father P. F. O'Reilly, specialized in land law. Another lawyer, Frank Ryan, became chairman of the Democratic State Committee. His father, John Ryan, had served in the state legislature.

Many other St. Louis Irish entered politics. Before the war, William Patrick had won a seat in the Missouri legislature on the Whig ticket. After the conflict, he became police commissioner in 1871 and served on the school board. Integrity lost Judge James Moody his seat on the St. Louis Circuit Court. When he denounced the infamous Drake Constitution and the "Iron-clad Oath" that had sent Father Cummings to jail, the state legislature threw him out of office. Thomas Carney moved to St. Louis after a war-time term as governor of Kansas. John Martin practiced law in St. Louis after three terms in the Missouri House. After election to the St. Louis City Council in 1866–1868, Richard Lancaster went on to serve two terms in the Missouri Senate. Dan Kerwin of Kildare, a manufacturer and police commissioner, also won two terms in the state senate (1887–1890).

William Keating, a contractor and builder, served as justice of the peace for sixteen years and as a member of the city council for two terms. Colonel Nicholas Bell, an outstate Scotch-Irish legislator, was elected to the state legislature in 1870. Bell worked to win state support for the Lincoln Institute, an African American college in Jefferson City. In St. Louis, Bell promoted Forest Park.

Another noted Democrat, Edward Aloysius Noonan, born in Pennsylvania of Irish immigrant parents, attended law school in Albany and moved to St. Louis. Twice assistant circuit attorney and twice judge of the Court of Criminal Correction, he was mayor from 1889 to 1893. During his term the Union Station opened. John J. O'Neil served three terms in the state legislature and five terms in the National Congress in the 1880s and 1890s. John F. O'Brien was speaker of the Missouri House of Delegates from 1905–1907.

M. J. Murphy served the public well. As president of the school board, he supported Susan Blow in her efforts to promote the kindergarten. As commissioner of harbors and wharves, he wrote extensively on river transportation. Mayor Edward Noonan then raised him to the position of commissioner of streets.

Irish architects had their part in two of the area's finest churches. John Haynes of the firm of Barnett, Haynes and Barnett, worked with his partners on the New Cathedral on Lindell. Following his father's career as an architect, Thomas W. Walsh of Kilkenny planned St. Francis Xavier Church on Grand

and Lindell, the Saint Louis University Du Bourg Hall next to it, the Lindell Hotel, the Pyrotechnic Building, Four Courts, the jail, and many public schools. With a quick eye for selecting desirable locations, he often suggested public projects.

As a young editor in pre–Civil War Illinois, Robert E. Tansey of Glenarm in County Antrim, supported his friend Stephen Douglas in his campaigns. After the conflict, Tansey moved to St. Louis and invested in river transport. He was president of the St. Louis Transfer Company and director of the Wiggins Ferry Company. In 1871 he was elected president of the Merchants' Exchange. One of the organizers of the Veiled Prophet Parades, he also headed the Knights of St. Patrick. But even while engaged in business in St. Louis, he preferred to reside on his farm in Illinois.

Ringrose John Watson, the son of an immigrant from Limerick with the same name, worked for his father in glass and queen's ware, and later dealt in real estate. Frank Phelan, an alumnus of both Saint Louis and Notre Dame Universities, began to sell paint in 1892 and in a few years developed an annual sales figure of a quarter of a million dollars. Later, he reorganized his firm as Phelan-Faust Paint Company, one of the largest in the West.

The father of John Ring of County Cork manufactured lard oil. During his years at CBC, young John majored in chemistry and developed an interest in the refrigeration of lard. He patented an ice-making machine used by meat packers. He married Kate, the daughter of Judge Joseph O'Neil. Their descendants remained active in St. Louis Catholic activities.

John Scullin spent some of his early years in the West building railroads. He constructed the central section of the Union Pacific in 1866. He built forty miles of the Rock Island line and two-thirds of the Missouri-Kansas and Texas. After moving to St. Louis, he invested in street railways, became president of the Wiggins Ferry, and served on the boards of many corporations. His son, Harry, followed his father in street railway development and produced steel.

Julius Walsh, the eldest son of Edward and Isabelle (De Mun) Walsh, had in youth attended Saint Louis University and St. Joseph's College in Kentucky. A distinguished-looking man, he studied law, was admitted to the bar, and received a Masters of Arts degree from the university. He took his father's place on the boards of banks, railroads, and street railway companies, serving as director of three banks and five railroads. In 1870 he became president of the Citizens Railway Company. As head of the fairground on North Grand at Natural Bridge Road, he improved the area for use during all seasons and opened a zoological garden. In 1890 he organized the Mississippi Valley Trust Company. Later he became president of the firm. He supported all civic ventures, especially the World's Fair of 1904. Saint Louis University recognized his contribution to his school and his city and conferred upon him an honorary doctorate of letters on that occasion.

In the field of entertainment, Joseph K. Emmet led the way. Gifted with dark-Irish good looks, an appealing voice, a winning manner, and a graceful dancing style, he could captivate Irish audiences in Dublin, New York, or St. Louis. But he was more popular with Germans everywhere with a routine called "Fritz, our cousin German." A master of dialect, he depicted a poor, confused German immigrant who won the hearts of all his "German cousins." Emmet even sang an aria to sauerkraut on one program. He reached the top in 1870 and retained his popularity for twenty years.

Patrick Short, an immigrant from Armagh who attended Christian Brothers College in St. Louis, also moved into the entertainment field, but on a different level. He managed the Olympic Theatre and handled finances for the Grand Opera House. A good manager and an urbane gentleman, he was described as "one of the best-known men in the theatrical field."[5] He promoted open-air productions during the summer months, such as Gilbert and Sullivan operas.

The skilled trades also welcomed many Irish. They worked as bricklayers, carpenters, plasterers, steamfitters, steelworkers, railroaders, as well as policemen, firemen, and other public servants. They welcomed the rise of the union movement and took active roles in the American Federation of Labor as it grew in the late years of the nineteenth century. When the workingmen of St. Louis prepared for the Washington Day Parade in 1874, John Donnelly of the Stone Mason's Union was one of the two marshals. John McCarthy was secretary of the Railroad Workers.[6]

When the Great Strike of 1877 erupted, socialist-leaning German workers commanded the operation. The strike leaders, in fact, set up their headquarters in a turner hall. Nonetheless, seven men with Irish surnames—Francis McGee, Barney Coyle, Jerry Denny, Jerry Cowery, C. Holland, Ted Stock, and Chris Henry—won places on the executive committee. On one occasion during the tension, J. J. McBride exhorted the strikers to avoid violence and hold firm for their rights.

The workers had many grievances. The year before, the railroads had lowered wages arbitrarily. In 1877 a strike began on the railroads in Baltimore. At the outset, the workers asked for a restoration of the wage cuts, but they enlarged their goals to include fair treatment of black workers, an eight-hour day, and the prohibition of child labor. The strike spread west.

Easy-going Henry Overstolz, St. Louis's first German mayor, urged the railroad to cancel the wage cuts. Instead, their spokesman asked the Secretary of the Interior to send one hundred thousand troops, more than Grant had at Richmond twelve years before, to keep the peace. The workers held torchlight parades, appealed to black workers to stand with them, and provoked walk-outs at thirty factories. Then they stopped. The leaders had no further plans. The owners of the turner hall ordered them out. They met in a room above a saloon. A small contingent of regular army arrived from Fort Leavenworth to bolster local peacekeeping forces. They fixed bayonets and charged the headquarters of the "High Command." The workers gave up peacefully. No blood was shed, and the strike ended.

On April 8 of that same year, the Irish got their own folk-hero, a firefighter with the unforgettable name of Phelim O'Toole. Born in Kingstown, six miles from Dublin in 1848, O'Toole had gone to sea at the age of twelve and had visited many distant places, from Liverpool to Valparaiso, Chile. After six years on the sea, he had come to St. Louis in 1866 and worked with the Northern Packet Line on the Mississippi. In the meantime, he had married a childhood friend, Anna Doyle. They made their home at 210 N. Seventh Street and had a son and a daughter.

In 1872, O'Toole joined the fire department. A wiry, athletic young man who stood five feet ten and weighed 160 pounds, he first gained public notice when a fire broke out in the courthouse dome. He clambered to the top cornice, cut a hole in the roof, and put out the flames. He showed continual bravery in other fires.

On April 8, 1877, fire gutted the Southern Hotel and trapped serving girls at a window one hundred feet above the ground. The only available ladder failed to reach their level. O'Toole climbed to the top and threw a rope into the window. He told the girls to tie one end securely to a bedpost. He went hand-over-hand to their level and calmly and steadily helped the girls to safety. He then came down himself. In another part of the building, three Irish young women of the hotel staff, Abbie Moran, Mary Dolan, and Kate Reilly, perished.[7]

*When fire gutted the Southern Hotel in April 1877, Irish St. Louisans got their own folk hero, firefighter Phelim O'Toole, who through resourcefulness, strength, and courage rescued servant girls from a window a few feet above the tallest available ladder.*

Seven years later, on July 6, 1884, O'Toole led his fellow Irish team of Thomas Finnerty, Austin Shay, and Barney Kearn into the rear of a cellar where a fire raged. As he was about to douse the flames, a defective fire extinguisher blew up and critically injured him.[8] His teammates carried him to a safe place, but to no avail. Arriving physicians, Drs. John H. McIntyre and P. H. Cronin, pronounced him dead. A large crowd attended his funeral at St. Francis Xavier Church. Fire Chief H. Clay Sexton said at the time, "He was one of the bravest men who ever lived—the bravest of the brave."[9]

On December 16, 1877, Bishop Patrick Ryan caught the attention of all St. Louisans when he spoke on the subject "What Catholics Do Not Believe," to an overflow crowd at the Mercantile Library Hall. In a jovial opening, the bishop told the story of a man who learned "the truth" about the Democratic Party from a Republican. Ryan recommended that people hear a Democrat on the Democrats, and a Catholic on what Catholics believe.

Bishop Ryan claimed that those hostile to the Church opposed something they mistakenly thought was the Catholic Church. He looked at the contemporary charges that the Catholic Church enslaved the human intellect by holding the doctrine of infallibility, relied on sentimentality rather rather than reason with art in churches, demeaned the divinity by devotion to the saints, and put man in the place of God by confession. Then, as a teacher of Catholicism, he answered those objections clearly and tersely. His explanation of devotion to Mary and the saints had special appeal—"Is an artist annoyed when someone acclaims his work? Why, then, should God be annoyed when we honor his great creatures, Mary and the Saints?"

The bishop spoke simply and concretely. He illustrated his message with dramatized stories, some contemporary, some from history or scripture. At least one of them provoked resounding laughter from his audience. He quoted historians and statesmen of his day, such as Lord Macauley, who wrote in admiration of the Catholic Church; James A. Froude, who hated it, but was amazed to find that when the world became totally secularized, the Church, "like a kite against the wind," flourished; and François Pierre Guizot, French Protestant statesman and historian, who, while he could not accept the Church's dogmas, recognized its influence over the years.

Bishop Ryan's listeners heard none of the classic flourishes of Daniel Webster. Instead, he spoke with the straightforward terseness of Lincoln's Second Inaugural Address. The people of St. Louis, Irish and others, happily could look forward to more wisdom from Patrick Ryan and rejoice that the greatest pulpit orator in the country was their auxiliary bishop.

Joseph McCullagh, the Dublin-born editor of the *St. Louis Globe-Democrat*, used this speech as a means of increasing circulation dramatically by starting the "Great Religious Controversy" that for several months in the winter gave every fluent churchman a forum for his beliefs.[10] Many did, and all met their match in young Father Cornelius O'Leary of Mexico, Missouri.

Even though many other priests, including David Phelan and "an anonymous Jesuit," entered the McCullagh lists, O'Leary spearheaded the Catholic forces. He could write both thoughtfully and objectively, as well as belligerantly and subjectively with equal force. Well-versed in theology and church history, he gave a clever, witty, and learned discussion of British history and undercut Anglicanism with quotations from English historians. He quoted Martin Luther extensively. He challenged Protestantism philosophically, theologically, and historically.[11]

Everyone had a chance to air his views. Interest in religious discussion, if not in religion itself, gripped the people for a time. No great Christian accord came as a result, but at the same time the two Christian bodies came to know more about each other's beliefs and continued the St. Louis tradition of tolerance.

Bishop Ryan had enhanced his reputation as a speaker and a man of deep charity. Several Protestant ministers spoke and wrote excellently, such as W. C. Falconer and R. A. Holland. Young Father O'Leary in Mexico, Missouri, made his name known. The *Globe-Democrat* gained many subscribers, and for a long while kept the title "The Great Religious Daily" that McCullagh had given it during the lively and vocal winter of 1877–1878.

*Dublin-born Joseph McCullagh built the* Globe-Democrat *circulation by good editing and promotions such as the "Great Religious Controversy" that he stirred up in the winter of 1878–79.*

# XVI

# Irish Parishes, Organizations, and Colleges

The St. Louis Irish opened many churches shortly after the Civil War. Father Thomas Bonacum, a native of Tipperary who had studied theology at the University of Wurzburg, opened Holy Name Parish on North Grand Boulevard. He could preach to his Irish and German parishioners, the Hannegans and Hauschultes, the O'Hearns and Openlanders, the Walshes and Wagners. Later Pope Leo XIII appointed him bishop of Lincoln, Nebraska.

The Holy Angels Parish at La Salle and St. Ange Streets on the near southside, mentioned in the earlier parochial school discussion, was tri-national, enrolling Papins and Boislinieres, Damhorsts and Trolichts, Keatings and Delaneys.

Other new parishes were predominantly of one nationality. Among the Irish, St. Teresa's opened at Grand and North Market in 1865 shortly after the end of the Civil War. In 1871 the archdiocese sent Father James McCabe, ordained in Baltimore five years before, to open a shrine at Twentieth and University dedicated to the Sacred Heart. Eventually the parish built a beautiful, gray stone building of unusual architectural style. The statue of the Sacred Heart surmounted a large central dome. Twin open towers graced the front of the church on the west.

In 1870 the city annexed Carondelet, a village almost as old as St. Louis, and adjacent to it on the south. Two years later, the Irish in the area began a parish at Michigan Avenue and Davis Street. They named it St. Columcille, in honor of the Celtic monk St. Columba of Iona.

Other Irish parishes opened in quick succession: St. Kevin's at Cardinal and Park in 1875, St. Cronan's at Boyle and Swan in 1879, Visitation at Easton and Taylor in 1881, St. Thomas of Aquin at 3949 Ohio on the southside in 1882, St. Leo's at Twenty-Third and Mullanphy in 1888, Holy Rosary at Margaretta and Newstead in 1891, St. Agnes in the western section of Assumption Parish on the near southside in 1890, and four parishes in 1893—St. Matthew's at Sarah and Kennerly, St. Mark's on Page at Academy, Holy Innocents on Reber Place near Kingshighway, and St. Edward's at Clara and Maffit. St. Kevin's became Immaculate Conception after the turn of the century.

Many pastors besides Fathers Phelan, Bonacum, and McCabe left their mark in the succeeding years. One of the most colorful, Father William Walsh, succeeded Father David Lillis who died young. The new pastor shepherded the people of St. Bridget's for twenty-six years. Born in County Limerick in 1829, he made his studies at the seminary in Carondelet. During his years in St. Louis, he saw to the completion of the church and built schools and a rectory so large that it could accommodate as many priests as ever came to any ceremony in St. Louis. The appreciative priests dubbed it "Father Walsh's Hotel."

The list of Father Walsh's assistants—all Irish—reads like a roll call of the Ancient Order of Hibernians: Edward F. Fitzpatrick, James Archer, Edward Fenlon, J. J. Ryan, Jeremiah J. Harty, F. P. Gallagher, E. A. Casey, J. A. Connolly, J. P. Tuohy, John O'Shea, J. Gavin, C. F. O'Leary, J. Cooney, Thomas J. Walsh, and O. J. McDonald. St. Bridget's Parish weathered many a storm over the succeeding years.

At the east end of "Kerry Patch," Father Martin Brennan combined the posts of St. Lawrence O'Toole's Church pastor, master of ceremonies for the archdiocese, and professor of science at Kenrick Seminary. Born in St. Louis of parents from Tipperary, he attended Christian Brothers College and developed an interest in astronomy. He was a member of the St. Louis Academy of Science, and wrote books in the field.

While recognizing that a few small Irish parishes, such as St. Thomas of Aquin and St. Columcille's on the southside and Mt. Carmel in Baden on the northside, stood in heavily German neighborhoods, three distinct Irish pathways fanned west from the Cathedral on Third and Walnut Streets. The early established families marched with the old-line Anglo-American families straight west from the Cathedral to Saint John's on Sixteenth and Chestnut Streets, later to the new St. Francis Xavier on Grand at Lindell, and, after the turn of the century, to the New Cathedral on Lindell at Newstead.

A slightly larger thrust, mostly of working people, followed the northern rim of Mill Creek Valley, through St. Malachy's, St. Cronin's, St. James's, and later to Maplewood and beyond. By far the largest group of Irish seeking new homes moved west between Delmar and West Florissant Avenue.

Several entirely Irish Catholic organizations began shortly after the Civil War. As already mentioned, the Irish-American Revolutionary Society, commonly known as the Fenians, pursued questionable policies. The Fenians planned an uprising in Ireland, an attack on Canada, and other quixotic ventures. Further, they required a secret oath outlawed by the Church. When Archbishop Kenrick forbade a Catholic funeral for a member of the order,[1] few other American bishops followed his example. But the Fenians sprung their ill-advised actions and brought opprobrium on the Irish community that had just won wide acceptance throughout the North for its contributions to the success of the Union cause. Finally the bishops of Ireland prevailed upon Pope Pius IX to condemn the Fenians. Other less militant Irish societies took root.

In St. Louis, Dr. W. H. Brennan, James Bligh, and others, under the spiritual direction of Father James Henry, promoted the United Sons of Erin for mutual assistance in 1866. This was an exclusively local organization. In one of its early years, the officers were M. Whalen, president; John Costello, secretary; and Richard O'Neil, treasurer.

In 1870, a group of Irishmen that included John Tigh, Andrew Ferry, Peter Leonard, and Patrick Coughlin began the first St. Louis division of the Ancient Order of Hibernians. Irish immigrants on the eastern seaboard had started this organization in 1847 to relieve the distress of their countrymen hurt by the famine. The Ancient Order grew rapidly. Within a year of the initial unit in St. Louis, two others began. Every district of the city wanted a division. Eventually, there were ten in all, ranging in size from 58 members to 150. Prospective members had to be Irish or of Irish descent, and Catholic. When other units formed outstate, P. J. Kelly was the St. Louis delegate to the state division; Charles Landers of St. Louis was state treasurer.

Father Mathew's Young Men's Total Abstinence and Benevolent Society began in 1870, named for Father Theobald Mathew, Irish Temperance promoter. The founding group included James Hagerty, Martin Duddy, James McGraw, James J. McGeary, Jeremiah Sheehan, Matthew Bond, Patrick Cassidy, and Thomas Fox. By 1873, the society numbered thirteen hundred members, but membership declined in succeeding years.

A second temperance group, the Knights of Father Matthew began on May 9, 1872. Father P. F. O'Reilly, pastor of the newly formed Immaculate Conception Parish, was spiritual father. Except for President Thomas Fox, member of the earlier society named for Father Matthew, the founding members included no names connected with the earlier group. Thomas E. Phelan was vice president, John Rohlf, corresponding secretary, John McGrath, financial secretary, and John B. Hagerty, treasurer. Other founding members were John McGrath, John Hagerty, Michael Ratchford, and Patrick Mulcahy. "Total Abstinence" cornerstoned the organization. The knights had a distinct uniform, drilled regularly, and marched on appropriate occasions. They also promoted literary and debating programs. Twelve councils developed, generally connected with Irish parishes, and the organization won a charter from the state in 1881.

In 1874, a former St. Louis pastor, Bishop Patrick Feehan of Nashville, sponsored the Catholic Knights of America, with wider goals and without restrictions on national background but maintaining some parochial affiliation. The order flourished like daffodils in March. Many Irish joined, soon, thirty-four branches numbered 2,819 members in St. Louis. The order served the interests of the individual members and of the Catholic Church in the area. All the members publicly demonstrated their faith by taking part in festive occasions, such as cornerstone layings, church dedications, papal and episcopal jubilees, and St. Patrick's Day Parades.

All the Irish societies—the United Sons of Erin, the Hibernians, and others—celebrated March 17 with a St. Patrick's Day Parade. Several hundred marchers started from St. Patrick's Hall at Seventh Street near Biddle and marched in good order on the near northside toward St. Lawrence O'Toole's Church. The day ended with a banquet at the Southern Hotel. Alderman John

*The St. Patrick's Day Parade in 1874 started from St. Patrick's Hall on Seventh near Biddle Street and marched through the near northside. In the evening, the Knights of St. Patrick sponsored a banquet at the Southern Hotel.*

Finn led the parade one year. His son, Francis, destined to be America's leading juvenile Catholic novelist, was at that time a student at Saint Louis University. Young Finn's career arises in a later chapter on Irish writers.

Father Thomas Ambrose Butler founded a different type of organization. Known as "Father TAB," because he always signed his name by using only his initials, Father Butler had worked near the Potawatomi reservation in Kansas, ninety miles west of Kansas City, before locating permanently in St. Louis. As pastor of St. James Parish in the area known as Cheltenham south of Forest Park, he noted many newly arriving young Irish country lads who had not yet rooted themselves in American soil.

Determined to promote an Irish colony in Kansas, Father TAB won the support of a group of wealthy Irish businessmen. They set up a Colonization Board, organized a stock company, and purchased twelve thousand acres from the Union Pacific Railroad. The site was in Potawatomi County, fifteen miles north of the Jesuit college at St. Marys, Kansas, originally the site of the Potawatomi tribal mission. They put out a brochure that advertised land for $3.60 an acre with an eleven-year payment option. The board also offered loans to purchase tools and seed to help young Irishmen get started. Father TAB and the Colonization Board had a final meeting with the soon-to-be Kansans on the night of February 1, 1887, at St. Patrick's Hall in St. Louis. The next day the young men took the train west. Eventually, six hundred accepted the offer.

The brochure also listed another benefit of the plan—it assured mothers that their sons would find good Catholic wives on the plains. The Osage and Potawatomi girls learned their Catholic religion at the mission schools and were as pretty as colleens. What more could a devoted Irish mother ask?

The area's central town won the title Butler City but later became Blaine, the name it now holds. Although Father Butler made his presence felt more as a colonizer, he was eminently successful as a pastor as well. His tombstone stands high in the priests' lot at the north end of Calvary Cemetery, directly in front of those of Archbishop Kenrick and his successor, Archbishop John Kain. Rightly does the stone belong in such illustrous company. Father TAB's one-time plan had lasting benefits.

While Father TAB's boys plowed Kansas fields, the Irish who stayed behind began to get their exercise on the soccer field. Just as the sport of football tremendously influenced the University of Notre Dame forty years later, so in the 1880s the sport of soccer galvanized Irish Catholic parish loyalties in St. Louis. A few years before, several clubs on the northside in St. Louis had formed soccer teams, among them the "Thistles," made up of the few newcomers from Scotland. A British team challenged the Scots.

On the Sunday after Thanksgiving in 1881, Tommy O'Hanlon led the Irish against the "English." Gradually northside parishes taught by the Christian

Brothers—St. Patrick's, St. Bridget's, St. Malachy's, and St. Teresa's—developed teams. The college named the team it sponsored the "Paulian Club" after Brother Paulian Fanning. A native of Ireland, young Fanning had grown up in St. Louis, attending CBC before he joined the brothers. One of the original incorporators of the college, he headed the school, and later the St. Louis District of the Congregation. A man of patriarchal presence, he represented the American Brothers at General Congregations in Europe.

The Paulian Club played in the Sodality League, the best-managed league in the city, under the leadership of William Klosterman. In the 1890s, Frank P. Furlong managed the St. Teresa's team that dominated the sport. Ten of the eleven starters were Irish. The nicknames of the players—"Tiger" Daly, "Elbow" McNamara, and "Hustler" Finnegan—in a style played that brought a one-year suspension in 1897. While restricted at home, they played out-of-town teams from Indiana and Ohio and beat them.

Early in the twentieth century, the St. Leo's team led by Jimmy Donoghue and "Bull" Brannigan won the championship of the Sodality League ten times, and it beat the champions of other leagues. Paul McSweeny, a local star, won a national reputation as a referee. During World War I, the CBC team excelled. Youthful enthusiasm enhanced the team's loyalty to the parish. Many St. Louisans came to identify where they lived by their parish.

Only many decades later soccer clubs grew up on the southside. These, such as the Carondelet Sunday Morning Club, were not parish-based. A group of Spaniards from Catalonia who came to work in St. Louis just before World War I and located in Carondelet played excellent soccer. They recruited one Irish neighbor, Harry Keough, later the "number one" soccer personality in the city.

*The St. Theresa's Soccer Club dominated the scene in the 1890s. Pete Finn captained this championship team of 1894–95.*

Years later, a successful high school teacher of Irish background, historian James Robinson, a star himself on the baseball field and baseball coach at Saint Louis University High School, wrote a treatise titled *A History of Soccer in the City of St. Louis.*[2] Dr. Robinson credits the Christian Brothers with the development of the sport and emphasizes the influence of soccer in the growth of vital parochial life in the city. It was predominantly an Irish-American phenomenon. Young men in the German parishes tended to get their exercise in hard work in the family enterprise or at the gymnastic societies introduced by the liberal Germans who arrived in the middle of the century.

By this time, Brother James Carney had chosen a new site for Christian Brothers College on the northwest corner of Kingshighway at Easton in the western flow of Irish parishes. Architect James McGrath planned "a splendid school" on that gradually ascending land. The projected building won wide support even beyond the Catholic community. Civil War hero General William Tecumseh Sherman and woodenware magnate Samuel Cupples, among others contributed to the building. The magnificent, five-story, cross-shaped structure facing south had four wings leading to a grand glass-roofed rotunda, sixty feet square, the same dimensions as that of the rotunda of the Old Courthouse in downtown St. Louis. The south wing contained classrooms, and the east wing housed student dormitories. The top floor offered a commanding view of northwest St. Louis. The school opened in the fall of 1882 and the college library gained recognition, listing forty thousand volumes, more than that of the University of Missouri.

Though not aspiring to be priests themselves, the Christian Brothers always had a great record for preparing men for the priesthood. During a period of slightly over 75 years (1849–1926), 165 men became priests—92 diocesan priests, 43 Redemptorists, 19 Vincentians, 6 Jesuits, and 5 Passionists. Four became bishops—Jeremiah Harty of Omaha, Joseph Chartrand of Indianpolis, J. J. Hennessy of Wichita, and James Schwebach of La Crosse. The vast majority of the brother teachers were from Ireland.

Washington University professor Marshall Snow wrote of CBC in his *Circular on Higher Education in Missouri*, commissioned by U.S. Commissioner of Education, William Torrey Harris: "For fifty years the College of the Christian Brothers has been an important factor in the up building of the fame that belongs to St. Louis as an educational center. . . ."[3]

While CBC moved west, Saint Louis University remained downtown twenty years after Father Thomas O'Neil, the first Irish-born president, bought property at Grand and Lindell. In 1880 the school discontinued its residential facilities. A large percentage of its local students were Irish. During the eighties, a historian of Irish ancestry but English birth, Father Thomas Hughes, set out to put the university back in the public life of the city. He promoted evening lecture programs in history, science, and philosophy for adult men. A surprising number of prominent physicians, among others, attended these courses. Such programs had led to the development of graduate schools at Harvard and Yale a decade before.

When the Jesuit provincial superior sent Thomas Hughes to another Jesuit school, the program ended. A later provincial Father Edward Higgins sent Father Hughes to Rome, where he completed a four-volume work on the Jesuits in Colonial and Federal North America that won national acclaim. It was the first scholarly work by a priest to earn such recognition.

By the late eighties, Saint Louis University stood in an expanding clothing district along Washington Avenue. The school finally decided to move in 1889 to a new location on Grand Avenue between Lindell and Baker (later West Pine), on the fourth terrace of the city, the land purchased by Father O'Neil twenty-five years before. A student at the time and later Jesuit Bishop of Belize in Central America, David Hickey, recalled that most of his classmates were Irish. Class lists of the time show McMenamys, Butlers, Dillons, and Kanes. The faculty, too, had a heavy Irish cast with Jesuits Father Laurence Kenny teaching history and Father Joseph Murphy, who also would be bishop of Belize, drilling his students in English grammar.

While the Jesuits moved their school to the center of a developing parish, the Visitation Sisters anticipated western growth by building beyond Union Boulevard on the south side of Cabanne at Belt. Shortly before the school moved, Madeline Kerens, daughter of railroad tycoon Richard Kerens, who became America's ambassador to the Austro-Hungarian Empire, led her class in all subjects.

*Tom Sherman, Francis Finn, and Festus Wade were among the many sons of Irish immigrants in this 1874 photograph at Saint Louis University.*

# The City's Most Popular Irishman?

Who was St. Louis's most popular Irishman during the 1870s and early 1880s? Was he Phelim O'Toole, folk hero and firefighter, born in Kingstown near Dublin, who risked his life often in performing routine work and—by his resourcefulness and bravery—aved the lives of young women during the great fire at the Southern Hotel in 1877?

Or was he Joseph K. Emmet, the nation's leading Irish entertainer who charmed audiences from coast to coast singing Celtic ballads and presenting comical dialogues of the plight of an immigrant landing confused in Manhattan?

Or was he Dublin-born Joseph McCullagh, the flamboyant editor of the *St. Louis Globe-Democrat*, who brought his paper into prominence by inaugurating the "Great Religious Controversy"? Possibly, was he Father James Henry, beloved pastor of St. Lawrence O'Toole's large Irish parish, revered by countless of his countrymen throughout the nation for facing up to the Know-Nothing rioters of the 1850s? Or maybe Father John B. Bannon, former pastor of St. John's Church and chaplain of the State Militia and then of the First Missouri Confederate Brigade, who, though gone from the city for twenty years, was still regarded as one of St. Louis's most prominent citizens? Or was he the venerable archbishop of the West, St. Louis's own Peter Richard Kenrick, called "the Lion of the West," the leading theologian of the American Church who had served close to forty years in St. Louis?

The St. Louis Irish of the 1870s included no public

benefactor comparable to John O'Fallon, Bryan Mullanphy, or John Thornton of the 1850s or to English-born Henry Shaw, who gave to his fellow St. Louisans the Missouri Botanical Garden and Tower Grove Park in the 1870s.

The Irish community had no great athletes at the time as it would have in the next century, like Harry Ratican and Harry Keough in soccer, "Easy Ed" Macauley in basketball, or Bob O'Farrell and Mark McGwire on the diamond. Sport was not such a predominant factor on the last frontier. St. Louis produced more great hunters than hard-ballers in those days.

John O'Fallon, the popular Irishman of the 1850s, had lived in a community that grew in his lifetime from a town to a large city on the Mississippi. Many of his fellow Irish merchants, Catholic and Protestant, made their fortunes supplying needed commodities for the many groups in the growing West. Even before their fortunes were relatively large, they looked to helping others, both newcomers in the area and those who stayed behind in Ireland.

The post–Civil War environment was more constrained. The frontier had moved into the sunset. The days of the *Grand Republic* and other palatial steamboats had given way to the railroad's Pullman cars. The Irish community was strictly Catholic now. Many of its heroes were clergymen, and the most popular was Bishop Patrick Ryan.

Interestingly, both John O'Fallon and Patrick Ryan were friendly, approachable men, handsome of feature, quietly impressive rather than

*Father Patrick Ryan, who came to St. Louis as a seminarian before the Civil War and was pastor at Annunciation and later at St. John's, soon won a deserved reputation as an orator. Named bishop of St. Louis in 1872, he ran the archdiocese in the name of Archbishop Kenrick until 1884, when Pope Leo XIII named him archbishop of Philadelphia. He was universally loved.*

dominating, wide of vision, and wise and conciliatory in dealing with others; they won praise from all who spoke or wrote of them. O'Fallon was born in America, and Ryan in the town of Thurles in Tipperary. As a young man in school, Patrick Ryan had won recognition as a speaker. On one occasion, the school authorities chose him to give an address to the "Great Liberator," Daniel O'Connell.

Ryan studied at St. Patrick's College in Carlow, where Cardinal Paul Cullen and Bishop John England of Charleston, South Carolina, had gone to school. In 1852, at the age of nineteen, he had come to St. Louis and continued studies for the priesthood. Before ordination, he assisted Father William Wheeler at St. Patrick's Church and was invited to speak at the Cathedral. After his ordination, he taught English at the seminary in Carondelet, became pastor of Annunciation Parish on the near southside, and looked to the spiritual needs of Confederate officers at the Gratiot Street Prison.

"Many of these unfortunate men," local historian Logan U. Reavis wrote twenty years later, "who by the vicissitudes of war had been inmates of the place, now broadcast over the South, remember with feelings of gratitude his humane ministrations, his acts of kindness, and kindly words of cheer."[1] As a result, many turned to God. Father Ryan baptized hundreds at the prison and at the hospital. As mentioned earlier, Major General Francis Blair offered to get him an official chaplaincy, but he preferred to work as a civilian pastor.

After the conflict, he impressed the assembled bishops with his preaching skill at the Plenary Council of Baltimore in 1866.

A man of medium height, broad shoulders, with a pleasing voice, he made a deep impression on those who heard him speak. When he warmed up to his subject, contemporary St. Louis historian Logan U. Reavis wrote, "His eloquence is like an avalanche in the Alps, irresistible, and sweeping every obstacle before it."[2]

In the fall of 1866, he traveled with Archbishop Kenrick to Dublin. There, he accepted an invitation from a pastor to address his congregation. The *Irish Catholic Directory* recorded that he "preached a magnificent sermon before a densely crowded congregation of parishioners drawn together by his fame as a pulpit orator."[3]

He became pastor of St. John's in 1868. Even though routine administration of a large westside parish taxed most pastors' energy, the new bishop answered the call to pulpit and podium. In 1868 Pope Pius IX invited him to give the English lenten series in Rome. Previous speakers had been Cardinal Wiseman of England, the American Archbishop John Hughes of New York, and the Dominican, Thomas Burke, Ireland's greatest orator at the time. On a visit to America later on, Father Burke spoke of fellow Dominican, J. B. H. Lacordaire, a fixture in the pulpit of Notre Dame in Paris. "When I heard Lacordaire in Paris," Burke stated, "I thought the whole Church could not produce his equal, but now that I have heard your good and great assistant bishop, I do not hesitate to say that as a pulpit orator he immeasurably surpassed that celebrated preacher." [4]

After his consecration on April 14, 1872, and in spite of his additional duties as administrator of the archdiocese, Bishop Ryan preached at St. John's Church on the first Sunday of each month, and lectured on the sanctity of the Church in leading cities of the country. He addressed the state assembly in Jefferson City. Twice he went to Columbia to address the students of the University of Missouri. He presided at vow ceremonies at convents, and he confirmed countless Catholics. He was at home with the elementary school girls at Visitation Academy and with his fellow bishops in Baltimore and in Rome. He was welcomed everywhere as a loving person, not just as a churchman of distinction.

"Those of the Catholic faith," contemporary historians Howard Conard and William Hyde wrote, "have come to look upon him as a kind father and counselor in whom they may repose confidence and from whom they may always go for a gracious welcome."[5]

When Bishop Ryan gave a famous lecture on "What Catholics Believe," *Globe* editor Joseph McCullagh sent his reporters throughout the city to interview more than thirty clergymen.[6] The following Sunday issue of the *Globe-Democrat* gave a full page of responses, twenty-eight in all. A rabbi, Doctor S. H. Sonneshein, wrote, "I believe it to be the best rhetorical as well as scientific effort that has ever been produced by a modern Catholic priest to apologize for, and to correct the many prevailing errors in regard to the Catholic Church."[7]

The vast majority of the twenty-eight ministers who commented, including Bishop Thomas Bowman of the Methodist Church, spoke favorably of the positive presentation of Bishop Ryan. In the same issue, Bishop Ryan had a letter that told of the projected publication of his lecture at the request of several important citizens, including General William T. Sherman, Civil War hero, Pierre Chouteau, descendant of Creole pioneers, and Major H. S. Turner, Mexican War veteran, banker, and son-in-law of Theodore Hunt and Ann Lucas Hunt.[8]

In looking at this interchange, the observer finds the conciliatory tone on both sides surprising, more attuned to the late-twentieth than to the late-nineteenth century. Part of the credit, certainly, goes to Bishop Ryan. Even though he spoke informally from the pulpit, this speech tells many things about the speaker himself and also points to the many excellent features of his oratory. In a notable way, it shows his conciliatory spirit. He had extensive experience in inter-group activities. Like Pope John a century later, he looked to what united people.

Ryan also endeared himself to his co-workers in the Catholic clergy. On one occasion late in his years in St. Louis, Archbishop Kenrick threatened to remove a priest from his parish for alleged misconduct. Many priests spoke out against the archbishop's decision in support of their fellow pastor. Bishop Ryan stood in the middle. With his calm conciliatory manner, he studied the case carefully. Eventually, he found a loophole that eased the matter. The priest had been a member of a religious congregation and had not been released fully from his previous commitment when he took the pastorate. So technically, he had no right to the pastorate but still had the right to his good name. He could take a new assignment in another diocese without umbrage.

Eighteen Eighty-Three was Bishop Ryan's last year in St. Louis. On July 8, 1884, Pope Leo XIII named him archbishop of Philadelphia. The *Western Watchman* predicted that Ryan's appointment to Philadelphia would be "a blessing to the whole country."[9] His voice was to ring clearly for liberality and moderation in the councils of the American hierarchy, but the country's gain proved a severe loss to the people of St. Louis, Irish and others. "Seldom has any event so stirred Saint Louis society to its depths as the departure of Archbishop Ryan," Father Phelan wrote. He described the mood of the people as "a feeling of regret so deep and profound, shared by Protestant and Catholic alike."[10]

St. Louisans, without regard to religious affiliations or ancestral backgrounds, gave him a notable farewell. Hundreds of admirers gathered at the station in Indianapolis as his train passed through. An entire trainload of Philadelphians went to Pittsburgh to accompany him on the last stage of his journey. The public reception in Philadelphia outstripped the celebration at the centennial of American independence in 1876.

In 1886, two St. Louis Irish clergymen—Archbishop Kenrick and controversialist Father Cornelius O'Leary, pastor of St. Rose of Lima Church in

*Father Cornelius O'Leary's strong jaw reflected his total personality. A trenchant penman, he proved a match for anyone who entered the "Great Religious Controversy" in 1878. A decade later, he defended the Knights of Labor before the Curtin Committee of the House of Representatives. He was the first American priest to speak out for justice of the laboring man.*

De Soto, Missouri—became entwined with the rise of labor unions, an excellent example of new issues that rose during the archbishop's later years. The archbishop's contribution to the labor unions was a negative one; the pastor's was most positive.

At that time, workers of the industrial northeast, most of them Catholic, formed the first great labor union, the Knights of Labor. Misunderstanding the secrecy of an oath the knights took, Kenrick looked upon them as a condemned "secret society." He met with a representative of management, but with no labor leader. At the meeting of archbishops, he refused to approve the union. Only the archbishop of Santa Fe supported him, but that was enough to send the issue to Rome. Fortunately, the newly created cardinal of Baltimore, Archbishop James Gibbons, won approval for the knights.

Then, in 1886, nine thousand railroad workers went on strike. A number were members of Father O'Leary's parish in De Soto, a division point on the Missouri Pacific Railroad. They quit work and set out to stop all trains by removing small but essential parts from the engines.

When the strike broke out, Pastor O'Leary was lecturing in the East. He returned and began to attend to relief work for the families of the strikers. Gradually, he took a more active part in the struggle and unlimbered his guns. He denounced the railroad barons, and he organized a committee of five to help poor families. He prevailed upon lawyer Richard Graham Frost, a former member of Congress and a son of General Daniel Frost, to defend the railroad workers.

While no other Catholic clergymen spoke on behalf of the workers, O'Leary testified before the Curtin Committee of the House of Representatives sent to investigate labor troubles "in the Southwest," on May 12. He explained his concern for the working man. He described how company policies goaded the men to violence, and he pointed out that some corporations wielded a power that overshadowed state and federal authorities. He gave evidence of gross inequities in pay scales, condemned the use of gunmen as strikebreakers, and denounced the "blacklist," whereby one employer passed to a fellow employer the list of men who favored unions and excluded them from work.[11]

During that same summer (1886), a representative of Pope Leo XIII, Monsignor Germano Straniero, came to the United States to bring the symbols of his new dignity as cardinal to Archbishop James Gibbons of Baltimore. Church historians such as Gerald P. Fogarty, S.J., have recognized Straniero as one of the few representatives of Rome who understood America.[12] Before he left, Monsignor Straniero said words in favor of the Knights of Labor. O'Leary admitted publicly that he had conferred with the papal representative.[13]

The De Soto pastor had little support from his fellow priests, even from Father David Phelan, the editor of the *Western Watchman*, ordinarily a defender of the underdog. The strike had dispersed the congregation of St. Rose

Church, crippled the resources of the parish, and almost ruined the town of De Soto. Some of the residents turned against Father O'Leary. He lost his parish and spent some time in Ireland, vacationing and giving home missions.

In his memoirs, *The Pathway I Trod*, Terence Powderly, the grand master of the Knights of Labor, listed the names of several bishops and many priests who supported the Knights *after* Cardinal Gibbons returned from Rome with the approval of the order in 1887. Powderly named only one priest who spoke out in favor of the knights *before* that papal endorsement, Cornelius O'Leary of the achdiocese of St. Louis. This is the Grand Master's tribute: "No man in or out of the organization did greater service to the men than Father O'Leary."[14] This was no accolade.

At the same time, two organizations that had started up several years before, the St. Louis Trades Assembly and the Central Labor Union, combined in the St. Louis Labor and Trades Assemby. The American Federation of Labor, an association wresting national leadership from the Knights of Labor by working for narrower and attainable goals, granted the new St. Louis organization a charter in September 1887.

Even though so many of his flock were union men, Archbishop Kenrick left no record of his views on the American Federation of Labor. His attack on the Knights of Labor had been one-sided and led to a church action that conflicted with his lifelong insistence that local matters be handled locally. This was the one bar of inconsistency on his otherwise proud escutcheon.

# Twilight of the Lion

When Archbishop Peter Richard Kenrick celebrated his episcopal jubilee in 1891, he was the first American to serve as bishop for half a century. No archbishop in the Christian centuries had lived to see so many dioceses created from his original territory. He had towered like a mighty oak over the midwestern Church. He had a large part in training and choosing the bishops who directed the many sees in the mid-continent, and he had consecrated most of them.

In St. Louis itself, he opened a seminary and many new parishes. He sent priests to recruit priests, brothers, and sisters from Europe. He welcomed religious congregations of men and women in education and health care. He promoted a bank where poor people could get needed loans, and for a time he took part in the day-to-day running of the institution. While scholarly by inclination, he made himself available to his flock. He lived frugally, more like a Trappist monk than a Renaissance prelate.

His jubilee in 1891 would have been an appropriate time for Pope Leo to name the St. Louis prelate a cardinal. Archbishop Ryan recommended to Cardinal Gibbons that he seek the "red hat" for Archbishop Kenrick. No evidence indicates he did so. Sixty bishops gathered from all over the country. Cardinal Gibbons celebrated the Pontifical Mass on December 1, 1891, and Archbishop Ryan gave the sermon.

In the afternoon the assembled bishops and all the priests of St. Louis gathered for a banquet in honor of the "Old Lion." Speaking in the name of the non-English-speaking priests,

Father Francis Goller of Sts. Peter and Paul Church praised the veteran churchman in these words: "Archbishop Kenrick discovered in Catholic immigration not a danger to the republic, but a priceless acquisition. Our noble prelate welcomed all the children of the Church, unconcerned about their disparity in language and manner, for he based his hope of a bright future upon the unifying bond of faith."[1]

The people of St. Louis planned a parade that took two hours to pass the residence at 3810 Lindell that they had given the archbishop as a jubilee gift. Archbishops Kenrick and Ryan watched from the window. Governor David Francis and Mayor Edward Noonan rode in this last great torchlight parade in the history of St. Louis. The spontaneous outpouring of acclaim from the people matched anything given anywhere at the time to any prelate of the Church.

The city officials set aside three-fourths of an acre of land immediately across Lindell for a park, called Kenrick Gardens. Later it gained the name "Kenrick Square," even though it is a triangle bounded by Vandeventer Avenue on the west, Lindell Boulevard on the south, and McPherson Avenue that converges with Lindell on the north.

A half-century had gone by since Kenrick came west as auxiliary to Bishop Rosati. The nation of that time numbered only two states totally west of the Mississippi. Only one other churchman, the bishop of Dubuque, shared responsibility for that vast territory between the mighty river and the Rocky Mountains. Eventually, sixteen other bishoprics grew up in the original territory that Peter Richard Kenrick guided. Seventeen priests, diocesan and religious, who had worked in St. Louis under his leadership had gone out to guide dioceses throughout the country.

He held a steady course during the war that split his people and he brought them back together after the conflict. He gave the governor no guidance in running Missouri and told the state authorities to stay out of church affairs. He held for a collegiate view of the hierarchy that suffered eclipse at Vatican I but came to shine clearly at Vatican II. Above all, Archbishop Kenrick set an example of what a shepherd should be. "The morality of the people," a St. Louis journalist wrote, "received a tonic from his holy and devoted presence that has had an appreciable effect on the manners and modes of our people."[2]

Had the post–Vatican II discipline been in order in the last century and had Archbishop Kenrick retired on his seventy-fifth birthday in August 1881, he'd have left in glory. Instead, new issues baffled him. Nonetheless, he truly merited Patrick Ryan's great tribute: "Most Reverend Peter Richard Kenrick will survive in the ecclesiastical history of America as, in many respects, the greatest of her bishops—in profound and varied learning, in marked individuality and fortitude of character, in enlightened and tender piety, and with all in practical judgment and financial ability and foresight. In each of these qualities, he was the equal of any one of them, but in their unusual combination he stood alone."[3]

All Catholics—Irish, German, and others—faced a resurgence of Nativism during the early 1890s from the group called the American Protective Association. Its members, like the Know-Nothings before them, began to harass the Church by blacklisting Catholic businessmen and aspirants for political office. One Irishman decided to do something about this ugly un-American threat. Father Phelan made the APA his special target. He had two not-too-Irish-looking members of his parish gain offices as sergeants-at-arms for a chapter of the APA. On one occasion, as the sergeants-at-arms escorted the secretary of the unit to his residence, a mishap occurred. In the morning, the secretary could not find the list of names of his members. He did not have to worry. They were available in the next issue of the *Western Watchman*. Surprisingly, the list included the names of a Murphy and a Marquette. This ended the danger of any further APA activity in St. Louis.[4]

The one Irish mayor of the city in the last half of the nineteenth century, Edward Noonan, led the people of St. Louis in applauding the completion of Union Station in 1894. It outranked the London and Paris terminals with fifty-four trunk lines converging and four hundred passenger trains arriving and departing daily. America's three larger cities, New York, Philadelphia, and Chicago, dispersed their passenger traffic to several depots. Architect Theodore Link modeled the beautiful building after the Castle of Carcassonne in southern France.

As in the 1880s, the Irish parishes supported their soccer teams. Attendance at parochial schools grew. New churches opened, and among them, these had predominantly Irish or Irish-American parishioners: St. Matthew's on North Sarah, St. Paul's on Page, St. Mark's farther out on Page, St. Edward's on Clara and the Cathedral Chapel on Lindell in the West End, Holy Innocents on South Kingshighway, and Our Lady of Good Counsel near old St. Michael's on the northside.

In addition to the new parishes, many Irish continued to live in the Kerry Patch district. By 1880, St. Lawrence O'Toole numbered six thousand parishioners and St. Bridget's had five thousand. As a result, on Cass Avenue just to the north of Visitation Academy, many Irish families opened St. Leo's Church on Mullanphy Street in 1888. The parishioners invited the Sisters of St. Joseph, now almost entirely Irish or Irish-American, to staff a school that soon numbered 813 pupils.[5] The Josephites already had staffed five parish schools in that general area, and they resided at a central convent in the old Clemens Mansion on Cass Avenue, next to Visitation Academy. They hoped to open a central high school for girls on the former Clemens property.

The Sisters of the Visitation secured the McPherson Residence at 4012 Washington Avenue, three blocks west of Grand Boulevard in 1887, for a second academy. All of the nuns teaching at their thirty-five-year-old school on Cass Avenue anticipated the westward movement of St. Louis and purchased property west of Union Boulevard on Cabanne at Belt. They would move to a castle-like structure there in 1892.[6]

In the early 1890s, the Christian Brothers, who had taught so many Irish young men in St. Louis, faced an unexpected in-house struggle with their French superiors. To prepare for the canonization of their founder, St. John Baptist de la Salle, the leading brothers in France had worked to have his original intent honored, namely that they teach only in elementary schools. In St. Louis, New York, and elsewhere in America, the brothers had taught on the elementary, secondary, and collegiate levels. Unfortunately, the brothers lost the permission to teach the classics which they had gained in Kenrick's time. As a result, during the ensuing years, they no longer could train young men for the priesthood, and they lost those students who planned careers in the professions, except in architecture and engineering.

All the while, the Daughters of Charity, most of them born in Ireland, kept at their many avenues of concern. St. Vincent's Institution for psychiatric care in Soulard had expanded steadily over the years adding a special floor for the chemically dependent. During the Civil War, when the state asylum at Fulton had closed temporarily, St. Vincent's took sixty-seven more patients. As the needs continually rose, Sister Magdalen Malone purchased a large farm in suburban Normandy and commissioned a large, castle-like building. The sisters moved the patients there in 1895.

During the last half of the century, the Mercy Sisters had continued to grow, with boatloads of candidates still coming from Ireland. They set up a novitiate that sent sisters to start convents in Louisville and New Orleans. They undertook Sunday religious instruction at Immaculate Conception and St. Charles Borromeo Parishes. They also continued health care at St. John's Hospital where, since 1873, they had worked closely with the doctors of the Missouri Medical College a few blocks away on Twenty-Second Street. When the Sisters of Mercy celebrated the silver jubilee of the hopsital, they reported that they had treated nearly eleven thousand patients, men and women, at the hospital and more than eight thousand others, free of charge, at the Infirmary. They set up a small infirmary for black women when segregation became the norm.

When the St. Louis College of Medicine (the original Saint Louis University School of Medicine) joined Washington University in 1891, the Missouri Medical College sought affiliation with Saint Louis University. It had worked closely with the Mercy Sisters' Hospital and its prominent Catholic physicians. However the Jesuit president at the time, Father Joseph Grimmelsman, failed to see his way clearly and turned down the offer. Thereupon the Missouri Medical College joined Washington University in 1892, as the St. Louis College of Medicine had done the year before.

# XIX

# New Irish Names Surface

A ll the while in 1893, when no one knew who was in charge of the Catholic community religiously, Archbishop Kenrick had wanted Vicar-General Father Thomas Brady to follow him as archbishop. Father Brady's fellow Irish priests questioned his capacity to guide the large archdiocese. In those days the priests had the right to submit a *terna*, which contained the names of three agreed-upon nominees for their bishop. The bishops of the area could submit a terna as well. Rome made the final decision.

Two of the Irish priests, James and Michael McCabe, drove from Irish rectory to Irish rectory drumming up support for Bishop

*Bishop John J. Kain was the priests' choice to succeed Archbishop Kenrick. He supported the Christian Brothers and gave full pastoral rights to foreign-language parishes.*

John J. Kain of Wheeling, their classmate at St. Mary's Seminary in Baltimore. They enlisted the support of one of the few American-born priests, Father Charles Ziegler of St. Malachy's Parish. He invited all the non-English-speaking pastors to a meeting. They went along with the majority of the Irish. Only two priests, both Irish, Fathers Jeremiah Harty and Joseph Connolly, refused to sign a letter to Cardinal Gibbons recommending John Kain.

Rome acceded to the request and named Kain coadjutor, but failed to clarify his actual power in relation to Archbishop Kenrick. To everyone's dismay, the old archbishop refused to welcome him. Two years of embarrassing uncertainty followed. On his part, Kain made several misjudgments. He turned against those who had welcomed him: the McCabe brothers, Father Ziegler, and Father Phelan, the editor of the *Western Watchman*, who then was squelching the bigots of the APA by using humor against them. His humor also forced the archbishop to revoke the censure of his paper. Kain gained full power in 1895.

Sedate Republicans and the vibrant Populists chose St. Louis for their conventions the following year. The weatherman must have been a Democrat. By late May 1896, he had sent out numerous forebodings. On the twenty-first a hailstorm came from the south, rather than from the north, and caused extensive damage to windows. St. Louis had its first warning. On May 25, tornadoes in Iowa wiped out six towns and killed thirty-five people. On May 25, a tornado hit Victoria, British Columbia, and another left forty dead and one hundred injured in Michigan and Western Ontario.

At noon on May 27, a heavy thunderstorm hit St. Louis. That afternoon a funnel cloud swept in from the southwest and unleased its full fury in the Lafayette Park and Soulard areas, damaging eight thousand homes and four thousand other buildings and killing more than three hundred people. The worst damage occurred near the corner of Seventh and Rutger. The tornado smashed beautiful Annunciation Church, where Father Patrick Ryan had been pastor and previously mentioned Mary Christy Scanlan[1] had worshipped. Three other Catholic churches sustained damage.

Since the targeted blocks housed only one Irish parish, the list of the dead and injured included a small proportion of Irish names. On the east side of the river, however, half of the first individuals listed as fatalities had Irish surnames.[2] The displaced residents of the demolished areas, non-Irish and Irish, set about to rebuild.

The damage to the four churches and the homes of so many Catholics thwarted plans for a new cathedral, although Archbishop Kain did choose the eventual site at the northwest corner of Lindell and Newstead. This caused one mainline Protestant congregation to seek a site farther west, not wishing to build in a future "Irish slum," as one of its elders allegedly remarked at the time.

In spite of the disaster on the southside, the political conventioneers came during the summer. Since most of the St. Louis Irish were Democrats, not many of them had an active interest in the Republican convention, except Richard C.

Kerens, a Republican committeeman, and Marion Reedy, the political analyst, who was highly critical of Republican imperialistic policies. The delegates chose Governor William McKinley of Ohio. The Populists, on the other hand, caught the attention of the Democratic Irish by pledging support to the nation's leading orator, William Jennings Bryan, as the Democratic nominee.

The tornado of 1896 had done structural damage to St. Patrick's Church. A new tornado, Father J. H. Tuohy, hit the parish the following year. At first sight, Tuohy did not seem to be the type to give editor Joseph McCullagh of the *Globe-Democrat* an opportunity for another paper-selling controversy. A scholar, not a provocateur, Tuohy seemed to be a tabby cat, not a timberwolf. He had edited a publication, *Church Progress,* and had taught at the Catholic University of America in Washington, D.C. When he returned to the archdiocese, Kain named him pastor of St. Paul's (later St. Ann's) Church on Page Avenue, a few blocks west of Grand . Not being adept at budgeting, he shortly had the finances of the parish in disarray.

Instead of letting Tuohy find his niche teaching at the seminary or in editorial work, Kain sent him to St. Patrick's, presuming Tuohy could do less harm in the old Irish parish. Shortly, Tuohy repeated his financial mistakes. Kain urged him to resign in June 1897. Tuohy refused and metaphorically filled

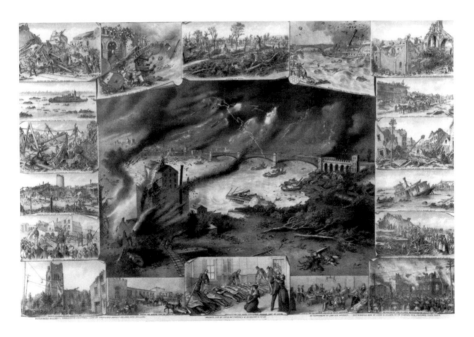

*The 1896 tornado killed more than three hundred individuals on the near southside and destroyed Annunciation, one of the most impressive churches in the country at the time of its erection.*

the moats, pulled up the drawbridges, and barred the gates to the rectory. But he did not presume to say Mass.

Twelve hundred Irishmen petitioned the archbishop for a peaceful solution. Archbishop Kain left for his biennial visit to Rome, required of all bishops, without responding. A thousand Irish women and six hundred Italian residents of the area signed a letter to the new Apostolic Delegate, Sebastian Cardinal Martinelli, in support of Tuohy. The *Globe-Democrat* gave the matter sufficient play and gained more subscribers. Finally, in 1898, the Apostolic Delegate brought a quiet solution to the long siege. Tuohy resigned and accepted a country parish.[3] His name never again reached the pages of the *Globe-Democrat*.

St. Louis African American Catholics faced a major setback in 1896. Their new status provided a challenge to Irish religious leadership and was destined to affect Irish parishes in the century ahead. When Missouri emancipated slaves in 1865, Archbishop Kenrick had set up St. Elizabeth's black parish, not as a segregation measure but as a place of identity and security. African Americans could attend any church, but whites could not fulfill their religious duties at St. Elizabeth's. Kenrick looked on St. Elizabeth's as a home base for black Catholics, much as he had when he set up St. John Nepomuk for Bohemians and St. Stanislaus for Poles.

St. Elizabeth's Parish was alive. It took part in all local Catholic activities and in the five national congresses of black Catholics held between 1889 and 1894. However, the decision of the U.S. Supreme Court in *Plessy v. Ferguson* of 1896, with its questionable "separate but equal" doctrine, served to harden and extend segregation. After Kenrick, Irish church leaders accepted segregation.

Late in the century also, a French writer accused American Catholics of emphasizing natural virtues over the supernatural, and minimizing errors of Protestants in order to convert them. He lumped his views together under the principle of Americanism. Soon, controversy raged. As a result, in an encyclical, *Testem benevolentiae*, of January 22, 1899, Pope Leo XIII condemned what Europeans unjustly called "Americanism." While at least one archbishop on the Atlantic seaboard and a prominent St. Louis Catholic editor[4] thanked the Holy Father for his wise admonitions, Kain and three other archbishops, including Cardinal Gibbons, denied that Catholics held such views.[5] Kain urged Catholics, further, to recognize that Protestants adhered to many Christian truths. The apostolic delegate thought this a dangerous view.[6] It seemed as if Archbishop Kain could do nothing right.

In the meantime, the end of a century approached. The Census of 1900 showed that 575,238 people resided in St. Louis. The percentage of Irish-born citizens stood sixth in the nation. The number of natives of Ireland numbered 19,421, or 7.5 percent of the immigrant population, more than all of the Eastern and Southern European countries together.[7] The percentage of those with Irish-born parents stood even higher.

Those years of the late nineteenth century and early twentieth century brought St. Louis its only political boss. In the 1890s Edward Butler came to control a two-thirds majority in the municipal assembly, and could override any veto by the mayor. A blacksmith as a young man, Butler moved "behind the scenes" in politics. By bribery, political manipulation, and preferential contracts, he became a millionaire. His leadership brought no significant forward thrust to the city. Rather, it called forth widespread reproach in national journals of opinion. While gray skies clouded the political scene, business flourished.

In 1901 Assemblyman E. J. Simmons of Shelby County introduced a compulsory public education bill in the Missouri legislature that threatened to curtail drastically parochial education throughout Missouri and put private religious colleges under the Board of Education. Deaf children were forced to attend the State School in Fulton. State authorities had sponsored nuns from France to teach deaf children in 1838. Now state authorities wanted to close the school's door.

Nothing ever brought the Irish and German Catholics closer together than this attack from outstate. Catholics of all the parishes held a mass meeting at St. Bridget's Church on Jefferson Avenue. Judge Daniel Dillon presided. Speakers agreed that the bill forbode trouble. Fortunately, it failed to win needed support. The Catholics of St. Louis, of all national backgrounds, had won. Parochial education continued to flourish.

The mere relocation of Saint Louis University to the top of the central ridge of the city did not revitalize the institution. That came with the selection of William Banks Rogers as the first American-born president since Father Verdin in the days of the Know-Nothings, and the first of Irish ancestry since Father Thomas O'Neil during the Civil War. Father Rogers moved with the energy of his contemporary, President Theodore Roosevelt, introducing American academic terminology, separating the high school department from the Arts College, and recruiting a board of advisers. Among his advisers were Francis Drew, Festus Wade, and Richard Kerens, all born in Ireland, and Julius Walsh, David D. Walker, and John Scullin, all Irish.

As president, Rogers brought the university into the mainstream of the city by preparing for and participating in the World's Fair. He welcomed President Roosevelt to the dedication of the site of the fair, a full year before its official opening. He encouraged a sports program and recruited Coach Eddie Cochems, who brought the university to a recognized position on the gridiron.

Rogers was determined to bring a medical school into the university's orbit. After considerable reflection and negotiation, he purchased two small medical schools that had recently banded, the Marion Sims and the Beaumont Medical Schools. The latter institution bore the name of Dr. William

Beaumont, who had been on the board of the original Saint Louis University Medical School, but otherwise had no connection with either institution.

The Jesuit officials of Saint Louis University wanted their faculty members to work with the Mercy Hospital. The impasse caused great unpleasantness for the Sisters of Mercy, who long had worked with the physicians at the Missouri Medical College. These physicians had sought unsuccessfully to affiliate their school with Saint Louis University ten years before. Now they faced a different rejection. Archbishop Kain intervened in this issue, writing directly to Mother Bentley, the superior of the Sisters of Mercy in America, and the officials of Saint Louis University worked out a detailed agreement.[8]

That was the last and one of the few successful efforts of Archbishop John J. Kain in St. Louis. He had lived his first few years in the city in the shadow of a great oak, Peter Richard Kenrick, and he sat out the last years under a willow of illness. He had to call on Bishops George Montgomery of Monterey, California, and John Hennessey of Wichita, Kansas, to come at various times to ordain new priests. Facing up to his declining health, Archbishop Kain asked Rome to appoint Father Connolly as auxiliary bishop. Rome refused to act on his request. Next, the archbishop submitted the name of Father Jeremiah Harty, the other priest who had refused to sign the letter to Cardinal Gibbons asking for Kain's appointment to St. Louis. This time Rome said "No" by means of a decree listing procedures required for such a request.[9] Harty shortly became archbishop of Manila, and later of Omaha, Nebraska. Auxiliary Bishop John J. Glennon of Kansas City, who had impressed the local Irish with his fluent oratory during a Eucharistic Congress at St. Francis Xavier College Church in 1901, became coadjutor of St. Louis on April 23, 1903. Archbishop Kain died on October 13, 1903.

Even more than Kenrick in the previous century, tall, boyishly handsome John J. Glennon would dominate the local Irish scene for many years to come.

**XX**

# St. Louis Irish Writers

etween 1890 and 1920, three natives of St. Louis gained national and international prominence in the field of creative literature: an Irish-French woman in short stories and the novel; an editor of Irish ancestry in political analysis, literary criticism, and creative editing; and an Irish-American priest in juvenile fiction. The first and third spent some time in other parts of the country and located their stories there. The second rarely strayed far from his home at 3501 Washington Avenue. Three other writers gained local recognition.

Kate Chopin was the daughter of Eliza Faris, of French–St. Louis background, and of a prosperous immigrant

*Years as a young wife in the Bayou Country of Louisiana gave Kate O'Flaherty Chopin the setting for her great short stories that are masterpieces of fiction.*

businessman, Thomas O'Flaherty, who was killed in the Gasconade Bridge disaster on the trial run of the Pacific Railroad in 1858. As a girl, she attended both Visitation Academy and the Academy of the Sacred Heart. There, Sister Philomena was her favorite teacher.

Kate met and married a Saint Louis University student from Louisiana, Oscar Chopin, in 1870 and moved to Evangeline County. She immersed herself in Creole and Cajun folklore. Shortly after the death of her husband in 1882, she returned to St. Louis and began writing short stories that won gradual notice. A book of stories, *Bayou Folk*, published in 1894, won acclaim from reviewers in the *Atlantic Monthly*, the *Nation*, and the *New York Times*. In the short-story section of the *Cambridge History of American Literature*, critic Fred Lewis Patee agreed with them. "No more exquisite work," he wrote, "may be found in the whole range of local color school than in Kate Chopin's (1851–1904) 'Bayou Folk' (1894.) . . . She was of Celtic blood and spontaneously a story-teller. Such stories as 'Desiree's Baby,' the final scene of which grips one by the throat like a sudden hand out of the dark, and 'Madame Celestin's Divorce,' with its delicious humour and its glimpse into the feminine heart, are among the few unquestioned masterpieces of American short story art."[1]

Kate soared in popularity toward the close of the nineteenth century. Then her novel, *The Awakening*, offended Victorian sensibilities and brought mixed reviews from critics. She had to wait until after World War II for readers to accept her novel. In recent years, scholars at Louisiana State University renewed an interest in her work. At the time of her death, however, another significant literary figure of St. Louis, critic and editor William Marion Reedy, called her a "true literary genius."[2]

*William Marion Reedy took two avenues to editorial prominence: he discovered and published new writers in his magazine* Reedy's Mirror; *and he wrote stinging editorials against the imperialism of the late 1890s that betrayed American principles by annexing Puerto Rico and the Philippines.*

One of three sons of Patrick Reedy, a police captain, and his wife Ann Marion, William Marion Reedy was born during the Civil War and baptized at St. Lawrence O'Toole Church. He attended Christian Brothers College and Saint Louis University before becoming a reporter for the *Missouri Republican*. He soon displayed a clear, vivid, and unfailingly interesting way of writing. He began to freelance. Among other magazines, he wrote for the *St. Louis Mirror*. The owner, James Campbell, whose career graces a later chapter, offered him the editorship in 1893 and three years later gave Reedy the paper. Advertisements for railroads that Campbell controlled kept the paper afloat financially, but Campbell never attempted to dictate policy or position. Jack Sullivan managed the advertising department.

A master of incisive style, with a clear vision, an acute view of people and policies, and a relentless hold on reality in the face of popular opinion, Reedy wrote articles, essays, and editorials dealing with a variety of subjects, with heavy emphasis on literature and politics. While his views on the state of the nation grabbed the attention of his contemporaries, people today remember him more for his influence on writers of the time.

"One of the chief factors in the growth of Reedy's reputation," librarian and critic Clarence Miller wrote, "was his quick recognition of significant new talent in the literary world."[3] He was the first to publish American writers Sara Teasdale, Zoë Akins, Fannie Hurst, and Edgar Lee Masters, and he introduced John Galsworthy, Joseph Conrad, and Lord Dunsany to American readers. He soon made the *Mirror* a critical journal known throughout the English-speaking world.

"Our town has its authentic great man, William Marion Reedy," St. Louis journalist Orrick Johns (who also owed a gratitude to Reedy) wrote. "Reedy was the only figure to give St. Louis a literary character in the eyes of the rest of the country between 1900 and 1920. . . . During those years, Reedy was known to every critic in the English language."[4]

While Reedy's biographer, Professor Max Putzel of the University of Connecticut, questioned some of Johns's opinions, he concurred with that view. Putzel wrote of "Reedy's influence on his own and succeeding generations. He had a lofty conception of literature and a superbly independent recognition of its bearing on political and private life. . . . He was a spokesman for a kind of individual and civic dignity. . . . Scholars who want a new insight into our culture in its political and economic, or its aesthetic and literary ramifications, can do worse than turn to the files of the *Mirror*."[5]

In the political arena, Reedy, a liberal Democrat, fought land monopoly and supported the single tax, as proposed by economic theorist Henry George. He had harsh views on the Republican candidate in the election of 1896. The Republicans met in St. Louis and nominated Governor William McKinley of Ohio for the presidency. Instead of coming to St. Louis to give an acceptance speech, McKinley stayed in his rocking chair on his front porch in Ohio.

Reedy asked if Governor William McKinley really existed. In turn, Reedy appreciated the oratorical power of William Jennings Bryan, the Democratic nominee, but questioned the soundness of his political views.

Two years later, during the presidency of William McKinley, whom he regarded as a "puppet of Big Business," Reedy criticized the annexation of Hawaii. He looked upon this action as a departure from the traditions and practices of the country. Reedy opposed America's meddling in Cuba; he opposed our war with Spain and the annexation of the Philippines.

To Reedy our unprovoked attack on Spain was not the "pretty little fight" Theodore Roosevelt and his friends had sought. It broke with our tradition and altered the fabric of our national life for all time. Reedy saw no reason for a mighty navy. Imperialism, he insisted, opposed the American spirit. As a result of this stand, the circulation of the *Mirror* soared to a high of 32,250, overshadowing the 7,000 circulation of the prestigious *Atlantic* and the 13,000 of the influential *Nation*.[6]

The world of William Marion Reedy was remote from the routines of St. Louis Irish parish life. While he remembered the lessons of unity, coherence, and emphasis that his Christian Brother and Jesuit teachers had inculcated in his younger days, he neglected early the rules of the Young Men's Sodality. A tall, robust, physically impressive man, with surprisingly small hands, he too often wrapped them around glasses of Irish whiskey. He presumably was influenced strongly by drink, as when he undertook his first marriage. His wife's manner of making her money, however, had been in public disfavor since the Book of Leviticus. She and Reedy lived together only a short time. He then hoped to marry Eulalie, the daughter of Dr. Jerome Keating Bauduy, a prominent St. Louis physician of French West Indian ancestry.

Reedy had greatly admired Archbishop Peter R. Kenrick and felt he would have been a cardinal of the Church but for his stand against papal infallibility. Reedy lacked similar regard for Archbishop John Kain who saw no grounds for declaring his first marriage null and void.[8]

The union of Eulalie and Reedy failed to win the blessing of the Church, but the years of their marriage proved highly productive for the editor. When Eulalie died at the age of thirty, Reedy found a third wife, Margie Rhodes. Like his first wife, she ran an establishment frowned upon by the Chamber of Commerce, the League of Women Voters, and the Council of Churches. Surprisingly, this marriage endured. They settled down on an estate on Manchester Road that Reedy named Clonmel after his father's birthplace in Ireland. On one occasion in 1907, when the *Mirror* reflected only red ink, Margie loaned the *Mirror* five thousand dollars of her hard-earned money, without Reedy's knowledge.[9]

At his sudden death in San Francisco, Reedy apparently received the last sacraments. Archbishop John Glennon approved his funeral at the College

Church and his burial in Calvary Cemetery.

Unlike Reedy, Francis Finn followed the Sodality rules all his life, but he did not heed his Jesuit English teacher as Reedy had done. The reverend gentleman told Finn that his story "Tom Playfair" lacked merit. His advice: young Finn should stick to teaching English, not writing English. Fortunately, one afternoon when Finn lacked time to prepare his class, he read the story to the boys. They loved it. So, eventually, did boys in nine other countries over the years.

The son of a St. Louis alderman who once ran for mayor of the city and on one occasion was Grand Marshall of the St. Patrick's Day Parade, Francis Finn attended Saint Louis University and then entered the Jesuit seminary in Florissant. Ill health regularly forced him to interrupt his seminary course. Assigned to St. Mary's College in Kansas to teach English, he began writing stories of the everyday experiences of American Catholic boarding-school life. Benzinger Publishers in Cincinnati agreed with the boys who liked Finn's stories rather than the English teacher who downrated them. That firm published *Percy Wynn*, structurally the best of his stories, in 1889. Others followed at regular intervals.

Finn placed some sections of his stories, especially the most popular one, *Tom Playfair*, in St. Louis, but he himself would have little identification with the city after completing his theological studies at Saint Louis University and

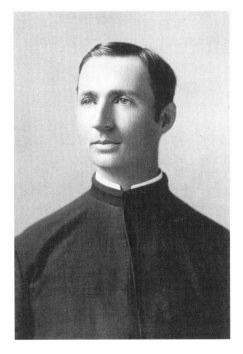

*Juvenile novelist Father Francis Finn, S.J., son of a public official of St. Louis, advised the staff of* The Dial, *the student publication at St. Mary's College in Kansas, where he taught in his early years as a priest. His three most popular books,* Tom Playfair, Percy Wynn, *and* Harry Dee, *recently came out in a paperback edition one hundred years after their debut.*

his ordination at St. Francis Xavier Church. He spent most of his priestly life in parish work in Cincinnati. Each summer he spent his weeks of vacation at Campion Jesuit High in Prairie du Chien, Wisconsin, writing stories.

Eventually he published twenty-seven books. Fifteen went into French editions, eighteen into Flemish, six into German, four into Italian, Polish, and Bohemian, and several into Hungarian, Spanish, and Portuguese. Thirteen came out in Braille editions. In 1911 the *American Catholic Who's Who* singled him out as "the foremost writer of fiction for young people."[10]

During all these years, Father Finn fulfilled his duties in the parish of St. Francis Xavier in Cincinnati. He directed the parish school, built an endowment of one hundred thousand dollars, and made the school tuition-free.

Besides these three creative writers, Irish St. Louis boasted a scholarly writer of distinction in the field of history and theology. Father William Fanning of Saint Louis University wrote for far different readers than any of the other three. He published a history of the university to commemorate the 75th anniversary of Jesuit education in St. Louis. He also contributed one hundred short articles on theological issues for the *Catholic Encyclopedia*, and two long articles, one on the life of the missionary Peter De Smet, and the other on the place of woman in the modern world. The latter anticipated women's advances by half a century. Few contemporary articles matched it, none by men.

St. Louis novelist Mary C. Dillon grew up in Pennsylvania, moved to St. Louis, married an Irish-American, and developed a great interest in the French heritage of the area. Her best novel, *Rose of Old St. Louis*, attracted favorable attention when published at the time of the World's Fair. It remained on St. Louis booklists throughout the 1920s. Though a popular author in the St. Louis Irish community, Mary Dillon was Anglo-American by birth. It was her husband who was Irish.[11]

Another writer of the time, Jane Frances Winn, "the dean of newspaper women in St. Louis," was of Irish parentage on her father's side, and Anglo-American on her mother's side. As a young woman, she taught school in her native Ohio and cultivated a scholarly interest in botany. She sent a series of articles on flowers to the *St. Louis Globe-Democrat*. One of her talented pupils, William Ireland, illustrated her articles. As a result of these articles, the editor of the *Globe* offered her a position on the paper in the late 1890s. Her student illustrator went on to become a cartoonist for the *Columbus Dispatch*. Jane Winn accepted the offer and moved to St. Louis, and she resided with her brother next to Forest Park University, across from the park on Oakland.

During the World's Fair five years later, among other events, she covered the dinner given at the German Hall in honor of Archbishop Joseph Satolli, the representative of Pope Pius X. The local archbishop introduced Miss Winn to the pope's representative. Archbishop Satolli autographed her program with these words: *"Honestas, Veritas, Caritas,"* and said to her, "Be honest always in what you write, tell only the truth, and love your profession so dearly that you will never fall short of your ideal of perfect fairness."[12]

She made that statement of Archbishop Satolli the norm of her work. Every Sunday she featured "Women the Wide World Over." She called her readers' attention to the positive achievements of women everywhere. Her message stood in striking contrast to the usual column that told of the club activities of society women.

XXI

# An Amasser of Money
# and a Martyr for Justice

At the turn of the century, a group of business leaders, among them Governor David R. Francis, Julius Walsh, John Scullin, and Adolphus Busch, combined such political and economic power that they enjoyed instant community recognition. "The towering figure of this group was James Campbell, a major stockholder of the Mercantile Trust," historian James Neal Primm wrote. "Dubbed by the press, the 'Morgan of the West,' . . . by 1900 he was a multimillionaire with a palatial home on Westmoreland Place. Having little education, and less social finesse, Campbell was contemptuous of society, but he enjoyed making money with its representatives."[1] A social observer agreed: "Without leaving St. Louis," he wrote, "Campbell, utilities and traction financier, became a power to reckon with in Wall Street."[2] Like John Mullanphy and John O'Fallon, among early Irish immigrants to St. Louis, he deserves lengthier consideration.

James Campbell was born on a twelve-acre farm near Mullrick, County Galway, Ireland, in 1848. Two years later, his folks crossed the Atlantic and settled in Wheeling, West Virginia, where his father worked as a drayman. When James, one of six children, was only eleven years old, he began working at a grocery store. During the Civil War, General John C. Fremont noticed Campbell delivering groceries to the military camp and hired him as a messenger. When Fremont left the army after the war to take up railroad enterprises, Campbell accompanied him and came to St. Louis in 1866.

The young Galway man joined the surveying party that laid out Fremont's Atlantic and Pacific Railroad. For seven years, he worked with a crew. By the age of twenty-one, he headed the surveying team. With his wages, he took options on inexpensive Missouri "wildlands" and sold them to settlers. Seventy-four Missouri counties had issued millions of railroad bonds that became almost worthless in the Panic of 1873. Campbell invested all his money, and some he borrowed in the bonds, on a hunch they would eventually be redeemed. His hunch proved right. In 1876 Campbell started a stock and option business in St. Louis. Appointed receiver of a little street railway company that went to the Fairgrounds on the nouthside, he eventually gained ownership. In association with John Scullin, he improved and enlarged the lines.

Campbell continued to branch out in railroads, traction companies, and street lighting and other utilities. In politics, he cut his own path through the thickets. Long before modern businesses began to give money to rival candidates, Campbell helped set up a satisfactory slate for both parties, often with strategically placed political donations. Throughout his life Campbell checked carefully every business situation. His study of the electrification of the railroad led him to value electricity for other purposes. When electric utilities in St. Louis were in their infancy, he invested in plant after plant until his holdings brought profit. When a friend, Festus Wade, laid the foundation of the Mercantile Trust Company, Campbell, among others, backed the enterprise. All the while, Campbell never lost his first love of the railroads and continued his investment in stocks and bonds of systems that grew with the

*"The Towering Figure" among St. Louis business leaders at the turn of the century, enterprising James Campbell amassed many millions in his journey from a twelve-acre farm in County Galway to a palatial home on Westmoreland Place.*

great Southwest. On boards of directors, Campbell kept silent, waiting for sentiment to crystalize. Believing that no man can buck the direction of his fellow men and succeed, he usually stood with the majority.

Campbell married Florence A. Van Platner, a daughter of a noted New York attorney, on November 5, 1887. They had one surviving child, a daughter Lois. A son and daughter died as infants. The Campbells moved from the northeast corner of Grand and Washington to a palatial home at 2 Westmoreland Place. They also enjoyed a country estate near Greenwich, Connecticut, known as Mullrick, after his home village in Ireland. While Campbell and his wife shared many interests, especially the theater, he found his greatest happiness at home.

A social observer described Campbell as a "short, solid Irishman . . . with a silvery laugh and an air of pugnacious scepticism."[3] Friends felt that he could have been a good mixer if he had thought it worthwhile. Apparently, he did not. He was cordial to individuals on occasion, but generally he was businesslike. He wanted the visitor to come to the point and present facts and proposals at once. As soon as he heard them, he dismissed the caller with these words: "Come again in the morning." Those who took this as a dismissal made a mistake. Those who returned to his office the next morning generally found him accessible and knowledgeable. Rough with the rich, he dealt sympathetically with the poor, especially those he had dealt with for a long while. He was always ready to give them a sympathetic hearing. Newspaperman Walter D. Stephens stated that Campbell was one of the frankest men he ever had to interview as a newspaper reporter; the tough Irishman never dodged a question.

Campbell avoided committees. Many of his fellow Irish served on the consultative committee of Saint Louis University President Father William Banks Rogers, or on that of Archbishop John J. Glennon; but Campbell did not. He made only one exception. In preparation for the World's Fair, he was a forceful factor. He gave his time and thought with a measure of public spirit not hitherto in evidence.

In 1909 Campbell became president of the North American Company that controlled the United Railways and the Union Electric Companies. He served as president for five years and was succeeded the next March by James B. Mortimer, whom he had trained for the position. Campbell became chairman of the board of directors. In 1912, by pressing a four hundred thousand–dollar claim, Campbell's company, the North American, forced the Frisco Railroad into a receivership. He was then the largest stockholder, with forty thousand shares of Frisco.

On December 17, 1912, five hundred guests from St. Louis and New York came to 2 Westmoreland Place for the debut of Lois, Campbell's daughter. Later, they assembled at the University Club. While at his summer estate in

Connecticut in 1914, Campbell contracted blood poisoning following an operation to remove a carbuncle from his neck. Pneumonia set in that May. James Campbell died five weeks later on June 14, 1914, at sixty-six years of age. His widow and daughter accompanied the casket to St. Louis in a private railway car. Close to a thousand people thronged Union Station for the arrival of the train.[4]

Since the New Cathedral was under construction, the pastor, Father Francis Gilfillan, a fellow Irish immigrant, soon to be named bishop of the diocese of St. Joseph, Missouri, conducted the funeral ceremonies at the Cathedral Chapel on Newstead behind the growing new structure. The list of honorary pallbearers included almost every important businessman of the city.[5] Newspapers spoke extensively of Campbell's wealth. The *Post-Dispatch* stated, "In that year, 1914, Campbell had been assessed at $2,888,270 for real and personal property in St. Louis, almost a million dollars more than any other St. Louisan pays taxes on. His fortune was estimated at more than $20 million."[6] In his will, James Campbell provided that his wife should receive the income of the estate for her life and that their daughter should receive the income after Mrs. Campbell's death. Eventually, the will stated, the Campbell estate would go to Saint Louis University for the creation and support of a hospital, even though Campbell had no previous association with the university.

The years of James Campbell saw the nation go from the age of empire builders to that of the "Robber Barons" and on to that of the money manipulators. The soldier returning from the Civil War battlefields, or the immigrant arriving soon after, looked to building "a little gray home in the West," or starting a business in the city. By the end of the century, the frontier no longer beckoned. The younger sons of farmers and the immigrants alike looked for that job in the crowded city. Few young men saw a fortune awaiting them.

Instead of the sixty neighborhood breweries of 1860, by 1890 four plants monopolized beer bottling in St. Louis. One employed four hundred workers. Neighborhood stores continued: groceries, pharmacies, and hardware stores. Gradually, however, large chains came on the scene and won a good share of their business. New industries arose, such as automobile manufacture. At first many firms built autos, but gradually a few big firms controlled the assembly lines. Other industries walked the same route. Such firms grew and production expanded, but working conditions deteriorated. Hours were long, wages low. Management ignored the basic rules of safety; fire escapes were inadequate, the facilities unsanitary. Workers lacked security, and they depended entirely on their wages. Police protected the property of the owners but cared little for the needs of the workers. Laboring people languished, powerless against bosses.

In a small magazine, the *Iconoclast*, a writer using a pseudonym, attacked the business leaders of St. Louis, including Irishmen James Campbell, Julius Walsh, and John Scullin, as well as Anglo-Americans David R. Francis, Edward Whitaker, and Thomas West, of controlling everything worth owning in the city. While religious and moral men, their commerce and politics caused concern. William Marion Reedy stressed that their wealth was based not on earned income but upon monopoly of what the community's growth had created.

A transit strike broke out in 1900. Union members sought recognition of Local 131 of the Street Railway Employees of America and demanded that they be required to work no longer than ten hours a day. When bosses reneged on promises, 2,325 transit workers struck. Edward Whitaker of the St. Louis Transit Company brought in strikebreakers from Cleveland. Violence broke out and vandalism came next. The north and south sides of the city supported the strikers, while the wealthy west of Grand Avenue deplored their action not those of the owners or the "scabs."

Federal Judge Elmer Adams enjoined fifty strike leaders from further action and authorized a *posse comitatus*, a special force of the "better elements," to act on the side of the owners. On June 10, a battle between the posse and the strikers left three dead and fourteen wounded. Eventually, destitution and misery forced the workers to give up, but the strike was not totally in vain. Historian James Neal Primm summarized the results: "The six-month confrontation had highlighted the poor municipal services, corporate arrogance, legislative corruption and the need for fair taxation of utilities, with public ownership as an alternative."[7] But many years elapsed before the city faced up to these needs.

The Knights of Labor, and then the American Federation of Labor, worked to improve the lot of the work force. Courts favored big business, however, even when the legislators ruled in favor of the worker. The organized workers chose good leaders. All of them were Irish or Irish-American, except American Federation of Labor Chief Samuel Gompers. Notable among them were Terence Powderly of the Knights of Labor, John Mitchell of the Mine Workers, John Fitzpatrick, president of the Chicago Labor Federation, Peter James McGuire, who gave the nation Labor Day, and Dublin-born Joseph Patrick McDonnell, who pioneered in labor editing in the New York area.[8] None of these great individuals made St. Louis the center of their activities. However, the city would have its own great labor leader, Fannie Mooney Sellins, an Irish woman who died in the cause of social justice.

Early in the century, business interests marshalled young women on the assembly line. The garment industry lured many of them into working conditions that recalled the words of Pope Leo XIII's encyclical *Rerum Novarum* of 1891: "A yoke little less than slavery itself." The entire nation realized the awful conditions a few years later when a fire at the Triangle Shirtwaist Company in New York in 1911 incinerated 146 women workers, mostly girls.

In St. Louis, years before that terrible fire, hundreds of women workers labored in equally poor conditions at Marx & Haas Clothing on Washington

Avenue, but a change was coming. Women in the garment industry set up their own Local 67 of the United Garment Workers of America. Local President Hannah Hennessey had worked in the garment trade from the age of thirteen and had lived a life of low wages and little leisure. She had started working sixty hours a week, ten hours each day for six days.

In 1907, when the work week was fifty-four hours and the minimum wage was five dollars a week, Hennessey traveled to Chicago for a conference of the Women's Trade Union League. Becoming convinced in Chicago of the power of women's networking, Hennessey organized a chapter of the WTUL in St. Louis and set out to develop other woman labor leaders, among them another young woman of Irish ancestry, Fannie Mooney Sellins.

In her early years, Fannie Mooney worked as a dressmaker in her rented home at 962 Chouteau Avenue in Annunciation Parish. She married Charlie Sellins, a garment worker. They had three children. When her husband died, Fannie moved to 1432a North Garrison Avenue and worked downtown.

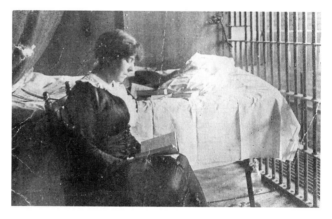

*Fannie Mooney Sellins led the successful struggle of St. Louis garment workers in St. Louis that ended long hours, low pay, and unsafe working conditions. Later, as union organizer for the mine workers in Appalachia, she was jailed for picketing in New Jersey and shot fatally in the back by three mine guards in Pennsylvania in August 1919. Sadly, St. Louis forgot her.*

## POST CARD

PUT ONE CENT STAMP HERE

Your Excellency:

I herewith respectfully petition you to release Fannie Sellins, at present confined in the Marion County Jail, Fairmont, W. Va., under a six months sentence inflicted by Judge A. G. Dayton.

She is not charged with the violation of any law of the state or nation, but with the alleged violation of Judge Dayton's own injunction, which has been appealed. She is the only woman in a jail containing no provisions for women, and this makes her imprisonment simply torture.

(Signed) .........................

(Address) .........................

36

**Hon. Woodrow Wilson,**

President of the United States,

WASHINGTON, D. C.

On September 13, 1909, the firm of Marx & Haas, located at the southwest corner of Thirteenth and Washington, locked out hundreds of its employees, members of UGWA Locals 23 and 67, ostensibly because some of the workers objected to walking up six flights of stairs. The management at Marx & Haas obviously believed that higher profits were more important than the humane benefit of elevators for their wage-earners.

The women workers, many of whom did not speak English, worked fifty hours a week—nine hours a day, Monday through Friday, and five hours on Saturday. The standard wage at the time was nine dollars a week. One worker complained that the high-speed machines shattered nerves in a few years. Further, the company ignored safety procedures. In one year, for instance, five hundred minor accidents occurred, chiefly to fingers caught by needles and in machines.[9]

The management apparently was trying to destroy the local garment workers' union and institute an open shop. The lockout notice went out in English, Jewish, Italian, and Slavic languages. The women struck in response. The Matthew Kiely Detective Agency, hired by Marx & Haas, brought in strikebreakers from Chicago and New York. As chief of police a few years before, Kiely had given an order during a strike to "shoot and kill." That order so outraged the public that he had to resign. His company soon became known as a "thug" agency.[10]

A month into the strike, Hannah Hennessey died of tuberculosis. Fannie Sellins took the lead of Local 67. Negotiations between Marx & Haas and leaders of the UGWA locals, among them Fannie Sellins, broke off after a two-hour meeting on October 12, 1909. Judge George C. Hitchcock of the Circuit Court of the City of St. Louis, following the usual court procedure of favoring management rather than looking to justice for workers, granted a temporary injunction against picketing.

In response, Fannie Sellins undertook a nationwide speaking tour to tell the world of the wrongs of the underpaid and overworked garment workers. That action transformed the local struggle into a national campaign for the rights of labor.[11] Fellow Irish garment worker Kate Hurley, who lived at 3708 Laclede in St. Francis Xavier Parish, joined her. Together they ranged the country, raising money for relief of the striking workers and promoting a national boycott of Marx-made clothes among the women of the country.

Sellins gained national recognition over the course of the strike, which lasted for twenty-five months. She and Kate Hurley went to Chicago to visit every union on behalf of St. Louis garment workers. The Chicago Women's Trade Union League and nationally known social reformer Jane Adams supported their cause. On the front page of the November 6, 1909, edition of *St. Louis Labor*, the editor featured the help miners gave to the garment workers. He expected help and expressions of concern also from Archbishop Glennon, since the two young women who headed the fight for justice were Catholics, as were so many of the garment workers. Instead, on the following Sunday, the archbishop spoke on two topics: the cost of the New Cathedral and the evils of European Socialism. "In his sermon," the editor wrote, "the archbishop showed what great service he can be to the capitalist class."[12] Fannie talked the mineworkers' union in Illinois into assessing its members a token sum to support the strike. In Des Moines, Fannie talked before the Iowa State Convention of the Socialist Party. "It was a fiery speech of an almost Socialist trend," a Des Moines newspaper stated. "Time after time she was interrupted by cheering from all corners of the auditorium."[13] Rural Iowan Republicans rarely heard such advanced social thinking.

In August 1910, Sellins made the Sixteenth Annual Convention of the United Garment Workers aware of her presence. Even though many UGWA members were women, few held leadership positions. Fannie sponsored several resolutions. One called for a prompt release of funds voted for the St. Louis strikers. The boycott continued, and in the end, Fannie won. On October 13, following two weeks of negotiations, Marx & Haas signed a closed shop agreement, with wage issues to be settled by negotiation and, if necessary, by third-party arbitration. While she was on the tour, incidentally, vandals smashed Sellins's home on Garrison. Many wondered if the perpetrators worked for the Matthew Kiely Detective Agency.

Fannie refused to let terrorism hold her back. By the end of the year, she had launched another strike: this one against Schwab Clothing Company at 2649 Locust Street. The Schwab owners resisted all UGWA organizing efforts among their five to six hundred workers. The union boycotted Schwab's products, picketed the Schwab factory on Market Street, and sent Sellins and Hurley on another national speaking tour. They appealed for support from the United Mine Workers at their convention in Indianapolis.

In the meantime, in the Danbury Hatters' Case, the U.S. Supreme Court ruled a secondary boycott unconstitutional. The central office of the UGWA repudiated Fannie and Kate's efforts to solicit funds. At this juncture, the United Mine Workers wanted her as an organizer. She went to the coal fields on the West Virginia–Pennsylvania border. Fannie stated that her decision to work with the miners came while traveling in the interests of the garment workers in Pittsburgh. A miner on strike by the name of Paul Scoric had invited her to visit his family in Colliers, West Virginia. When she saw the conditions in the town, she knew her destiny lay in the mine camps.

Her early work in Appalachia consisted of bringing food and clothing to women and children in need, rather than organizing workers. During a confrontation with miners, someone shot a guard. Judge Alston G. Dayton, who had already declared the United Mine Workers Association unlawful, sentenced Fannie and ten other union organizers to jail for sixty days. The judge personally warned Sellins "not to emulate Mother Jones,"[14] an already famous Irish labor leader who agitated tyrannical mine owners and their friends on the bench for many years.

Fannie Sellins went to the Marion County jail in Fairmont, West Virginia. The UMWA produced hundreds of postcards with a gripping photograph of her reading in her cell and sent large numbers to President Woodrow Wilson. Even with the intervention of the president, two years went by before the West Virginia courts acceded to his wishes and removed the penalties. Sellins began more organizing activities in Pennsylvania. Owners brought in black strikebreakers from the South, without telling them of the situation that confronted them. Fannie explained to many that they had been recruited as "scabs" without their knowing it, and helped them to return to their homes.

At the end of World War I, employers in many industries began to clamp down on their workers. A major steel strike was imminent. On August 26, 1919, Fannie Sellins picketed a mine in an area where violence broke out. A hired guard pushed Fannie. As she ran for the safety of Constantin Rafalko's backyard nearby, three hired gunmen shot her from behind—a horrible deed against the code of any cold-blooded gunman of the West. One bullet hit her in the back of her head and came out her forehead. A nephew of Constantin, Stanley Rafalko, saw the shooting. No judge sentenced her murderers. Instead, the Allegheny County Coroner's Jury ruled that the deputies had acted in self-defense and denounced "the Alien or Foreign agitators who instill Anarchy and Bolshevist Doctrines into the minds of unamericans and uneducated Aliens."[15]

Thousands of people attended her funeral Mass at St. Peter's Church in New Kensington, Pennsylvania, three days later. No memorial Mass was held in St. Louis. The city forgot her. Even when James Cassedy, a historian at the National Archives, told her story in the winter 1992 issue of *Labor Heritage*,[16] few St. Louisans became aware of Fannie Mooney Sellins. Fortunately, local historian Rose Feuer learned her history, wrote about it, and told it to her classes, union editors, and others interested in labor history. No St. Louis battler for justice matched the zeal and self-sacrifice of Fannie Mooney Sellins, a martyr for the cause.

# World's Fair and World War

Many Irish, both in St. Louis and in Ireland, had their part in planning for the World's Fair to commemorate the centennial of the Louisiana Purchase in 1904. Among St. Louis Irish participants, business leader James Campbell strongly supported the proposal to locate the fair at the west end of Forest Park, and John Scullin and W. F. Boyle served on the Executive Committee. The planners wanted the famous tenor, John McCormack, to grace the Irish village with his presence and his voice. They negotiated with the Irish theater group to present one of William Butler Yeats's plays, either *Cathleen Ni Houlihan* or *Diedre*.

*At the 1904 Worlds Fair, Ireland's presence was most noted at the "Irish Village," at the east end of the Pike, the entertainment district of the exposition.*

Lady Aberdeen, the wife of the Lord Lieutenant of Ireland, promoted the Irish Pavilion at the fair and urged the Fay Theater group to play in St. Louis. Unfortunately, James Reardon, Commissioner of Ireland in St. Louis moved ahead with plans before clearing copyright arrangements with Yeats. The playwright-poet wrote on April 8, 1904, insisting on a competent Irish or American company to produce the plays.[1]

Myles J. Murphy, the general manager of the Irish Industrial Exhibit and director of Amusement, described the potential St. Louis audience in a way that might have better fit the attendance at the Pendelton Round Up or Frontier Days in Cheyenne. He bracketed the Irish plays with Will Rogers's lariat twirling. Yeats ultimately did not approve of the Irish company that went to St. Louis. He called some of them "more politicians than players," and expressed regret that they were to be Ireland's representatives. He did not attend the fair.[2] This was unfortunate both for the visitors to the fair and the Irish themselves. However, John McCormack came to the Irish Village and sang *Macushla and Somewhere A Voice Is Calling*, two of his all-time favorites. He also visited the Irish Sisters at the Visitation Academy, fifteen blocks north of the fairgrounds.[3]

The World's Fair board of directors had sent to Rome a committee, headed by local newspaperman Walter Stevens to borrow art objects for display and to ask the newly elected Pope Pius X to send a representative to St. Louis. The pope agreed on both accounts and designated Francis Cardinal Satolli, the former apostolic delegate, as his special envoy in 1904. Governor David R. Francis, president of the exposition, welcomed the cardinal on the steps of Brookings Hall, the headquarters of the fair. St. Louis's new archbishop, John J. Glennon, joined him in greeting Pope Pius X's representative. Glennon had come from Kansas City the previous year as coadjutor to ailing Archbishop Kain and succeeded him when Kain died that October.

Archbishop Glennon joined the four thousand guests who came to Festival Hall on "Saint Louis University Day," October 18. Governor Francis congratulated the university and singled out alumnus Julius Walsh, among others, for special thanks for helping make the celebration a success. The participation of the university in the fair stemmed from the coming of the already mentioned Father William Banks Rogers, who lifted the "beleaguered citadel" and monastic spirit of the university and turned it into an American institution by adopting American educational terminology and procedures. He invited Catholic educators to meet at the university during the year of the fair, welcomed President Roosevelt to the campus, and enlisted prominent businessmen as consultants. Among them were Irish individuals: banker Julius Walsh; John Scullin in steel; Francis A. Drew in glassware; Richard D. Kerens in mining and railroading; Daniel C. Nugent and David Walker in merchandising; and Festus Wade at Mercantile Trust.

To head an already successful athletic program, Father Rogers recruited an outstanding coach, Eddie Cochems, who brought Saint Louis University's predominantly Irish-American team led by Captain Jack Kenney into prominence in midwestern football. Over the years, the Saint Louis University eleven beat Nebraska, Iowa, and Arkansas, and held the powerful Carlyle Indians, led by Jim Thorpe, the famous Olympic star, to a tie. The forward-looking legacy of Father Rogers carried on during the terms of his immediate successors.

The same outstanding laymen who advised Father Rogers, as well as John Leahy and W. J. Kinsella, rallied to the call of Archbishop Glennon when he announced his plans for a magnificent cathedral on the site his predecessor had chosen, the northwest corner of Lindell and Newstead. No one doubted the wisdom of the new location. The former cathedral on the waterfront hardly breathed in the impacted area of cobblestones and warehouses. With the

*Coach Eddie Cochems led the predominantly Irish Saint Louis University football team of 1908 to its most successful season by introducing the forward pass, an innovation that caught opponents off balance. All but one of the sixteen players shown here became physicians. The other chose dentistry.*

approval of the archbishop, the architects—Barnett, Haynes and Barnett of St. Louis—chose to combine Byzantine and Romanesque features. The Catholics of St. Louis responded generously to his call for funds.

Several Irish priests moved beyond traditional parish programs. Father Peter Dunne, one of the first priests Archbishop Glennon ordained, had been orphaned on a Kansas farm at the age of nine. He set out to help orphan boys, especially those who sold newspapers or shined shoes. Soon thirty-five boys came under his guidance. After several attempts at finding a satisfactory residence, he began a drive for permanent quarters. Archbishop Glennon released him from parish duties and dedicated "Father Dunne's Newsboys' Home" at Washington and Garrison on November 10, 1907. Some decades later, his successful story became the basis of the film "Fighting Father Dunne."

No movie mogul chose to film the life of a far more colorful personality, Father Tim Dempsey, pastor of St. Patrick's Church since 1898. As robust and hearty as Father Dunne was trim and reserved, Father Tim found that many Slavic and Italian families had moved into the once all-Irish parish. Some Irish were still there and many old families came back to celebrate St. Patrick's Day. But vagrants came, too. Many homeless drifters, migrant laborers in off-season, rivermen, and roustabouts wandered through the old Irish ward.

After planning carefully, Father Tim opened a "Hotel for Workingmen" with 68 rooms and 207 beds. Archbishop Glennon blessed the building on May 5, 1908, before a distinguished gathering that included Mayor Rolla

*Versatile Father Tim Dempsey, pastor of St. Patrick's Church and social reformer, opened homes for workingmen and working women, settled strikes, calmed gang warfare, and assisted the African American community.*

Wells. During the following year, Father Tim won a donation of ground from the directors of Calvary Cemetery to provide graves for the indigents of all national backgrounds. Such was Father Tim's appeal that the Bensiek-Niehaus Funeral Home provided caskets and hearses free of charge. In due course, the zealous priest opened a residence for women. He put out the *Hotel Magazine* to keep everyone apprised of coming events. Father Tim made newspaper headlines regularly in the succeeding decades.

Over the years, Archbishop Glennon excelled in the pulpit or on the platform. Whether he was blessing a local Catholic enterprise, such as Father Dempsey's "Home," or gracing the dedication of the great cathedral of Denver, he early gave an indication of the quality of oratory that earned him the reputation as the premier orator of the American hierarchy after the death of Archbishop Patrick Ryan of Philadelphia.

The following excerpt from his St. Patrick's Day speech in Kansas City in 1908 illustrates well the flow and beauty of his messages:

> That mystic light that comes from the wild sea that washes the Irish coasts; from the heather that covers its hills; from the moaning winds that crowd its woods; . . . from the open meadows and the summer nights; from out of the scenery and association and life that becomes a part of the Irish character, there comes that strange yearning, . . . that unwillingness to be part of the commonplace, that restlessness, energy and fire, that, as a dissolvent set here in American life, makes crass materialism impossible and sets across the face of our land a rainbow . . . of hope that . . . tells us of the better things and the brighter land.[4]

When the time came for the laying of the cornerstone of the New Cathedral on Sunday, October 18, 1908, the apostolic delegate, Archbishop Diomede Falconio, O.F.M., led a group of five archbishops and many bishops from all over the country for the ceremony. The delegate brought a special blessing from Pope Pius X.

Since the Christian Brothers no longer offered Latin courses at their academy, the Jesuit Fathers opened two more preparatory academies in the city, along with Saint Louis University High School on Grand at West Pine. Gonzaga opened adjacent to St. Joseph's Church on the near northside, and Loyola Academy, which welcomed many Irish students, opened in the old Eads mansion on Compton, two blocks north of Lafayette Avenue.

While the Jesuits expanded their educational efforts on the secondary level, the Daughters of Charity drew back. A few years before they had moved St. Vincent's Free School from an inner-city location to Grand Avenue a few blocks north of Saint Louis University. The school flourished as St. Vincent's Seminary and drew the wealthy Irish in the area as well as the less affluent. The sisters gradually came to realize that the school did not meet their vocation to work with the poor, and they closed it in 1909.

The Census of 1910 registered 14,268 St. Louis residents of Irish birth. The heaviest concentrations found 1,302 in the 20th ward, 845 in the 27th, and 704 in the 19th.[5] During those first years of Archbishop Glennon's leadership in St. Louis, many new parishes opened. These had a heavy Irish constituency: Immaculate Conception in Maplewood in 1904, Nativity in 1905, Blessed Sacrament in 1907, St. Roch's in 1911, Epiphany in 1912, St. Luke's in 1914, and St. Rita's, Our Lady of the Presentation, and Our Lady of Lourdes in 1916. The old Irish neighborhoods, whence these westward-moving Catholics came, filled first with immigrants from Eastern and Southern Europe, and then with African Americans who moved in from the rural South looking for jobs.

When European leaders and people rushed blindly into war in 1914, many St. Louis Irish as well as local Germans opposed U.S. entrance into the conflict, as did organized workers of all nationalities. The people of Ireland long had sought their own parliament. When they had almost reached that goal, the British government used the outbreak of the war to shilly-shally. Popular pastor Father Tim Dempsey railed against England for tyrannizing Ireland. The St. Louis Irish had sympathy for invaded France and Belgium, but not to the extent of wanting to go to war.

Father Tim had other concerns besides the European war at that time. One of these was the conflict between Capital and Labor. He set out to improve labor-management relations. In his *Hotel Magazine* he often gave his views on the rights of workingmen and, in turn, spelled out their duties. In 1910 he had talked to a thousand members of the Workingman's Welfare Association at Goller Hall in Sts. Peter and Paul Parish on South Seventh Street at Allen.[6] A year later, several members of the Teamsters' Local 700 carried two fatally wounded strikers, Paddy Kane and Mike Kane (not related) into Father Dempsey's rectory for first aid and the last anointing. In an altercation on the work site, strikebreakers had gunned down both of them. Such experiences increased the priest's concern for organized labor and his aversion to bloody strikes.

In mid-August 1915, the Teamsters again went on strike for better wages and working conditions. Among their immediate goals, they did not want to be forced to work more than ten hours a day. Rugged Father Tim waded right into the fray. Unable to reach John Duggan, the business agent of Local 700, or its president Tom Coyne, the priest got in touch with Dan Murphy, the vice president. Dan was willing to talk with whomever Father Tim suggested. George Tansey, the head of the Transfer Company, one of the main firms involved, would talk issues with Murphy, accepting Father Tim as a "go-between." When Tansey agreed to reasonable demands, Father Tim went to the

Central Trades and Labor Union Hall and persuaded the rank-and-file to accept.[7]

At that juncture, he went to city government with an idea unique for its time, namely the setting up of an Industrial Dispute Commission. The city fathers failed to catch the pastor's far-sighted view. A quarter of a century later, however, such ideas came to prevail.

In February 1916, Father Tim mediated disputes between the Stove Mounters' Union and Louis Stockstrom, head of the American Stove Company, and a short time later, between the leaders of the Building Trades Council, Maurice Cassidy and Steve McCoy, and the officers of the Fruin-Colnon Construction firm.[8]

On the morning of October 6, 1916, a deadly disaster struck Christian Brothers College. While the boarding students left the school in order, a fire trapped Brother Cormac and Brother Clement in the infirmary and took the lives of seven firemen and the night watchman. The Jesuit community at Saint Louis University and pastors throughout the city housed the surviving brothers. Chancellor Robert Brookings of Washington University allowed the brothers to use without cost the spacious Smith Academy and the Manual Training School buildings, later Blewett High School. CBC continued there until June 1917. In the meantime, the brothers sold the campus, which later became Sherman Park.

The Shepherd Goes, the Flock Remains — By Bishop

*Daniel Bishop, cartoonist for the* St. Louis Star, *caught the sorrow of the depression-hit St. Louisans at the death of Father Tim Dempsey.*

Over in Europe the terrible year 1916 had seen countless men slaughtered on both sides, with little effect. When Emperor Franz Joseph of Austria-Hungary died that fall, Archbishop Glennon presided at a Requiem Mass on December 2, 1916, in the presence of priests and people representing six different language groups. All of these nationalities joined the Irish in their hope to avoid war. When war did come, however, they all served loyally. A recent historical survey shows that the view of these St. Louisans reflected the views of the majority of Missourians who opposed American intervention.[9]

On Palm Sunday in 1917, Archbishop Glennon severely criticized the determination of Congress to vote on war on Good Friday. Along with many midwesterners, Congressman William Igoe, representing a heavily Irish district of north St. Louis, voted against America's declaration of war. With the conflict still raging, his constituents re-elected him in November 1918. Kate O'Hare, editor of the *National Rip-Saw*, a socialist paper published in St. Louis, strongly opposed American's declaration of war. Federal authorities sent her to the women's prison in Atlanta for her "traitorous" remarks. Her revelation of the horrid conditions there brought on prison reform. She became a national heroine as a result of her disclosures, but the Irish community could not claim Kate as its own, except by marriage. She was a Kansas Protestant of Anglo-American ancestry; her husband was Irish Catholic.

Literary and political pundit William Marion Reedy saw the causes of the war as economic. All nations, he said, held the same economic fallacies and shared responsibility for the outbreak. After the terrible slaughter of 1916 at Verdun and on the Somme, Pope Benedict XV offered a plan for peace. In a similar vein, Reedy wrote an editorial he called, "Still Hope for Peace." "Both sides made war inevitable," he began. "Both sides are wrong. And neither side can win save at such cost as may well give it pause."[10]

Unfortunately, Europe did not have statesmen of sufficient wisdom and courage to react to the call for peace of Pope Benedict that many men like Reedy supported. As the struggle continued, and revolution racked Russia, many Americans wanted our country to intervene. Reedy finally acquiesced in this decision but gave wise and courageous advice: "We should not make war on German music, art, letters, philosophy, and language. Our business is to smash German autocracy. And we should be as kind as possible to our own German-Americans while we are doing it. Now is the time to show what American liberty means."[11] Even though he had finally come to accept the fact of our involvement before the war was over, Reedy began to question the rightness of our taking part.

Prohibition and the economic adjustment after wartime prosperity brought problems. Returning veterans found few jobs. The government provided little help for their return to civilian life, as it had done in earlier wars by land grants, and would do after World War II with the G.I. Bill. A few frustrated veterans on the near northside, some of them Irish, unable to find good jobs, turned to the illegal "booze business." This brought rivalries between gangs. When Willie Egan, the leader of one gang, was taken to a hospital mortally wounded, Father Dempsey was called to his bedside.[12]

The Egans blamed the murder on a rival gang, the Hogans. None of either gang lived in Father Dempsey's parish, but he did know many of them personally and called them to his rectory and urged them to make peace. Other murders followed beyond the Irish community before peace eventually came.

# The St. Louis Irish in a Melting Pot

The excessive nationalistic propaganda of wartime carried over into the twenties. During the years before the conflict, when an increase occurred in numbers of immigrants from Eastern and Southern Europe, the St. Louis newspapers acclaimed the diverse practices of people who made up our community, and told of the marriage customs of the Slovenes in Soulard or of the variety of ethnic restaurants there. After the First World War, the newspapers no longer heralded the hyphenated Americans.

America became a "melting pot," producing one people, "not a salad bowl" of many cultures, a term that became popular decades later. The Germans felt the brunt of this new spirit. People did not heed the warning of editor William Marion Reedy to avoid demeaning German music, culture, and literature. They chose to consider Germans "Huns," barbarians, or descendants of Attila, not of Barbarossa or Bach. A chance visitor from Germany was a pariah. People of other nationalities, including the Irish, felt the changes of the times, but in a neutral, not hostile, way.

St. Louis had no great Irish-American hero returning from the war, no Father Francis Duffy or General "Wild Bill" Donovan, as New York did. It was not a time when groups of Irish men or women joined strictly Irish organizations with a specific goal. John Dinan or Dan Stack of Epiphany Parish, a new, heavily Irish community at the southwestern edge of the city, more likely belonged to the De Smet Council of the Knights of Columbus rather than to the Kenrick Chapter of the Ancient Order of Hibernians. St. Louis had no Irish political boss, such as Mayor Ed Kelly of Chicago or Tom Pendergast of Kansas City. But a historian who preferred to remain anonymous claimed that St. Louis did have a political boss, Archbishop John J. Glennon. Certainly he wielded tremendous influence in civil life, but deftly and behind the scenes.

Ireland was in the final stages of its drive for freedom from foreign oppression. That freedom, however, was coming in such a way that Irish, disappointed with the conditions Britain insisted upon, were soon at each other's throats. But Oliver Swift and Pete Flaherty in Epiphany Parish were more interested in the struggle between St. Louis Browns' pitcher "Schucks" Pruitt and Yankee slugger "Babe" Ruth at Sportsmen's Park on North Grand Boulevard than in the rivalry of Eamon de Valera and Michael Collins in the land whence their grandparents came in the days of the Great Famine. And Father Joseph English, pastor of Epiphany Parish, concentrated more on building an adequate church for his growing flock than on the happenings near his native Cork.

The young people who grew up in that parish, with its Irish-born pastor and with Irish-American Dominican Sisters as teachers, found almost no mention of "Irishness" or contemporary Ireland. The pupils sang "Oh Blessed St. Patrick, who brought to our mountains, the gift of God's faith and the sweet light of his love," every St. Patrick's Day, but it was a school exercise, not an Irish effort. Agnes Stovicek and Bob Seitz sang along with Catherine Dinan and Jimmy Leahy. Father English's St. Patrick's Day talk was exuberantly and patriotically American, with much on Bunker Hill and little on the Battle of the Boyne.

Even with its Cork-born pastor and its large percentage of Irish parishioners, Epiphany was not as exclusively of one nationality as St. Lawrence O'Toole's or St. Bridget's had been fifty years before, or as its neighbors St. Aloysius on Reber Place was German and St. Ambrose "on the Hill" was Italian. The population of Epiphany Parish was 45 percent Irish, 35 percent German, 14 percent Slavic, and 5 percent Italian, but, nonetheless, was thought of as Irish.

"Irish" parishes had changed, and so had the city of St. Louis. By the 1920 census, the city, with 772,897 residents,[1] had dropped in population two places, behind Cleveland and Detroit, while suburbs such as University City, Wellston, and Kirkwood had grown by 22 percent, from 82,417 to 100,737. By 1930, 28,353 St. Louisans had come from Ireland,[2] and 48,617 had parents who had been born there.[3]

The postwar period spawned many studies of civic life. The Chamber of Commerce sponsored an industrial survey that started a trend. A school survey followed, then a study of charitable agencies, a city planning survey, and a religious survey sponsored by the St. Louis Metropolitan Church Federation.

This last moved far beyond theological reflection to present valuable information on city growth patterns that significantly affected many Irish parishes. Churches on the northside and the southside stayed where they were, both mirroring and abetting the stability of the homeowners, while those in the central city tended to move west at regular intervals. African Americans followed this westward movement and at times anticipated the general movement. St. Lawrence O'Toole Parish, once Irish but multinational in the late 1920s, would be a heavily black neighborhood by the 1950s. Eventually, the Irish of St. Leo's and St. Malachy's, the Anglo-Americans of First Presbyterian, and the Jews of Shaare Emeth Temple, moved west and African Americans took their places.

The 1923 bond issue brought electric street lamps, and "the old lamplighter" became a memory and the subject of a nostalgic song. The city widened Natural Bridge, Olive, and Gravois, facilitating movement northwest, west, and southwest. The city built a new Civil Courts Building and Kiel Auditorium. Daniel Fitzpatrick, the great cartoonist of the *Post-Dispatch*, called the city's attention regularly to the growing threat of smoke that was causing Dr. George T. Moore, head of the Missouri Botanical Garden, to consider moving Shaw's great legacy to the Arboretum at Gray Summit, forty miles out along what soon became highway U.S. 66.

Working men had enjoyed decent treatment during the war, with production high and with management anxious to profit from war sales. But once the war was over, owners began to retrench. In spite of the Clayton Anti-Trust Act of 1914, enacted during President Woodrow Wilson's first term, that excluded labor unions from prosecution under the Sherman Anti-Trust Act, the conservative courts continued to harass organized labor during the 1920s. A large percentage of Irish workers were organized, and in turn a good percentage of organized workers, except in brewing, were of Celtic ancestry. At least conditions were better for the American Federation of Labor members than for unorganized or unskilled workers.

During the half-century after the First World War, the Irish community had no pre-eminent businessmen as John O'Fallon and John Mullanphy were a century before, or James Campbell and Julius Walsh were at the turn of the century. It had no writers to match William Marion Reedy or Kate Chopin. The story of the Irish in St. Louis from 1920 to 1960 will not be the story of a group of Irish people working together for a specific goal. Rather, it will be the story of individual people of Irish background succeeding in various areas—in politics, education, labor leadership, or religious activities, such as Dr. R. Emmet Kane, Catholic lay leader in the 1920s and 1930s. Individual Irish will achieve during these decades but without a particularly Irish aspect to their achievement. Their careers come up under various headings: Irish in education, Irish in church activities, and Irish in organized labor.

XXIV

# Irish St. Louisans on the Political Scene in Washington

I n the first half of the century, the St. Louis Irish Catholic community sent three significant men into the House of Representatives and one into party leadership and a place in President Truman's Cabinet: William L. Igoe, John Cochran, John B. Sullivan, and Robert Hannegan.

While Igoe is not a common name, three Igoes, not closely related, one from Missouri and two from Illinois, served in the U.S. House of Representatives. William Leo Igoe of St. Louis was admitted to the bar in 1902 and served on the Board of Aldermen from 1909 to 1913. Elected to the U.S. House of

*William Igoe, four-term congressman from the Irish northside and president of the St. Vincent de Paul Society, takes the microphone at a meeting of that society.*

Representatives in 1913, he joined that group of midwestern legislators who worked to keep us out of war. When the issue faced Congress on Good Friday in 1917, he voted against the declaration. In spite of the war hysteria, Igoe's nouthside constituents re-elected him in November 1918 with the war still in progress. He did not run in 1920 and practiced law until 1928, when he ran unsuccessfully for the office of mayor.[1]

While the housing project named for William Igoe and Lieutenant Wendell Pruitt, a war hero, met the headache ball, the Veterans Hospital that bears John Cochran's name still stands proudly on Grand Boulevard in the old Vandeventer Place area.

John Cochran, a native of Webster Groves, who worked on a newspaper as a young man, had become secretary to Congressman Igoe in 1913. He studied law and, after Igoe left the House, was admitted to the bar in 1921. He then served as secretary to Congressman Harry Hawes until Hawes resigned in 1926. Cochran was elected to take his place. During Cochran's second term in the House of Representatives in November 1929, the stock market crashed. Soon, millions lost their jobs. Men accustomed to driving Cadillacs sought work as manual laborers. Hundreds sold apples on the streets of our big cities.

The value of stocks on the New York Stock Exchange slumped from a high of $87 billion in 1929 to a mere $19 billion within four years. Wholesale prices dropped 38 percent during that same time, and farm prices sank 60 percent below the levels of 1929. Within less than three years, national income plummeted to almost half of what it had been in the last boom year. The same was true of industrial production.

By September 1932, an estimated ten million people were unemployed. The great and mighty of the business world, who had insisted that the economic laws always brought prosperity, were mute. Millions of people who had bought on an installment plan—a new electric refrigerator, a new electric stove, a new electric clock, a radio—had no paychecks to pay off this debt.

President Herbert Hoover tried to reassure the people by saying that prosperity was just around the corner. There was no corner. Individuals who had insisted that government stay out of business now demanded that government do something about the economic decline. Hoover answered with the Reconstruction Finance Corporation to aid businesses. It was not enough.

Governor Franklin Delano Roosevelt of New York challenged him in 1932 and won. With the support of men like John Cochran of Missouri, Roosevelt began the New Deal that offered help to banks, young men, farmers, businesses, homeowners, and working men. In the campaign of 1934, Cochran ran for the Democratic senatorial nomination. He had two opponents. One he knew well, Jacob LeRoy Milligan, a fellow congressman. Milligan came from Richmond in the "Little Dixie" section of west central Missouri just north of Lexington on the Missouri River, forty miles east of Kansas City. A captain of infantry in World War I, he had won the Silver Star for gallantry and a Purple Heart. Milligan had the support of the eloquent Senator Bennett Champ Clark. They both ran against Harry Truman, a County Judge or Supervisor of Jackson County, whom many considered a stooge of Tom Pendergast, the political boss of Kansas City. In actuality, Harry Truman had been "Old Tom's" third choice. Even Pendergast had not fathomed Harry Truman's openness to growth.

Truman's award-winning biographer, David McCullough, described the favorite, John Cochran, as "a big, friendly, humorous, and honest man, . . . experienced in the ways of Washington . . . a 'congressman's congressman,' someone known to understand the 'wheels-within-wheels' intricacy of government, and who, importantly, also had the support of the so-called 'Igoe-Dickmann' organization."[2] When Senator Clark attacked Truman mercilessly for his Pendergast connections, Truman began to show the fire that later came to characterize him. "Jack Cochran to his credit," McCullough wrote, "tried to keep the debate on a serious level. 'Mud slinging,' Cochran said, 'was a luxury for prosperous times and had no place when conditions were so desperate and so many were suffering.'"[3]

The Pendergast machine got out the vote in Jackson County. Even though St. Louis was almost twice as large as Kansas City at the time, twenty-five thousand more Kansas City residents voted than St. Louisans. Two years later, however, his St. Louis constituents sent John Cochran back to the House of Representatives, where he continued his great work in promoting sound social legislation.

When the Tennessee Valley Authority proved the value of regional planning, Congressman Cochran teamed with Senator James Murray of Montana in co-sponsoring the Murray-Cochran Bill, which called for the creation of the Missouri Valley Authority. This proposal, widely acclaimed by populists, brought his name before the western public. While the total plan never carried, many features, such as rural electrification, became a part of the area. He served in the U.S. House of Representatives until January 3, 1947, a few months before his death.

A second Irish St. Louisan, Robert Hannegan, surfaced in the Truman story. When Governor Lloyd Stark challenged the incumbent Truman in the Democratic senatorial primary in 1940, Hannegan, according to historian McCullough, became "Truman's last minute savior. . . ."[4] The "handsome, gregarious" Hannegan, the son of a police chief, had finished law school after starring in football at Saint Louis University. He took part in Democratic politics and became city chairman of the party. At first he seemed to favor Stark, but two days before the primary, he came out strongly for Truman. As Governor Stark had weakened the Pendergast machine several years before and lessened its clout, Truman got fewer votes in Jackson County. He won on his St. Louis plurality, the result of Bob Hannegan's work.

As Hannegan moved on the Washington scene, he became Commissioner of Internal Revenue, and in the words of McCullough became "a first-rate head of the Bureau,"[5] chairman of the Democratic Party, and postmaster general in the cabinet of Franklin Delano Roosevelt.

As National Chairman of the Democratic Party, Postmaster General Bob Hannegan had a deciding part in one of the landmark decisions in modern American politics: the choosing of the nominee for vice president and heir-apparent of the ailing Franklin Delano Roosevelt. When Roosevelt sought a fourth term in 1944, forecasters saw a close race. If the party rejected the Vice President Henry Wallace, FDR, who never gave a clear indication of his choice, presumably favored former Senator James Francis Byrnes of South Carolina, the Director of the Office of War Mobilization. Many influential Democrats, especially in the South, felt Wallace too liberal on domestic issues and too friendly with the country's wartime ally, the Soviet Union.

Byrnes, Roosevelt's apparent choice, had supported Hannegan in his leadership of the IRS and his advancement to party chair. But the St. Louisan knew that organized labor, then at its height of power, did not want Byrnes, since he opposed its interests. African Americans, who had supported Roosevelt in key northern cities, also did not want Byrnes, a conservative Southerner. The powerful Irish Catholic city bosses—Ed Flynn of the Bronx, Frank Hague of Jersey City, and Edward Kelly of Chicago, among others— knew that many of their Catholic constituents might think twice before voting for Byrnes, an Irishman who apparently left the Catholic Church for political reasons. Roosevelt needed those city votes to win.

Hannegan had worked in Truman's interest in his 1940 senatorial re-election

*President Harry S Truman and his aide John Snyder, join leading St. Louisans, among them S. W. Fordyce and H. B. Deal, in honoring Robert Hannegan (second from left), chairman of the Democrat Party.*

campaign. The president had no objections to Truman as his running mate, but presumably he preferred Justice William O. Douglas of the U.S. Supreme Court. Hannegan made sure that the senator from Missouri topped FDR's approved list. The Roosevelt-Truman ticket won over the Republican candidates, Governor Thomas E. Dewey of New York and Governor Earl Warren of California. The popular vote was close, but the big cities gave the Democrats a wide margin in the electoral college. A year later Harry Truman was president of the United States. Hannegan died of a heart attack a few years later.

The fourth St. Louisan in Washington had less national impact but served his country and his city well. When John Berchmans Sullivan's parents moved to St. Louis in 1910 from Sedalia, Missouri, shortly after he finished St. Patrick's elementary school, they were undecided where to send their son for further education. At that time, a young Jesuit teacher, Father Laurence Kenny of Saint Louis University, visited the Sullivans.

"Since you have named your son after a Jesuit saint," Father Kenny insisted, "you should send him to a Jesuit school."

"Tell us about Saint John Berchmans," Mrs. Sullivan said. "We liked the name. We know that the Church recently canonized him but know nothing about who he was."

When Father Kenny told the story of the young Belgian who died in Rome as a Jesuit seminarian after winning respect as a living example of the Jesuit ideal of manhood,[6] the Sullivans registered John at Gonzaga Hall, a Jesuit prep school adjacent to St. Joseph's Church on North Eleventh Street. He went on to Saint Louis University, won his A.B. degree in 1918, and served in the infantry during the last months of World War I. When peace came, he finished

*Local Democratic leaders—Ralph Devereaux, Jim McNary, and James L. Sullivan—greet President Harry Truman.*

the law course at Saint Louis University, passed the bar exam, and entered politics as a Democrat. A strong supporter of people's causes, Sullivan served in the 77th, 79th, 81st, and 82nd Congresses.

All the while, Father Laurence Kenny, the Jesuit who had prevailed upon the Sullivans to send their son to Saint Louis University, continued to teach history at the school. Retired because of age before World War II, he came back to teach after the war when GIs filled the classrooms. The revered Father Kenny outlived the distinguished congressman. Further, even though Sullivan supported good causes, his record paled before the great acclaim that his wife and successor, Congresswoman Leonor Kretzer Sullivan, won as a "consumer's advocate" during the succeeding quarter of a century.

The Irish could claim Mrs. Sullivan, as they did Kate O'Hare, the great anti–World War I advocate and prison reformer, only because she married an Irishman. They accepted her leadership along with their fellow Democrats.

On the local political scene in the 1930s, Mayor "Barney" Dickmann had won the support of President Franklin Delano Roosevelt for the creation of a fitting memorial to President Thomas Jefferson's purchase of the Louisiana Territory in 1803. Thirty-plus years later, with County Supervisor James H. J. McNary and St. Louis Mayor Raymond Tucker, who had solved the smoke problem in the thirties, St. Louisans watched the Saarinen Gateway Arch rise along the riverfront. Mrs. Sullivan gave strong support from base to "topping out." MacDonald Construction carried the plans for this unique monument of the iron and steel age to completion on October 28, 1965.

Among other public servants of Irish ancestry in those years, Jack Keane served as deputy mayor of St. Louis, Georgia M. Buckowitz headed the city parks, Joseph Roddy was Clerk of the Circuit Court, and Donald Gunn was president of the Board of Aldermen and later a judge.

# Noted Irish Clerical Personalities (1920–1940)

A t regular intervals during the late 1920s and early 1930s, the *Globe-Democrat Sunday Magazine* carried sketches of Catholic personalities, many of them Irish: Father J. McGlynn on his 50th jubilee at St. Rose's; Father Daniel J. Lavery of Holy Rosary, who had gone back to Ireland twenty times since his arrival in the United States forty-five years before; Father Patrick Bradley, a master mechanic; Monsignor Martin Brennan, an astronomer; Father James Johnson, who took over Father Timothy Dempsey's projects for the poor and homeless with enthusiasm; Father John J. Butler, who expanded the work of Catholic charities; Mother Amadeus, an Ursuline nun who had mastered the ancient Irish art of illuminating books; Mother Annunciation, who had started a school for children with special needs on Natural Bridge Road; George T. Devereaux, who directed a fifty-six-voice choir at St. Francis Xavier Church; and the ladies of St. Roch's, who organized a sewing guild to help the poor. St. Luke's Parish had a splendid dramatic club—the young people's response to Archbishop Glennon's prohibition of dances in parish halls.

The Sisters of Mercy, originally an Irish congregation, by the end of World War I had become a predominantly Irish-American sisterhood. Mother M. Michael Fennell succeeded Sister M. Alacoque Kelly as superior of the Mercies in St. Louis in 1921. During Sister Alacoque's term, the sisters had moved into their new St. John's Hospital on Euclid and Parkview. Mother Michael added north and south wings to the hospital, a convent chapel, and the nurse's home. She stressed higher education for the sisters and sent a number to universities for degrees. Under her leadership the roster of novices rose from three to thirty.

St. John's Hospital had a highly deserved reputation for warm and kind health care. Bishops and priests of the area joined lay people in praise of many nuns. Among those singled out, many were Irish-Americans: Sisters John Conners, Xavier Kinsella, Antonia Galvin, Alphonsus Keane, Clare Morrisey, Theresa Gillis, Mary Magdalen Dowling, and Bernardo Mulligan.

The Sisters of Mercy had always looked to the welfare of young women coming to the city for employment. When St. John's Hospital found a new location at Euclid and Parkview early in the century, the Mercies turned the former hospital into a home for young employed women. Sisters Dominic Lynch, Josephine Forester, Michael Fennell, later regional superior, Austin Leonard, Regis Fitzpatrick, Scholastica Frawley, Agatha Campbell, and Patricia English had worked over the years under the direction of Sisters Angela Molloy, Vincent Carter, Nolasco Allen, and Cecilia Scanlan.

Back in the 1920s the Mercy Sisters had decided to build a fourteen-story home on the southwest corner of Sarah and Lindell, but depression thwarted those plans. An opportunity came in 1936 to exchange the Lindell property for the Governor David Francis Mansion in a quieter area, a block north of the Cathedral. Sister Xavier Halloran directed the new institution, called McAuley Hall. Sisters Luke Martin, Alacoque Murphy, Borromeo Albrecht, and Charles Whelan staffed the home. The Catholic Daughters opened a similar residence on Lindell just west of Spring. Many Irish-American young women resided at such homes, among them Rose and Jane Shea who came from Prairie du Rocher, Illinois, to work in the city.

*Archbishop John J. Glennon built the New Cathedral on Lindell Boulevard, opened Kenrick Seminary in Shrewsbury, and preached on many major occasions in the American church during his almost fifty years as archbishop. He became a cardinal shortly before he died in March 1946.*

Since 1913, laymen had made spiritual retreats annually at either Kenrick Seminary in Shrewsbury or at St. Stanislaus Jesuit Novitiate in Florissant. A small group of retreatants met once every month to freshen their religious outlook. They called these monthly meetings Manresa units. The leaders of this lay group asked Father Francis Xavier McMenamy, the Jesuit provincial, to provide a permanent retreat director. In 1921, he chose Father James P. Monaghan. It was a wise choice. An orderly man, he put the movement on a businesslike track.

Father Monaghan found an ideal location ten miles south of the city in Lemay. A Southern-style mansion called White House stood on the property overlooking the Mississippi River. When the original building caught fire, a stone structure took its place. Dayton Mudd of St. Louis gave money for a beautiful stone chapel. Director Monaghan ran a strict program. Attendance grew, and retreatants returned year after year. More Manresa units developed. White House soon won recognition as one of the leading retreat centers in the country; it remained so into the twenty-first century.

In 1925, Father Daniel A. Lord, a Jesuit of Anglo-American–Irish ancestry and Chicago native who spent his entire adult life in St. Louis, succeeded to the directorship of the National Sodality Service Center. Over the next quarter of a century, he wrote 42 books and 240 religious tracts for people of all ages. He redirected the slant of the magazine *The Queen's Work* to the needs and interests of youthful readers and increased the circulation. He began leadership schools in various parts of the country, called Summer Schools of Catholic Action. Pope Pius XI commissioned him to write the encyclical on movies *Vigilanti Curia*. The pope was so pleased with Father Lord's draft that he released

*Father Daniel A. Lord, S.J., sodality leader, pamphleteer, author of forty-two books, and songwriter, leads a sing-along of high schoolers. Pope Pius XI asked him to write the encyclical on the movies.*

the English edition unedited. It is the easiest to read of all the encyclical letters. Above all, Father Lord helped the nation, trying to escape from puritanical gloom brought on by propaganda for the Prohibition Amendment, to see that religion could be a source of joy.

In 1926 St. Louis prepared for the 100th anniversary of the establishment of the diocese by Pope Leo XII. Archbishop Glennon scheduled the consecration of the Cathedral for June 19 of that year, the 30th anniversary of his own episcopal consecration. Cardinal Patrick O'Connell of Dublin graced the occasion with his presence. All parishes took part. Several new parishes opened during the decade: St. Catherine's in Riverview Gardens in 1921; St. Stephen's just north of Carondelet Park in 1926; Christ the King in University City in 1927; and Annunziata in Ladue in 1929. Many Irish-Americans lived in each parish, but their lack of a distinct ethnic identification pointed to a growing trend in a multinational direction.

Over the years, the Boy Scouts of America program spread chiefly in Anglo-American areas. To many Irish parents it seemed a Protestant organization, much like the YMCA. Few Catholic parishes sponsored troops. St. Roch's Parish Hall in the Central West End was one that did. Dr. Forrest Staley led Troop 98, ranked high among those in the city. In the late 1920s, the Knights of Columbus promoted the boy scout movement by setting out to choose and train potential adult scout leaders. Among these were Knights Patrick Kelly and John Scott of Immaculate Conception Parish in Maplewood, who organized a heavily Irish troop, Maplewood 5. Thomas Durkin, destined to be the Monsignor Rector of the St. Louis Cathedral many years later, was one of the early members of that troop.

*The ladies of St. Gabriel's Parish lead the procession that welcomed the cardinal of Ireland.*

People called the time the "Roaring Twenties," but few knew what they were roaring about. During the election year of 1928, Governor Alfred E. Smith of New York, the first Catholic major party nominee for the presidency, briefly visited St. Louis in October. Smith was extremely popular with the Catholics of St. Louis and especially with the Irish, by tradition Democrats. Glennon was one of the few Irish Catholics in the city who favored the Republican Party. A meeting between the two might have proven awkward. The otherwise untimely death of Festus Wade, a leading Irish Catholic businessman, gave the archbishop a way to avoid what might have been an embarrassing meeting with Smith. Glennon presided at Wade's funeral.

When the once-Irish parish of St. Lawrence O'Toole on the near northside celebrated its 75th anniversary in 1930, the pastor boasted that children of fifteen different national backgrounds attended the elementary school. At the west end of the parish, where poor Irish had squatted during the famine, the section had gained the name "Kerry Patch." In the 1920s, the area became synonymous with brawling and boisterous conduct. To other Irish, the term "Kerry Patcher" was a derogation. Unfortunately, however, many non-Irish writers used the term indiscriminately for any Irish neighborhood.

At that time, too, the local Knights of Columbus, under the guidance of Father Lester Fallon, C.M., began a local, then national, program to clarify religious truths to the American public. The knights placed crisp, well-written columns of five to six hundred words on Catholic teaching, written by Charles Kelly, in a variety of magazines and newspapers.

In the summer of 1930, when Father Joseph P. Donovan, C.M., of the faculty of Kenrick Seminary went to Paris for the General Chapter of the Congregation of the Mission, he heard of a new organization, the Legion of Mary. It had taken root less than ten years before in Dublin, Ireland. Donovan stopped in Ireland on his return to find out about the Legion. He met the spiritual director and the founders, including capable Frank Duff.

Donovan heard the purposes of the legion: the spiritual advancement of its members and the general intensification of Catholic life. The legion gave great place to the initiative and the dependability of its members in the carrying out of a variety of highly personalized apostolic tasks. Every member recited a daily chain of prayers, with Our Lady's *Magnificat* as the core.

When Donovan returned to the States, he began to talk and write about the Legion of Mary. In the spring of 1932, he penned an article for the *American Ecclesiastical Review* titled, "Is This the long-looked for Church Society?"[1] While he left the conclusion to the reader, it was clear that Donovan warmly approved of the organization. Two months later, he started the first unit for women in Saint Louis at DePaul Hospital. A historian of the movement, Cecily Halleck, attributed the spread of the legion in the United States to "an American Vincentian Father."[2] The founder of the legion, Frank Duff himself, explicitly credited the growth of the movement to the energy and writings of Father Joseph P. Donovan. Soon the legion covered the nation, thanks to Father Donovan's conviction that it was truly the type of society that people needed.

In the late 1930s and early 1940s, Jesuit seminarians at Saint Louis University developed a fifteen-minute religious program on Radio Station WEW. It consisted of prayer, religious music, and a six-minute message by one of the Jesuit priests. They invited their assistant superior, Father Eugene Murphy, as guest speaker on one occasion. A devout priest, rather than a great pulpit orator, Father Murphy saw the potential of the program. Gradually, as each of the seminarians moved on to duties elsewhere, Father Murphy took charge of the program, named it the Sacred Heart Program, and invited other stations to carry it. The program soon went to all parts of the country and to the Armed Forces Network during World War II. Father Murphy enlisted the services of Father Hugh Harkins to recite the prayers. His voice matched that of the best contemporary radio personalities. Fred Waring, a popular orchestra leader of the time, wrote a hymn for the program.

The fifty-second religious congregation of women to work in the archdiocese, the Sisters of Charity of the Incarnate Word, came from Dunmore in County Galway to teach and care for the sick early in the twentieth century. They taught at Blessed Sacrament School on North Kingshighway, and later at Incarnate Word Academy in suburban Normandy. In health care, the sisters worked for hospitals managed by others until 1932, when they began Incarnate Word Hospital at Grand Boulevard and Lafayette Avenue. Sisters Joan Holder, an Irish American, and Maureen Wilson, a native of Ireland, excelled in this ministry.

# St. Louis Irish in Education

Late in the nineteenth century, when William Torrey Harris built the great public school system of St. Louis, he recruited many Irish teachers. This policy built in the system a high level of education for those Irish who did not attend parochial school. Congressmen James J. Butler and John Cochran, for instance, attended public schools. William Igoe attended both public and parochial schools. Since Susan Blow's kindergarten movement prevailed in the public school system long before it reached parochial schools, Bernadette Harris attended kindergarten at Woodward School before registering at St. Cecilia's Parish school for first grade, and Catherine Dinan attended Longfellow School, where her teacher was Miss M. Powers, an Irish-American Catholic, before entering the first grade at Epiphany.

The Irish in St. Louis enjoyed great educational opportunities, the result of many factors. Territorial Bishop William Du Bourg brought Italian Vincentians, French Sacred Heart nuns, and Belgian Jesuits to teach and engage in other ministries. Bishop Joseph Rosati welcomed the Daughters of Charity to staff a hospital. Over the years, they too taught at schools. Rosati invited the Sisters of St. Joseph to come from France and the Sisters of Loretto from Kentucky. Archbishop Kenrick asked the Visitation Sisters and the Christian Brothers to open schools.

During those years of the nineteenth century, over in Ireland the number of young men and young women willing to dedicate their lives to active religious congregations grew amazingly. Two originally French congregations, the Religious of the Sacred Heart and the Sisters of St. Joseph, accepted Irish and Irish-American candidates in large numbers in St. Louis throughout the century. Missouri Jesuits, originally Belgian and then multinational, welcomed a continually growing number of Irish and Irish-Americans. Eventually the midwestern Jesuit province was almost equally Irish-American and German-American in personnel; the Vincentians experienced the same pattern.

By 1910 thirty-four Irish parishes had schools. The largest, St. Leo's, a block north of Visitation Academy on Mullanphy Street, enrolled 791. Sixteen St. Joseph nuns taught there. The same congregation taught at eighteen other Irish parish schools. Lorettines taught at ten schools, the Christian Brothers at four, and the Sisters of Charity of the Blessed Virgin Mary at St. Francis Xavier. The Religious of the Sacred Heart taught at St. Thomas of Aquin and the Daughters of Charity at St. Malachy's. St. Vincent de Paul Parish had schools for German and Irish children.

After completing work at one of six academies, young men could attend Christian Brothers College or Saint Louis University. Twenty-five hundred young men took advantage of these opportunities for higher education. Young women had a choice of twenty-two academies or fifteen other specialized schools.

Catholic educators moved ahead with enthusiasm in the early 1920s. The Christian Brothers found a new site on Clayton Avenue just west of the city limits. It stood in the central corridor of the city-county growth. The brothers concentrated on secondary education and developed a more multinational student body than they had welcomed earlier, while situated among the predominantly Irish parishes of the northside. To improve the curriculum, those in authority allowed the brothers once again to teach Latin.

The archdiocese opened a school for high school boys on Kingshighway, one block north of the former CBC campus. The school bore the name of William Cullen McBride, who had prospered in the oil industry in Pennsylvania, moved to St. Louis early in the century, and donated the high altar in the Cathedral on Lindell. The school was a gift of his daughter. Situated north and west of many then flourishing Irish parishes, it welcomed a largely Irish student body. The colors of the school matched those of the Irish flag. The Marianist faculty, however, was largely German-American. The Marianists conducted elementary and secondary classes at Chaminade, a private residential school on Denny Road (later Lindbergh Boulevard) in West St. Louis County.

Back in 1911, the archdiocese had set up a girls' high school in St. Teresa's Parish, with a largely Irish-American student body, named for Archbishop Kain, and under the direction of the Josephites, and a southside school, Bishop

Rosati High, at Sts. Peter and Paul Parish in the Soulard District, with a largely German-American enrollment, staffed by School Sisters of Notre Dame. Applicants so crowded the two schools that in 1917 the archdiocesan school authorities looked for a new building. The spacious three-story St. Vincent's Seminary on Grand and Lucas was available, because the Daughters of Charity had closed their "select" school there in order to conform to their vocation to serve the poor. The combined Rosati-Kain opened there, and in the early 1920s a new Rosati-Kain High School went up on the northeast corner of Lindell at Newstead Avenue, just east of the Cathedral. The two congregations, the Josephites and the Notre Dames, shared duties, responsibilities, and honors.

When Mother Palma McGrath became provincial of the Josephites in the early 1920s, she moved the provincial headquarters to the convent on Cass Avenue. At that time, Sister Lucinda Savage published a history of the congregation, and Sister James Stanislaus Rogan put out textbooks for use in elementary schools. Mother Gonzaga Ryan had purchased property on Wydown at Big Bend in Clayton back in 1907, shortly after the World's Fair. In 1924 the Sisters of St. Joseph opened Fontbonne College there.[1] Over the years, a succession of Irish-American nuns directed the institution: Sisters Irene O'Hara, Palma McGrath, Pius Neenan, Bernice O'Neil, and Marcella Casey.

Dominican Sisters staffed an academy at St. Mark's Parish on Page and also taught at several heavily Irish parish schools—Epiphany, Holy Redeemer in Webster Groves, and at St. James south of Forest Park. Most of the sisters had Irish names, such as Sisters Aquin Riley, Mary Alice and Jane Dinan, Lenora Donahue, and Ann Celestine Devereaux.

*Nun-teachers gather to discuss educational issues.*

The Sisters of Loretto had opened Webster College on Lockwood Avenue in 1915. They kept their academy on Lafayette. In 1924 they opened a second academy in the old Lockwood Mansion a few blocks east of Webster College and called it Nerinx Hall. Maryville College stayed at its Carondelet campus on the old Withnell estate. All had a significant percentage of Irish-American students.

The Catholic colleges of the area, Webster, Fontbonne, and Maryville, and the Catholic community colleges—then called junior colleges—took an unprecedented step in uniting under the umbrella of Saint Louis University in 1924. While each school kept its internal administration, activities such as glee clubs and Latin academies were united, and all graduates received their degrees signed by Rev. Charles H. Cloud, Jesuit president of Saint Louis University.

Educational historians years later, looking back from the vantage of decades, wonder why the group failed to seek a common campus to forestall needless duplication.[2] The area adjacent to Fontbonne in Clayton was ideal. The area of Saint Louis University was overcrowded, and the authorities of the Jesuit High School looked to property on Oakland Avenue at the southeast corner of Forest Park. Either of these two locales, or property near Kenrick Seminary in Shrewsbury, offered space for a great Catholic university center.

Instead, while Fontbonne College opened on Wydown in Clayton, Maryville stayed in Carondelet and Saint Louis University built new buildings in its confined central city area. The Jesuit high school department, however, did move. Up to 1924, the Jesuits had staffed two high schools: Saint Louis University High School on Grand and West Pine and Loyola Prep on South Compton at Eads Avenue in the former James Buchanan Eads Mansion. Through the generosity of Mrs. Anna Backer, the two surviving schools consolidated into a new Saint Louis University High School on Oakland Avenue, across from the southeast corner of Forest Park, one block west of Kingshighway. Among the many Irish teachers, Father Laurence Leahy taught English and Coach Ed McCarthy taught geometry.

Sister Mary Joseph, S.L., of Webster College planned a special commemorative collection of books called the Gallery of Living Catholic Authors. She envisioned this treasury of contemporary writing as a means of alerting the American public to the high quality of contemporary Catholic writing in the English language, as a stimulus to aspire young writers, and as a focal point for Catholic writers everywhere. Father Daniel A. Lord was the only local writer whose works graced the collection.

The city of St. Louis lost one of its theological faculties in the fall of 1931 when the Jesuit School of Divinity moved from Saint Louis University to the campus of St. Mary's College in St. Marys, Kansas. A strengthening of other academic areas took up the slack at Saint Louis University. Father Raymond

Corrigan enlisted scholar-teachers, among them Thomas O'Connor, George W. Malloy, and others to build a strong history department. Marshall McLuhan joined Fathers William McCabe and Leo Forrey in the English department. Father William McGucken strengthened the School of Education with the addition of Dr. Leo R. Kennedy. Dr. Thomas E. Purcell became Dean of Dentistry.

From his office in St. Louis, Father Daniel Lord, S.J., National Promoter of Sodality of Our Lady, emphasized high schools in his efforts to spread the spiritual influence of the organization. He began leadership sessions of one-week duration at various points around the country during the summer months. Over the years, his team of teachers included Father Louis Twomey, advocate of social justice, and Herbert O'Halloran Walker, highly successful editor of the sodality magazine. Called Summer Schools of Catholic Action, these sessions emphasized Sodality organization, devotion to Mary, prayer, and Mass attendance, and offered classes on religious vocations, missions, evangelization, and leadership techniques. This traveling team covered all sections of the country, ending with a master rally in Chicago in August. Inter-ethnic in orientation, these leadership schools, nonetheless, had great influence on Irish young people.

In the spring of 1944, Father Peter Brooks, provincial of the Missouri Jesuits, urged youthful Father Patrick Holloran, the new president of Saint Louis University, to consider integrating the school. Father Holloran wrote to prominent members of the Laymen's Retreat League and other leading Catholic men of the difficulties black collegians had in getting a Catholic education. The response was overwhelmingly in favor of integration. The public relations director of the school, Father Claude Heithaus, gave a stirring sermon to the student body on the issue. The students looked ahead to an integrated school. Adults looked both ways. At the urging of the acting Jesuit superior general, the Very Reverend Zacheus P. Maher, Saint Louis University welcomed black students in the summer session. It was the first university in a former slave state to do so. Saint Louis University High followed the university's example three years later, leading the way in high schools.

When the war ended a year later, returning GIs sought homes away from the parishes of their birth in new suburban areas that lacked ethnic identification. Many took advantage of the G.I. Bill to enroll at Saint Louis University, a school moving into a significant era in its history.

Black GIs returning to the city found one improvement: they could enter Saint Louis University. Some did. Priests and nuns, engaged in the interracial movement in the city, credited Saint Louis University's action with defusing trouble locally at a time when riots swept through other cities. Its president, Patrick Holloran, was Irish, as were many of its distinguished faculty members, among them Professors James Collins and Father William Wade in philosophy and Dr. Thomas P. Neill and Father John Francis Bannon in history. With the death of Professor Herbert Bolton of the University of California, the founder of a school of historians specializing in the study of the Spanish Southwest, Father Bannon became the acknowledged leader of this group called, after their founder, the "Boltonians."

Father James Macelwane, one of the nation's leading seismologists, whose parents came from Ulster, began an Institute of Technology at Saint Louis University. At the same time, Oliver Parks, the founder of Parks College of Aeronautical Technology, one of the top schools of its kind in the nation, prevailed upon his fellow investors to affiliate Parks College in Cahokia, Illinois, with Saint Louis University.

While Parks himself was Anglo-American, the affiliation with Saint Louis University brought several Irish names, lay and cleric, onto the Cahokia campus. When Jack O'Reilly retired from his position as director of physical education, Jim Donohoo took his place. Dr. James F. Reagan headed the Department of Aeronautical Technology, and Bob Killoren taught aeronautical engineering. Frank D. Sullivan directed public relations. Father Edmund Burke, who had taught philosophy on the Grand Avenue campus before the war, returned from the Pacific where he had received the Silver Star for protecting a wounded man under enemy fire on the Island of Peleliu. He now taught on both sides of the Mississippi. Another Jesuit, Lieutenant Colonel Dan Campbell, returned from service with the Ferry command to work effectively in campus ministry. Called back to duty in Korea with the 51st Fighter Wing of the 5th Air Force, he never forgot Parks College and returned there after the close of that conflict. And Parks College never forgot him. He was especially successful in guiding the unchurched in religious matters.

Higher Catholic education had fresh new leadership for the postwar period, and so did the local Church itself. The century-long period of Irish

*Father John Francis Bannon, who taught the "History of the Americas" in the classroom and on a local PBS show, led an entire corps of western historians and wrote textbooks used widely in American universities from Berkeley to Chapel Hill, N.C.*

episcopal leadership ended abruptly in the fall of 1946. Archbishop Glennon had gone to Rome in February to receive the "red hat" as a new cardinal. He died in Dublin on his way back to the United States.

Archbishop Joseph Elmer Ritter of Indianapolis, a native of Indiana, succeeded him. Among his many policies, the new archbishop wanted Catholic education on all levels. A policy change brought co-education to new high schools: Bishop Du Bourg in southwest St. Louis, Laboure in the northwest, De Andreis in north city, Mercy High in University City, and Aquinas and Rosary High in North County. Diocesan priests and various congregations of nuns and lay teachers taught in these co-educational institutions. Previously, only parish high schools had been co-ed.

Acting on an even more dramatic decision, the new archbishop integrated the schools, a topic that comes up in a later chapter.

*Father James Macelwane, S.J., a pioneer in the study of earthquakes, was director of the Seismological Society in 1928 and president of the American Geophysical Union. In 1944 he was elected to the National Academy of Sciences.*

*Laymen and priests prepare to board the plane bound for Rome to accompany Archbishop Glennon to receive the "red hat" of a cardinal.*

# St. Louis Irish
# in Labor Leadership

The St. Louis Irish community had no nationally known labor leaders such as Terence Powderly, who headed the Knights of Labor in the 1880s; Peter McGuire, one of the founders of the American Federation of Labor (AFL) in the 1890s; John Mitchell, president of the Mine Workers early in the twentieth century; Philip Murray, who headed the Congress of Industrial Organizations (CIO) in the 1940s; or George Meany, president of the reunited AFL–CIO in the mid-1950s.

However, St. Louis did have three national labor leaders whose achievements merited inclusion in the *Biographical Dictionary of American Labor Leaders.*[1] These three men are James Patrick Noonan, John B. Haggerty, and Lawrence Raftery. The mature years of these three men covered almost a half-century: Noonan's from 1915–1930, Haggerty's from 1930–1945, and Raftery's from 1945–1960, and offer a framework for this chapter. These years saw organized labor move from a status of toleration to one of power, separation, and consolidation.

James Patrick Noonan, the son of an Irish immigrant farmer in St. Louis County, lost his parents at an early age. He held various manual labor jobs in youth and then enlisted as a private during the Spanish-American War (1898–1899). After his discharge from the service, Noonan became an electrical lineman in St. Louis and in 1901 joined the International Brotherhood of Electrical Workers (IBEW). A year later, he was elected president of his local, and in 1904 he became international vice president of the IBEW. He served as acting president in 1917 and was elected president in 1919.[2] Though he had his office in Washington, he kept his family home in St. Louis.

A man of common sense and wide interests, alert and energetic in manner, with an ability to adapt, he had an enormous capacity for work. He ran his office in a businesslike way. A good fighter when occasion called, he was also a skilled diplomat who won the respect of employers. The rank-and-file described his leadership as "pacific and progressive." He dealt frankly and candidly, and when he made a promise, he kept it. Physically, he was heavy-set, erect with broad shoulders, and almost completely bald.[3]

In 1922 he was chosen as the fifth vice president of the Building Trades Department of the American Federation of Labor, and in 1924 a member of the Executive Committee of the AFL. An authority on electric power, he was the only American delegate sent to the World Power Conference in London in 1924. He presented a paper on "Labor's Part in Power Production." In that same year, Secretary of Commerce Herbert Hoover appointed him to the St. Lawrence Waterway Commission.

The twenties gave laboring men a hard time. The courts turned against them in spite of the Clayton Anti-Trust Act of 1914, which the lawmakers had passed to protect unions from persecution as monopolies in restraint of trade. Firms wanted "company unions" of their own workers, not connected with national unions. Organized labor gradually declined in membership from five million in 1920 to close to three million by 1929.

Unemployment had risen steadily since the heady days of wartime economy. When President Coolidge called a conference on unemployment, Noonan accepted the invitation to participate. James Patrick Noonan rightly found his place among the men who built the nation and whose biographies appeared in the *Dictionary of American Biography*.[4] He died a few weeks after the Great Crash of 1929. St. Louis labor needed new leadership.

John B. Haggerty, a St. Louis native and an apprentice printer who learned his trade at George D. Barnard Stationery in St. Louis, joined Local 18 of the International Brotherhood of Bookbinders (IBB). A handsome man with a great capacity for making friends, he eventually became international vice president and served as a member of the IBB Executive Council from 1916 to 1926. The International Brotherhood of Bookbinders chose him president in that year. In 1929 he was an AFL delegate to the Canadian Trades and Labor Council.

In December of that year the stock market fell through the Wall Street pavement. Industry stagnated. Stores couldn't repossess the countless electric stoves, ice boxes, and other appliances purchased on installment plans. More than ten thousand deposit banks failed in the next few years. Then unemployment struck. Men drove Cadillacs to seek manual work at Walsh Stadium on Oakland. Others tried to sell apples on street corners.

The viewpoint of the Hoover Administration precluded direct relief action by the national government. The people of St. Louis helped their poor neighbors as best they could. By 1931, national unemployment stood at 15.9 percent, with St. Louis higher at 24 percent. The percentage among St. Louis African Americans rose to 42.8 percent, while that of whites, at 21.5 percent, was 2.5 percent below the national average. The percentage among the Irish was even lower, thanks to their membership in the building trades unions. Limited construction continued during the Great Depression. A heating contractor, for instance, who had work on new buildings at Washington University and in various churches, stated that a good pipefitter was never out of work during those trying years.[5] And most of them were Irish or had an Irish father, uncle, or in-law.

The AFL long had kept government at a safe distance, but after 1932 the Roosevelt Administration held out a welcoming hand. The National Industrial Recovery Act contained a clause, 7a, that guaranteed to workers the right of free choice of union and committed employers to dealing with such unions. As a result, unionization grew amazingly. John Haggerty served as printing trades labor advisor for the National Recovery Act.[6] He knew that labor at last saw the sunrise.

In a few years, however, Haggerty and other AFL leaders saw a new challenge. Their organization, concerned with the here-and-now needs of craft unions, had not given enough attention to the mass industries: steel, automobiles, aircraft, and others. In this impasse, John L. Lewis of the United Mineworkers made a call for concern for the unorganized. Convinced they had enough to do taking care of their own areas, the AFL leaders threw out every one of Lewis's proposals. In response, leaders of ten of the more aggressive unions gathered around the great mine chief to organize a Committee for Industrial Organization.

After a year, the Committee for Industrial Organization became the Congress of Industrial Organizations, independent of the AFL. Haggerty and his printers remained with the mother group. A local split matched the national split. In 1937 the AFL officials ordered the St. Louis Central Trades and Labor Union to dismiss its CIO affiliates. That left 178 affiliates with the mother body. Almost the same number formed the St. Louis Industrial Union Council.

Shortly, the country saw the organization of industries like steel, automobiles, textile, rubber, aircraft, and lumber—industries that had resisted the labor organizer for over a century. Violence erupted in many places, but eventually the union membership in the country rose from 3.7 million in 1935 to 8.5 million by 1940. Under the impact of the depression, the American labor movement had come of age.

When World War II came, Haggerty offered his expertise on the Labor Advisory Committee of the War Production Board. He was a member of the Democratic National Committee's Labor Committee. After the war, he chaired the Board of Governors of the International Allied Printing Trades Association. In his spare time, he enjoyed fishing and eventually moved to Florida, where sea-fishing always challenged him. He died in 1953 at the age of sixty-nine. He had seen labor advance from a struggling, barely accepted institution of America to a powerful force in national life.

Just as John B. Haggerty had moved into leadership when James Patrick Noonan passed, so a third St. Louisan was ready to move up. Lawrence Raftery, a graduate of Christian Brothers College School of Art and Interior Decorating, had joined St. Louis Local 115 of the Brotherhood of Painters, Decorators, and Paperhangers of America (PDPA) back in 1913. The second of ten children himself, he and his wife Enid King had nine children. He served in the Navy during World War I.

Between 1919 and 1923, he was the business agent of his local. He rose to leadership when the painters struck of 1924 for a five-day week; the strike lasted seven weeks. His leadership elevated him to the office of secretary-business agent of the St. Louis Painters District Council a year later. He became a member of the Executive Board of the Missouri State Federation of Labor and of the Advisory Board of the Missouri Unemployment Bureau in

*Exercising a different type of labor leadership, Father Leo Brown, professor of economics at Saint Louis University, gained recognition as one of the best labor conciliators in the country. Shown with him (from the left) are Joe Ferraro, organizer for the United Auto Workers, Wise Stone an official of the UAW, James Reynolds, Under-Secretary of Labor, and Robert Moore, assistant director of the Federal Mediation and Conciliation Commission.*

1929. He worked with his union throughout the early 1930s, and he was strong on apprentice training and emphatic on looking to the mutual interests of labor and management. He wanted vigorous unions in prosperous industries. After the expulsion of the industrial unions, Raftery became vice president of the Painters' Union, and in 1942 general secretary-treasurer.[7]

As at the end of World War I, the fall of Japan brought an end to a honeymoon period for organized labor. A long miners' strike in 1946 called forth national indignation. Over President Truman's veto, a conservative Congress passed the Taft-Hartley Act that outlawed the "closed shop," secondary boycotts and jurisdictional strikes. Several non-industrial states followed with Open Shop Laws, disguised as "Right-to-Work Laws." Labor's glory days had darkened.

These external pressures and the coming of new leadership brought the AFL and the CIO together in 1953 under the direction of George Meany, who had arisen step by step from apprentice plumber to president of the AFL. Rising to leadership with Meany in the merger was Lawrence Raftery. Elected head of the painters the year before, Raftery became a vice president and member of the Executive Council of the Building and Construction Trades Department of the AFL–CIO. In 1957 the International Brotherhood of Painters and Allied Trades of U.S. and Canada elected him president. He held that position until 1965. As president emeritus, he then returned to his home in Florissant. A member of the Knights of Columbus, he was active in the affairs of the Catholic Church and the Democratic Party, and he belonged to two service clubs. He had played baseball and soccer as a boy and remained a fan of both sports. He read widely, had a home workshop, and studied art, following the impressionistic school in his artistic efforts. He died in 1983.

In the meantime, the two local labor bodies, the Central Trades and Labor Union, and the St. Louis Industrial Council, followed the pattern of the national office and joined together in St. Louis Labor Council AFL–CIO with two hundred thousand members.

Many Irish union men were active locally in the ensuing years, especially in the Building Trades. Among them, Robert Kelly of the Commercial Workers presided over the Labor Council. Robert Young arose from leadership in the Pipefitters Union to a place in the national Congress. Phil Barry, of Local 35 of the Plumbers' Union, served on the Industrial Commission and was elected to the state legislature. Daniel "Duke" McVey rose from leadership in Local 562 of the pipefitters to be state president of the AFL–CIO for seventeen years.

# Irish Clergy and a German-American Archbishop

Shortly after the end of the war in 1946, Pope Pius XII named many cardinals from lands beyond Europe, among them John J. Glennon of St. Louis.[1] He was the seventh cardinal born in Ireland and the first from an episcopal see west of the Mississippi. The people of Ireland joined St. Louisans in celebration. The new cardinal received the "red hat" in Rome but died at the presidential palace in Dublin on his return. The people of St. Louis had festooned Lindell Boulevard west of the Cathedral to greet their first cardinal. Instead they welcomed dignitaries of Church and state for the Solemn High Funeral Mass.

Had Monsignor Mark Carroll of St. Margaret's Church, or Monsignor Dan Daly of Poplar Bluff, the leader of the Church in

*Parishioners and other friends of Bishop Mark Carroll bid him farewell at the door of the Old Cathedral as he prepares to leave for Wichita, Kansas.*

southeastern Missouri, been auxiliary bishop, he'd have won popular support to succeed the late cardinal. But Bishop George Donnelly held that post, a good pastor, like Philip Brady in Kenrick's late years, but lacking the stature to lead a great archdiocese. Monsignor John Cody, a master of Roman politics rather than a popular leader or zealous pastor, ran the chancellor's office with a rigid formality.

The people of St. Louis awaited a new religious leader. Some looked to Bishop Edwin O'Hara of Kansas City, a well-known advocate of social justice, especially for the farmers of the nation. Irish pastors gathered at Holy Name Church for Forty Hours Devotion, offered the name of Bishop Michael Ready of Columbus.

Had the priests exercised the same clout as their predecessors at the coming of Kain, the Irish leadership would have continued with O'Hara, Ready, Daly, or Carroll. To the surprise of most people, Pope Pius XII transferred Archbishop Joseph Elmer Ritter of Indianapolis to St. Louis in the autumn of 1946. A native of southern Indiana, of German-American ancestry, he was the first non-Irish archbishop and the first non-Irish bishop since the death of Joseph Rosati in 1843.

The new archbishop differed greatly from his predecessor, both in physical appearance and in personal qualities. Ritter was of moderate height while Glennon reached six feet four without his top hat. Ritter was more straightforward, easy of approach, and far more willing to listen. While Glennon spoke eloquently, Ritter had no illusions of oratorical skill. Instead, he spoke clearly and simply and let more inspiring speakers, such as Monsignor Charles Helmsing, preach on solemn occasions. Social analysts pointed out that Archbishop Ritter was to his predecessor what his contemporary President Harry Truman was to Franklin Delano Roosevelt.

Cardinal Glennon had reserved decisions to himself. His auxiliary, Bishop George Donnelly, officiated at religious activities, vow days, graduations and the like, but had no area of administration. Shortly after the new archbishop arrived, Pope Pius XII named Donnelly bishop of Leavenworth, Kansas, Monsignor Mark Carroll bishop of Wichita, and Chancellor John Cody auxiliary bishop of St. Louis. Archbishop Ritter set up Archdiocesan Councils of Men, Women, and Youth and gave the moderators, such as Monsignor Lloyd Sullivan of the Council of Youth, leeway to guide their groups.

The new archbishop shared with the people of St. Louis a vital concern for the spread of the Christian faith to distant lands, both by contributions and by actual presence. Among the missionaries from St. Louis, Father John Morrison went to India; the Prendergast brothers, George and Charles, went to Central America; and Father Morgan Casey went to Bolivia and was named auxiliary bishop. At home, Fathers Glennon Flavin and Edward O'Meara successively directed the national office of the Propagation of the Faith that sent help to the men and women in the field. They both later became bishops of midwestern dioceses.

Father Charles "Dismas" Clark, retreat master at White House in Lemay and then army chaplain during World War II, became involved in prison ministry after the conflict. He took the apocryphal name of the good thief "Dismas," prevailed upon Archbishop Ritter to name a new parish in Florissant St. Dismas, and opened a halfway house on the near northside to help parolees adjust to life outside "The Walls." "Dismas House" received wide areas of support in this venture, led by attorney Morris Shenker. Father Clark appeared widely on media presentations, among them the Art Linkletter Show. The movie "The Hoodlums' Priest" featured his career. Author Lisa Mulligan wrote an amazingly objective life of this controversial reformer. She called the Jesuit provincial superior, Father Joseph P. Fisher, the "true hero of the Dismas Clark story,"[2] for continually supporting the zealous and spiritually influential priest despite his sometimes irresponsible statements in press and pulpit.

Lisa Mulligan had many imitators in telling the story of St. Louis Irish achievers. Jesuit seminarian Harold McAuliffe wrote the life story of Father Tim Dempsey. Literary critic Max Putzel showed more concern for William Marion Reedy as a literary man than as an astute political observer in his book, *The Man in the Mirror*. Monsignor Nicholas Schneider told of the long career of Cardinal John J. Glennon. Father Thomas Gavin described the wide ministry of his fellow Jesuit, Father Daniel Lord.

In his book on St. Louis's first archbishop, Professor Samuel J. Miller concerned himself with the theology of Archbishop Peter Richard Kenrick, but he gives enough insights into Kenrick's character and personality that we know him as archbishop as well as a theologian of eminence.

Over the years, sisters of Irish-American ancestry wrote the histories of their congregations. Mother Louise Callen wrote a monumental life of

*Monsignor Lloyd Sullivan, chairman of the drive for the Cardinal Glennon Children's Hospital, welcomes Irish actress Maureen O'Hara, who came to highlight a benefit program for that cause.*

Philippine Duchesne that gave its readers a look at the work of the Religious of the Sacred Heart of various national backgrounds. Sister Dan Hannefin wrote *Daughters of the Church*, a popular history of the Daughters of Charity in the United States from 1807–1987. Sister Isadore Lennon wrote *Milestones of Mercy*, the history of the Sisters of Mercy in the United States from 1856 to 1956. Sister Liliana Owens researched the story of the Lorettines throughout the trans-Mississippi, and Sister Mary Magnan wrote a splendidly researched article of length on the Sisters of Loretto that appeared in the magazine *Gateway Heritage*.[3] Sister Dolorita Marie Dougherty wrote the history of her congregation, the Sisters of St. Joseph.

That a sister of Irish–St. Louis background wrote the history of the Sisters of St. Joseph of Carondelet points to the gradual change of the congregation from a French foundation to a heavily Irish-American sisterhood. The Sisters of St. Joseph originally came to the St. Louis diocese from France back in 1839 with a subsidy from the state government to teach deaf children. They also began to teach other children in Carondelet and welcomed candidates of other national ancestry. Between 1856 and 1929, 198 Irish young women entered the convent at Carondelet. During those same years, and on into the 1960s, Irish-American girls came in equal numbers to become nuns.

The Sisters of St. Joseph staffed elementary schools in many Irish parishes, Fontbonne College in Clayton and St. Joseph's Academy. During the provincialate of Mother Lilia Monaghan in 1953, the academy opened a new campus on the west side of Lindbergh Boulevard near U.S. 40. Sister Marie Vianney O'Reilly directed a splendid Sodality of Our Lady at the Academy, while Fontbonne College flourished in Clayton. The Josephites also agreed to staff a hospital in Kirkwood. In recognition of the great work of the Josephites in health care, the federal government deeded to the congregation the entire plant of ten buildings of the former Marine Hospital.

A succession of excellent provincials of Irish ancestry guided the sisters during those years: Sister Joan Marie Gleason, Sister Mary Laurent Duggan, Sister Mary Catherine O'Gorman, and Sister Donna Loretta Gunn, who previously had worked with the elderly through the Cardinal Ritter Institute.

Other sisterhoods that began in a different national community began to welcome Sisters of Irish-American background. The Sisters of the Precious Blood of Ruma welcomed Sister Pauline Grady, who wrote several books of interest in the history of her congregation. Sister Mary Timothy Ryan, of the Sisters of Notre Dame, took her doctorate in history at Saint Louis University and taught at Notre Dame College for a number of years, and Sister Pat O'Toole worked with the elderly. Sister Felicia McGalloway of the Franciscan Sisters of Mary headed Glennon Hospital, Sister Madonna O'Hara was President of the Ursuline Academy in Kirkwood.

Though not a member of Alcoholics Anonymous, Father Edward Dowling was the first clergyman of any denomination to encourage the movement. Father Dowling saw in the Twelve Steps of AA the same spiritual path that the Jesuit founder St. Ignatius Loyola used for personal religious development in his Spiritual Exercises.

Support of the AA movement, however, was not the only concern of the exuberant Jesuit. Father Dowling was a native of St. Louis, the son of the leader of the dissident parishioners who walked out on the pastor of Holy Cross Church back in 1870 when he asked prayers for the Prussian Army. Like his father, the Jesuit was an innovator. He began a program called the Cana Conference to gather lay and clerical experts to guide those about to enter into marriage. Later he stressed Cana Conferences for the fortyish, those married for twenty years whose children had gone on their own. Still later, Father Dowling began to counsel emotionally distressed people. On the day he died, quite characteristically, he had talked to AA members, married couples, and nervous people in Memphis at various informal gatherings.

As we shall see in a later chapter, Archbishop Ritter won national acclaim for the struggle for racial justice in 1947. During his years, American identity prevailed over ethnic diversity. There might be neighborhoods where one nationality predominated, but to him, there were no Irish parishes, no black parishes, no German, Italian, or Polish parishes, but only Catholic parishes. His openness to the new and forward-looking vision affected many areas of the life of all people of St. Louis.

# XXIX

# St. Louis Irish in Sports

T he great parish soccer tradition of the turn of the century continued during the European war. In the 1920s, St. Matthew's Parish on North Sarah succeeded St. Leo's and St. Teresa's as top eleven. The top local professional teams, such as the Ben Millers, that matched the best squads from other cities, transcended the parish level. The best center forward of the country between 1915 and 1922, Harry Ratican, was a native of St. Louis. He played at CBC and in the parochial league early in the century and starred on the Ben Millers from 1912 to 1915. Then he went to Pennsylvania and scintillated on an otherwise all-foreign team, the Bethehem Steel. During the years 1921–23,

*The St. Leo eleven dominated inter-parish soccer early in the century. "Bull" Brannigan was the best player, and Billy Monahan was the most dapper dresser.*

he coached soccer at West Point then returned to St. Louis.

In college athletics in the early 1920s, the Fighting Irish of Notre Dame University, among the top football teams in the nation, scheduled "home-and-home" games with the equally Irish players who wore the Blue and White of Saint Louis University. Steve O'Rourke, the Billiken coach, had two equally Celtic assistants, Dan Savage and Jimmy Finnegan. Leo Quirk captained a team that included Bob Hannegan and Bob O'Toole. A trainload of Billiken supporters went to South Bend in the fall of 1922 to see the SLU eleven play well in a losing effort to the powerful Notre Dame team.

During the following fall, Clarence Eggler and Frank Ramacciotti added non-Irish speed and offensive power to the 1923 squad. In spite of the rain, a sell-out crowd filled Sportsman's Park on Thanksgiving Day in 1923 to watch Elmer Layden, one of the legendary "Four Horsemen" of Notre Dame, lead the Indiana Irish to victory. Among the Billiken stars, Robert Hannegan went on to be national chairman of the Democratic Party, as mentioned in an earlier chapter; Tom Stanton starred in three sports at Saint Louis University, pitched for the Boston Red Sox in the American League, and then coached winning basketball teams at Saint Louis University High and at Beaumont High. His classmate and good friend Jack O'Reilly also coached successfully at CBC and SLU High.

The year 1922 almost brought glory to the St. Louis Browns. Two local Irish stars, Marty McManus and Johnny Tobin, had great years. Second baseman McManus drove in ten more runs than Babe Ruth, and right fielder Tobin's .331 batting average outranked Ruth's .315 average. Unfortunately, the Yankees led by one game at the end of the season.

The five-foot-eight, 142-pound Tobin had a lifetime average of .309 over a dozen years in the big leagues. Marty McManus managed the Red Sox in 1932 and then returned to St Louis.[1]

The Cardinals continually improved, moved into contention, and in 1926 won the National League title. They faced Babe Ruth and the Yankees in the World Series. The few Irish who cared little for baseball grew steadily more involved as the series went on—the result of the condescending attitude of the New York announcer, Graham McNamee. He continuously demeaned St. Louis. The normal response around town would not meet the current guides of "political correctness."

All sports fans remember that Grover Cleveland Alexander struck out Tony Lazzeri to end the seventh inning. Local fans recall, instead, catcher Bob O'Farrell's perfect throw to second base that cut down Babe Ruth, who unwisely tried to steal. That throw ended the game. St. Louis had its first World Championship, and Bob O'Farrell won the award as Most Valuable Player.

On the football field in the early 1930s, Coach Charles "Chili" Walsh steered the Billikens to repeated victories over in-state rivals, the University of

Missouri Tigers, the Rolla Miners, and the Washington University Bears. One of the stars Bob McCoole won All-American recognition from *Sports Illustrated* twenty-five years after he excelled in football at Saint Louis University. The magazine's editors selected outstanding players of the class of 1932 who achieved later in life.

During the 1930s many other Irish football players wore the Blue and White: John Conlon, Mike McDonough, Bill O'Brien, Frank Kennedy, Bill Montgomery, Tom Tierney, Bud Diffley, Lou Drone, Frank Hagan, and Bill and Denny Cochrane. Jack Joyce, who played a few years earlier, became a nationally known business executive.

Three St. Louis Irish starred on the Billiken basketball team: Frank Keaney, Bob Cochran, and John Flanigan. The first two excelled in a second sport: Frank Keaney in tennis and Bob Cochran in golf. Jimmy Manion already had made his mark on the links. John Flanigan returned ten years later to coach the Billiken cagers to their first Missouri Valley Conference championship. Classmate Bob Burnes began a great career in sports writing for the *Globe-Democrat*; he called his column "Bench Warmer." People credited the fluency of Bob Broeg, Burnes's counterpart on the *Post*, to his Irish mother.

In the 1944 all–St. Louis World Series, two Irish names made the headlines. "Blix" Donnelly won the second game for the Cardinals on Ken O'Dea's pinch-hit single in the eleventh inning. Terry Moore played in two World Series with the Cardinals.

While the St. Louis Cardinals—champions three times in the early 1940s—went without trophies during the late 1940s and throughout the 1950s, the Saint Louis University Billikens held the spotlight on the basketball

*Star center "Easy" Ed Macauley enjoyed a long career in the world of sport. He led the Billikens to the NIT championship in 1948. After many successful seasons with the St. Louis Hawks as player and coach, Easy Ed covered sports on radio and television.*

court. Alumnus John Flanigan coached the team to a double victory over the Oklahoma Aggies, previous national champions, and to its first Missouri Valley championship in 1947. Center "Easy Ed" Macauley led the Bills to the NCAA playoffs.

A new coach, Eddie Hickey, formerly of Creighton University, came the following year. He gave to Flanigan's defensive-oriented five a fast-breaking offense that brought them first place in the National Invitational Tourney in New York City, at that time equal in prestige with the present NCAA. "Easy Ed" made the All-American team, leading the nation in field-goal percentage with a .524 average. The following year the Billikens won the Sugar Bowl championship, beating Kentucky, the NCAA champion of the previous year.

"Easy Ed" played professional basketball with the Boston Celtics and St. Louis Hawks, and he coached the Hawks to the Western Division title in 1959–60. Chosen seven times for the National Basketball Association's All Star Games, he averaged 20.3 points a game during his ten seasons. He had a career high of 46 points against the Minneapolis Lakers on March 6, 1953.[2] On the college level, Macauley's former teammate, Tom Kavanaugh, who had captained the St. Louis U. High team to its first state title in 1945, led the Regis College Rangers in Denver to the Final Four in the National Association of Intercollegiate Basketball in 1951. Two other St. Louisans played on that Regis team, Tom Conlon and Eddie Kohl. When the Rangers won on St. Patrick's Day that year, Eddie insisted that the prayers of his maternal grandmother, who was born in Roscommon, carried the day. In an attempt to repeat its basketball success on the gridiron, Saint Louis University hired a professional-type football coach in 1948. In spite of the fine play of veterans Eddie Donahue, Tom Powers, Ed Shortal, Bill Cribben, and others, the

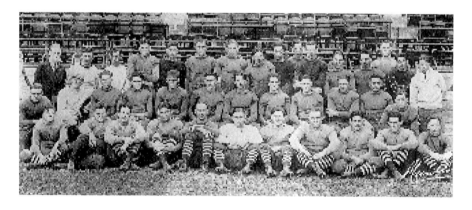

*Ed Quirk captained the Irish-German Billiken team. Seated at his left, the team punter, Robert Hannegan, went on to head the Democrat Party.*

footballers never matched the Billiken basketeers. A few years later the school dropped football.

Billiken basketball continued first-rate over the years. Bob Ferry led the team to many victories, won All-American rating, and, like "Easy Ed" Macauley, went on to star in the professional ranks. Other Irish players of the time were Jim Dailey and Pete McCafferty.

Soccer, such a great part of the athletic scene in St. Louis, was no longer an Irish dominion. When America's greatest World Cup team beat England in Brazil in 1950, Harry Keough of St. Louis was the captain, but the five other men of the first eleven who came from St. Louis were Italian.

The region of St. Louis developed an amazing number of professional ballplayers durint the immediate post–World War II period. Their names, however, were not Tobin and McManus, but Schoendienst and Garagiola, and Doby and Howard.

Many Irish athletes starred on the high school or neighborhood level. Among them, sports analysts rate two extremely high: Bob Murphy, who starred at McBride in basketball and baseball, and Bob Rooney at St. Louis U. High in football and soccer. Bob Rooney's brother Jack quarterbacked the Billikens in 1947, and Murphy's brothers, Glenn and Bill, also had noted careers in sports, Glennon as basketball coach at Spring Hill College in Mobile, and Bill in sports in military service.

The color green still waved on the field of sport.

*Defenseman Harry Keough (left) often challenged goalie Frank Borghi on local fields, but they worked together in World Cup competition in 1950, beating the British in Brazil, 1–0.*

# St. Louis Irish and the Black Community

I n colonial times, nearly all St. Louis African Americans belonged to the Catholic Church. During early American days the Reverend John Berry Meacham, a former slave, established a Baptist church and school. Sisters of St. Joseph also began schools for free black girls and another for the daughters of enslaved after normal school hours. Nativists harassed them, as they did Reverend Meacham. Missouri restricted the education of black children, slave or free. While Reverend Meacham reopened his school on a boat, the Sisters of St. Joseph continued their school "underground."

When emancipation came to Missouri in 1865, Archbishop Kenrick assigned a special parish for black Catholics, not as a segregation measure but to give them a secure sanctuary of their own—as the Bohemians, Poles, Croatians, and other nationalities had. The black parish, St. Elizabeth's, took part in all Catholic parades and demonstrations of solidarity.

With restrictions on African Americans coming from the "Separate but Equal" decision of the U.S. Supreme Court, *Plessy vs. Ferguson* (1896), security became seclusion and meant exclusion from "white" churches. Restrictions set in. St. Louisans voted on a segregation ordinance in 1916. State Senator Michael Kinney and twenty-three of the twenty-eight aldermen opposed it, as did political cartoonist Dan Fitzpatrick. Archbishop Glennon denounced its injustice too late to make any impact, and it passed.

Before the ordinance could be put into effect, however, the Supreme Court ruled such legislation unconstitutional.

Nonetheless, neighborhood segregation became a reality. The Church failed to call for fair treatment. Even after a remonstrance from the apostolic delegate in the mid-1920s, Archbishop Glennon did little to help black Catholics or the black community in general. His attitude seemed to suggest that African Americans tried to force their way into white parishes instead of building churches of their own.

A fit match even for Irish archbishops, Jesuit William Markoe became pastor of St. Elizabeth's Church in 1927. A descendant of wealthy French-West Indies planters who had made their fortune on slave labor, the tall, square-built Markoe had advocated racial justice in national magazines since his seminary days.[1]

Markoe purchased property on the northeast corner of Taylor and Cook in the Central West End, eighteen long blocks west and nine blocks north of his rectory at 2721 Pine Street. He planned to open a school for black children, 50 percent of them Protestants. The area had few black residents. Father Markoe might have opened his school successfully at other sites where black families lived. His choice of location seemed provocative.

On December 14, 1927, William W. Butts of the St. Louis Real Estate Exchange wrote to Archbishop Glennon protesting Markoe's chosen location, claiming, among other considerations, that it would ruin St. Ann's and Visitation's heavily Irish parishes.[2] Property owners of the area held a meeting of protest at Visitation Parish Hall on Taylor, near the site of the projected school. E. A. MacMahon of the Home Protective Association chaired the meeting. He spoke of the impending "invasion" of the area and predicted the depopulation of Catholic parishes. MacMahon had the support of the Baptist Hospital, Ranken Trade School, Catholic parishes, Protestant churches, Jewish synagogues, the Rice-Stix Shirt Factory, and the Boyd-Welch Shoe Company.

The host of the assembly, Father Joseph Collins of Visitation, questioned the alleged number of black Catholics living west of Grand. All three religious groups—Protestants, Jews, and Catholics—opposed the plan of Father Markoe. The opposition worried about the decline in the value of their property. They wondered why they should be the ones to suffer. Why not other neighborhoods? What had the wealthy employers who had lured African Americans from the rural south for war work done to help their workers? What had the government done? In short, few in St. Louis had done anything notable to help African Americans, except the Sisters of St. Mary, who opened a hospital for them and staffed it themselves. What surprises the social observer is the fact that neither these Irish-American pastors nor the archbishop did anything to challenge the *de facto* segregation installed by the Real Estate Exchange.

In 1932 Father Tim Dempsey began a new venture in housing: St. Patrick's Home for Colored on North Sixth Street. Despite the shortages all people endured during the depression, whites contributed mattresses, beds, stoves, coal, and other necessities to Dempsey's home, which welcomed 169 guests the first night. In its initial year, St. Patrick's Home provided 69,950 free lodgings.[3]

Missouri's first black congressman, William L. Clay of the First Congressional District on St. Louis's northside, praised Father Dempsey and Father James Maddigan for their positive influence in the black community.[4] Unfortunately, they had too few imitators among their fellow Irish priests.

Sodality leader Jesuit Father Dan Lord did his part in breaking down the racial barriers. He sponsored musical programs by the young people of St. Elizabeth's Parish before white audiences in the 1930s. Gradually, he integrated the cast to perform before an equally integrated audience.

During those years, black families steadily moved west, filling the central corridor to Grand Avenue. Saint Louis University and the theatre district held firm. As a result, the westward flow swung north a few blocks and continued west into once all-Irish parishes, such as St. Ann's, Visitation, and St. Matthew's. The percentage of Catholics among these newcomers was roughly 5 percent. Instead of welcoming the few Catholic families, the pastors of those churches refused to accept them and told them to go to St. Elizabeth's, the segregated parish on Pine, east of Jefferson Avenue.

Foreseeing a further influx of African Americans for war work in 1939, the provincial superior of the Society of the Divine Word offered to assign two black priests to St. Nicholas Parish and schools. The Archives of the Archdiocese of St. Louis and of the Society of the Divine Word contain no indication that Archbishop Glennon responded to this offer, even though the original is in the Archdiocesan Archives. Most of the clergymen at St. Nicholas's and St. Elizabeth's Churches were of ancestry other than Irish, as were the Franciscan Sisters of Mary who opened St. Mary's Infirmary on Papin Street for the black community in 1934.[5] Several individuals of Irish ancestry, however, took part in the education of black young men and women at St. Joseph's High School on Page at Whittier in the former St. Ann's elementary school building. Among them were Redemptorist Donald Corrigan, Kenrick seminarian Patrick Molloy, and Sister Ann Adelaide, C.S.J., principal.

When Cardinal Glennon lay in state at the Cathedral in March 1946, black Catholics paid their respects to an archbishop who had done little for them.

In the spring of 1947 the archdiocesan school authorities brought to the attention of the new archbishop, Joseph E. Ritter, the need of larger facilities for St. Joseph's High School for Blacks. The old St. Ann's school building had proven inadequate. The enrollment had continued to grow, with some high schoolers coming all the way from Kinloch near Lambert Field. Should the archdiocese build a new segregated school? The archbishop decided that African Americans could go to existing Catholic schools.

On August 25, the chancellor, Auxiliary Bishop John J. Cody, sent a confidential letter to all priests, at the direction of Archbishop Ritter. "The same principles for admission are to be followed in admitting colored children as for others," he wrote. "This is in keeping with our Catholic teaching and the best principles of our American form of democratic government."[6]

This decision had little effect on the southside parishes. A scattering of old black Catholic families always had lived in the area of Alexian Brothers Hospital on South Broadway. Other African Americans had resided at the northeast corner of Carondelet Park since Missouri's emancipation in 1865. While isolated, they formed an accepted part of the neighborhood. Some of them attended Sts. Mary and Joseph's Church on Minnesota Avenue. In the southwest section of the city, blacks had toiled in the clay pits "on the Hill" before the coming of the Italians. The two groups worked side by side until WWI, when most African Americans found work elsewhere. Only a few remained in the area. None were Catholics. Beyond that area to the southwest, one rarely saw a black person, except in city work crews.

African Americans had moved chiefly west toward areas predominantly housing Anglo-American, Jewish, and Irish families. Property values had deteriorated as neighborhoods changed. "Block-busters" took advantage of white fears. The integration of the swimming pool at Fairgrounds Park on the nouthside the year before had ended in fisticuffs. Few people in the area were ready for the archbishop's ruling.

Cardinal Glennon had accepted the "separate but equal" theory since the Supreme Court declared it during his early years as an auxiliary bishop in Kansas City. On one occasion, in correspondence at the time Webster College wanted to integrate, the archbishop had expressed his belief that the state law covered Catholic schools,[7] and prevented any Catholic move. Only a few priests—those of the archdiocese, Father Patrick Molloy, Cornelius Flavin, and John H. Smith, or of religious orders, among them Redemptorist Father Donald Corrigan, Divine Word missionary Charles Renault, and Jesuits William and John Markoe and Augustine Bork—had called for a change. Of the religious order priests, only Father Corrigan was Irish. The pastor of one inner-city area, descendant of an early Irish St. Louis family, looked at the matter from a different vantage: "My young black people," he insisted, "are not ready for the competition they'll meet in an integrated school."[8]

The new archbishop took the city by surprise. In retrospect, one can ask: "Might he have taken a wiser approach by ordering a year of reflection wherein priests and teachers could have prepared the Catholic people for this dramatic change?" That could be. The fact is, he chose to act. The action had an effect that recalled Pearl Harbor!

A group of Catholic parents at St. Edward's Parish in the northwest section of the city met to discuss the issue. Soon groups from nine mostly Irish parishes took part and then those from many more. They wrapped the scarlet robes of Cardinal Glennon around their shoulders and spoke of the Missouri laws that called for racially separated schools. No one spoke of church regulations regarding territorial parishes. They called themselves the "Catholic Parents Association of St. Louis and St. Louis County," elected John P. Barrett as chairman, and authorized him to request an audience with the archbishop.[9]

Barrett received the "bureaucratic run-around." Archbishop Ritter and Auxiliary Bishop John Cody were "out of town." Even the archdiocesan superintendent of schools, Monsignor Alfred Thomson, proved unavailable.

On September 20, Archbishop Ritter sent a letter "to the Reverend Clergy and Beloved Laity of the Archdiocese," calling attention to Canon 2341 of Church Law. Anyone who called his bishop before a civil tribunal for any action taken in administering his office incurred automatic excommunication.[10] Representatives of forty-nine parishes from various areas of the city and county gathered the next evening to consider the archbishop's letter. In a letter dated two days later to Archbishop Amleto Cicognani, the apostolic delegate in Washington, Chairman Barrett asserted that the group "actively desired Catholic education for the Negro," and that "it felt separate but equal facilities would be more advantageous for the Negro." The group pledged wholehearted support in any effort to provide such facilities.[11]

Despite these protestations of concern, no evidence exists that the group had done anything at all for the Catholic education of young blacks. Only after the archbishop's action did the Mothers Club of De Andreis Catholic High School offer to help in a campaign to provide funds for a new St. Joseph's High School for Blacks. The pastor of St. Matthew's Parish, Father Edward P. Ryan, partially defied the archbishop. He admitted black students but segregated them within his building and told them to attend Mass elsewhere.

When the parents of a boy and girl who were admitted but segregated at St. Matthew's notified Archbishop Ritter of the pastor's action,[12] Monsignor Charles Helmsing answered in Ritter's name. He gave Father Ryan the benefit of the doubt and challenged his priestly zeal to see the opportunities for good in the situation.[13] Father Ryan phoned in his full concurrence the next day.[14]

A few days later, the chancery advised Chairman Barrett to meet with Vicar General Monsignor Murray, his pastor at St. Edward's. The monsignor welcomed him as a parishioner, not as the leader of a group. Barrett accepted the advice of his pastor, and the protesting group disbanded. The Catholics of St. Louis accepted the guidance of their shepherd. Letters poured into the chancery; 401 favored the action, 71 dissented. Most of these dissenters lived in the area of St. Matthew's Parish. The chairman of the protest group, John P. Barrett, became an advocate of racial justice.[15] Archbishop Ritter rose from the status of an unassuming midwestern prelate to that of a nationally acclaimed social reformer. He never claimed this rating; he presumably looked upon this dramatic step forward as a routine action in archdiocesan administration.[16] Locally, it made all St. Louisans aware that their new archbishop possessed an inner strength that far outshadowed his physical presence. Nationally, he won the Thomas Jefferson Award from the Council against Intolerance in America.[17]

On the parish level, just as St. Joseph's High School for Blacks no longer existed, so no black parish existed, nor white parish for that matter, nor Irish, nor German, nor Polish, nor Italian, nor Bohemian. If a church remained Irish, German, Italian, or Polish, it simply meant that Catholics of that ancestry lived in that area. In the future, the pastor of St. Ambrose "on the Hill" might be Monsignor Adrian Dwyer, and Father Anthony Palumbo might serve the predominantly Irish flock at Holy Innocents not far away on South Kingshighway.

The archdiocese had no follow-up program of evangelization to tap the goodwill created in the black community. But it did set up an Archdiocesan Human Rights Commission, ably directed for many years by Monsignor Francis Doyle. It was the first diocese in the country to do so.

Few Irish leaders, clergymen or laymen, had taken the lead in the effort to bring better race relations to St. Louis. At the same time, the Irish Catholcs were not alone in opposing the advance of African Americans into once all-white neighborhoods. Protestant and Jewish groups had shared their fears of declining property values. As mentioned in an earlier chapter, while Cardinal Ritter's letter ultimately affected entire neighborhoods, it directly and immediately affected Catholic parishes and schools, and many of these happened to be Irish.

Archbishop Ritter did more than anticipate the integration decision of the Supreme Court that came seven years later. He led the dioceses of the country in promoting an archdiocesan mission band in La Paz, Bolivia. Named a cardinal by Pope John XXIII, Ritter took a significant part in the Second Vatican Council in the discussions on religious liberty and on ecumenic relations. He chose Monseignor Joseph W. Baker as one of his two theological consultants at the council. On his return from the council in 1968, to promote Catholic presence on the local radio scene, he chose Monsignor Joseph M. O'Brien as Director of the Archdiocesan Radio and Television Apostolate. As pastor of Ste. Genevieve du Bois Parish in Warson Woods, Monseignor O'Brien invited his fellow priests for an annual celebration of St. Patrick's Day. Still later he became director of Special Projects for Catholic Charities.

A navy physician from St. Louis, Dr. Thomas Dooley, wrote Deliver Us from Evil in 1956 and other books that alerted attention to the danger of Communism in Southeast Asia. After his term of service, he returned to the area and organized health programs.

# Moving into the Sixties

While St. Louis had its first non-Irish archbishop in a century, it got its first Irish mayor in sixty years. Raymond Tucker, a resident of Carondelet and professor at Washington University, had answered the call of the city fathers to mastermind a campaign for clean air back in the thirties. Dan Fitzpatrick, the political cartoonist for the *Post-Dispatch*, had dramatized the city's plight by showing the statue of St. Louis in front of the Art Museum lost in the smoke of a thousand chimneys. Dr. George T. Moore, director of the Missouri Botanical Garden, thought of moving the entire operation to the Arboretum at Gray Summit. But Tucker stayed at his task like a relentless beaver until St. Louis rode clear on Art Hill.

A grateful city then elected him mayor in 1953, and he served well into the sizzling sixties. One or two old neighborhoods retained their traditional identities—the Italian "Hill" and the predominantly Irish Dogtown, across the tracks and up the opposite rise. No new parishes among the three-a-year that opened during Archbishop Ritter's years had a distinctly ethnic flavor. Most of them, however, had some Irish parishioners.

Many long-standing Irish parishes lost their constituents—St. Lawrence O'Toole, Sacred Heart, St. Bridget, St. Malachy, St. Ann, and St. John, among others. St. Leo's grade school, which had the largest enrollment in 1910, lost its pupils and fell before the headache ball. No Irish parade marched up Market Street on March 17. The Ancient Order of Hibernians still carried on, but other organizations not based on nationality held the Irish interest and attention—locally the Laymen's Retreat League, and nationally the Holy Name Society, the Knights of Columbus, and later the Serra International. It was not that people were less proud of their ancestors. The time simply called for other rallying points.

The St. Louis Irish had welcomed Governor Alfred E. Smith back in 1928 when he ran against the Republican nominee Herbert Hoover. By 1960 a far more confident Democratic Party nominated Senator John F. Kennedy to run against Vice President Richard Milhouse Nixon. Kennedy came to St. Louis twice that fall. He spoke first to the delegates at the convention of the International Association of Machinists, held at the Kiel Auditorium on September 14. Union President Al J. Hayes presided, and Larry Connors, Chairman of the Host Committee and Head of Local District 9, welcomed the fifteen hundred delegates.[1] With his usual flair for the memorable quote, Kennedy stated: "In every area of our national life, we find the same story of a government 'frozen in the ice of its own indifference.'"[2] Kennedy returned to St. Louis a month later on Friday, October 21, for a number of speeches before large crowds in St. Louis County.[3]

Almost all St. Louis thrilled with the victory of Senator Kennedy in November. In response to threats from the Soviets, the young president challenged the National Aeronautics and Space Agency to "send a man to the moon and bring him back within a decade." The nation enjoyed a memorable moment called "Camelot," cut short by the tragic assassination of the president in November 1963.

The city celebrated its second centennial in 1964. The new Chief Executive, Lyndon Baines Johnson, visited the city on February 14 and planted a maple tree on the campus of Saint Louis University. The students gave him the first warm welcome that he had received as our national leader. At least one Irish undergraduate, Tony Harris, told of shaking hands with the president.

*In 1960 Irish Catholic John F. Kennedy made two trips to St. Louis.*

Johnny Keane, the Cardinals' manager who grew up in St. Louis, kept the team in contention until the final day of the season—and won. One star, like the manager, was born in St. Louis. Mike Shannon, a native of Epiphany Parish and a three-sports star at CBC, had signed with the Cardinals after a year of football at Missouri University. He played for nine years, hitting .308 in 1963. In the first game of the 1964 World Series with the Yankees, he tied the score with a homer in the sixth and the Cardinals went ahead in the late innings. In the fifth game, a graduate of CBC in Memphis, Captain Tim McCarver, hit a three-run homer in the tenth to give the Cardinals the victory.

In the series with the Red Sox three years later, both CBC alums would star again. In the second inning of the third game, Shannon homered to give the Cardinals the lead they kept. McCarver handled the pitchers well.[4] The pair went from the ball field to the broadcast booth, Mike locally, Tim nationally, and stayed in the world of sport.

In the field of radio administration, Bob Hyland, a vice president of Columbia Broadcasting Company, brought KMOX, "the Voice of St. Louis," to a new level of excellence. Talk-show hosts Jack Carney and Anne Keefe had their part in reaching that high plateau. A special favorite with senior listeners, Irish and others, was silver-voiced John McCormack, "the man who walks and talks at midnight." He also announced the Sacred Heart Program.

The field of church architecture, too, had its achieving Irish. Joseph P. Murphy and Associates looked in new directions with such churches as Resurrection of Our Lord on Meramec Street in South St. Louis.

In 1962 St. Louis–born writer Michael Harrington wrote a book that shook the country like an earthquake registering 9 on the Richter Scale. *The Other America* showed convincingly that poverty spread widely in the midst of a prosperous nation. With persuasive statistics, Harrington made his point. It

*Two heroes of the 1964 World Series were both natives of St. Louis, Manager Johnny Keane and third-baseman Mike Shannon. Keane later managed the Yankees and Shannon announced Cardinal games on KMOX Radio.*

could not escape the attention of Presidents John F. Kennedy and his successor, Lyndon B. Johnson. A "War on Poverty" followed; the administration tried hard, but the poor remained with us.

The first unit of the Citizens for Educational Freedom began under the leadership of newspaperman Martin Duggan and his wife Mae. The original unit included those of Irish as well as of other backgrounds. Among the Irish, besides the Duggans, were Judge Anthony Daly of Madison County, Illinois, Vincent Corley, St. Louis businessman, and the versatile writer Dr. Daniel McGarry, professor emeritus of history at Saint Louis University. Basing their position on the publications of Father Virgil Blum of Marquette University, a political scientist educated at Saint Louis University, they set out in the early 1960s to organize and work for the rights of children in parochial schools.

The group found little support beyond St. Louis in conservative Missouri. A small group that called itself Protestants and other Americans United had tried to block Saint Louis University's offer to buy property to expand its campus. At the time the Citizens for Educational Freedom began, the organization went as far as court in a vain attempt to block the salary of Christian Brother George McCarver, blood brother of the captain of the Baseball Cardinals, who had taught a night class at Lincoln University. The Citizens for Educational Freedom looked for and found a more fertile field for development in Wisconsin and Minnesota and began to sponsor a "Voucher Plan."

All the while, the Vietnam War had heated up, and protests grew more threatening against ROTC on campuses and other military establishments or symbols of military service. At Saint Louis University, protesters from off-campus threatened to burn down Cupples Mansion, then a student center, where the ROTC had its office. A young Parks College student successfully defended the ROTC program in a debate on that occasion with a pacifist professor. Neither was Irish.

In an entirely different mood, St. Louis Irish watched Rome for signs of dramatic changes in church life for the Irish and for all others. St. Louis's own Archbishop Ritter, by then a cardinal of the Church, upheld successfully the position of the bishops vis-à-vis the Roman Curia, in the tradition of his predecessor, Archbishop Peter Richard Kenrick. Two St. Louis prelates of Irish ancestry took an active role. Bishop Leo Byrne of Wichita served on the committee on the lay apostolate. Pope John XXIII named Archbishop John P. Cody of New Orleans to the Commission on Seminaries, Studies, and Catholic Schools. They supported Cardinal Ritter in his ecumenical effort that changed the Church's attitude toward other Christians, Jews, and Muslims. Not long after the council, Archbishop John Patrick Cody became the first priest born in St. Louis to become a cardinal of the Church.

On October 25, 1965, thousands of St. Louisans, without regard for national ancestry, watched the topping-out of the Gateway Arch, the greatest monument of the iron and steel age, designed by Finnish architect Eero Saarinen.

Three years later Missouri's Attorney General Thomas Eagleton set out to do what Representative John Cochran had tried to do in 1934, to take advantage of a split outstate vote for a seat in the U.S. Senate. He challenged incumbent Senator Edward Long and became Missouri's first Irish Catholic Senator. He began a long and distinguished career in Congress.

In the meantime, during the entire 1960s, the strong St. Louis soccer tradition reached great heights on a new level—college competition. The Catholic Youth Organization, under the direction of Monsignors Lloyd Sullivan and Louis Meyer, both of them star soccer players in their early years, had sponsored a program that brought five thousand boys and girls onto soccer fields. The athletic director of the Catholic Youth Council, Robert Guelker, trained the young athletes well.

Guelker's counterpart at Saint Louis University, Robert Stewart, discussed with him the development of a team of collegians to wear the Blue and White of Saint Louis University. After a trial year, Coach Guelker's charges took part in the National Collegiate Athletic Association's playoffs every year from 1959 to 1966, and they won the national championship five times.[5] The All-Americans from the Irish parishes were Pat McBride, Jack Gilsin, Bob Malone, Joe Hennessey, and Jack Kinnealy. The first two named also won the Most Valuable Player awards. Close behind them in soccer skills, Mike Shanahan went on to take a leading role in the local sport world and in university affairs as chairman of the board.

When Coach Guelker accepted the full-time position of athletic director and soccer coach at the University of Southern Illinois–Edwardsville, Harry Keough followed him at Saint Louis University in 1967. A successful coach at the community college level, and, as already mentioned, the captain of America's one great World Cup team in 1950, Keough led the Billikens to five more NCAA titles. He fielded many outstanding players from the Irish parishes. MVP Mike Seery was the son of Pat Seery, a Chicago White Sox baseball player who still held, with several others, a league record of four homers in one game. Another MVP, Pat Leahy, later place-kicked for the New York Jets professional football team for nineteen years. All-star Danny Counce starred in indoor professional soccer and, afterward, found a career in soccer management.

Twenty-one other Irish Billikens, including Mike O'Mara, Kevin Handlan, Chris Kenny, Denny Hadican, Bruce Hudson, Bob O'Leary, Joe Clarke, Pat Baker, and the brother combinations of John and Tom Hayes, Bill and Mike McKeon, and Tim and Dan Flynn, played in the pros. Three Dorans—Don, Dan, and Daryl—wore Blue and White jerseys. Daryl later starred as a player coach of the indoor professional soccer team, the St. Louis Ambush. Mike Sorber and Brian McBride played on the American World Cup team. Two

Billikens later gained prominence in the area of radio analysis for World Cup programs: Ty Keough, the coach's son, an All-American selection in 1976 and 1978, himself a successful coach at Washington University, and Bill McDermott, master of "one-liners," a player under both Coach Guelker and Coach Keough.

In the meantime, the Vatican Council had concluded its work. Changes were ahead in many areas of interest to St. Louis Irish. Then, on June 10, 1967, Cardinal Ritter passed away quietly.

Several months later, on February 21, 1968, Pope Paul VI named Bishop John J. Carberry, a native of Brooklyn, New York, then bishop of Columbus, Ohio, as archbishop of St. Louis. Once again, the Church in St. Louis had an Irish spiritual leader. A gentle, grandfatherly man, the new archbishop relaxed by playing the violin. While flying to Rome to receive the "red hat" of the cardinalate, he took out his harmonica and led the singing of "When Irish Eyes Are Smiling."

Cardinal Carberry lacked the theological background of Kenrick and the eloquence of Glennon. He reflected the "over-concern for continuity" of the eastern seaboard dioceses rather than "the receptivity to change of the heartland," but he vigorously supported the Pro-Life Movement throughout the state. Fortunately, he selected his co-workers wisely. Though generally conservative in approach, he appointed a popular young priest to guide the growing charismatic movement. In the overall running of the archdiocese, many rightly thought him less aware of what was going on than his predecessor. But he had great concern for the Church elsewhere. He prepared well for Synods. As a result, his fellow bishops chose him as vice president of the Conference of Bishops in 1974. He also participated in two papal elections and three World Synods of Bishops.

*Children greet Cardinal Carberry on his eightieth birthday.*

# XXXII

# The Tentative Seventies

While the sixties had roiled like the Mississippi at flood stage, the seventies moved as quietly as the Illinois in midsummer. Many Americans of various national backgrounds began to seek their "roots." Interest in genealogy grew. More and more St. Louisans began to visit Ireland, to look up relatives who stayed in Ballylanders or the Glen of Aherloe, or to go to the depositories of birth records at the Four Courts. *Aer Lingus* brought Irish from Chicago, Montreal, Boston, and New York to the homeland. St. Louis travel agencies arranged fine "packages" from any of these take-off points.

In the meantime, serious troubles broke out in Belfast and Derry. Militant members of the Orange Lodges paraded through Catholic neighborhoods, provoking trouble. The Reverend Ian Paisley used gutter language against the Pope and the Church. An Irish poet, John Montague, described the situation to American visitors in 1969: "To understand what is going on in the North, imagine Alabama's Governor, George Wallace, as President of the United States while the Ku Klux Klan has all the guns."[1]

Great Britain sent troops into the North to protect Catholics. They soon turned against Catholics and massacred a group of Derry Catholics during a religious procession. The perpetrators were never tried. All the while newspapers found it difficult to give the American public a clear picture of a regional situation that had economic, political, historical, and cultural aspects, as well as religious rivalries. It pitted the haves against the have-nots as well as Protestants against Catholics.

A detailed discussion of the origin of this provocative situation in Ulster strays far beyond the scope of St. Louis's Irish history. But it did have its repercussions throughout the United States and locally in St. Louis. Irish in America began to respond strongly to the mistreatment of their fellow Catholics in Ulster. The troubles in the North galvanized the attention of the dispersed Irish everywhere. One local response will come in the next chapter.

By the early seventies, psychologist Father Daniel O'Connell had established himself as one of the most popular teachers on the Saint Louis University campus. He had taken his doctorate at the University of Illinois and studied in the Federal Republic of West Germany. The Father General of the Jesuit Order named him superior of the Jesuit community at Saint Louis University. In the summer of 1974, the trustees of the university invited Father O'Connell to enter his name for the presidency of the university. He had not sought out the position. He was, in fact, a "person-to-person" rather than a "team" man, as the executive position seemed to require. Nonetheless, he accepted the invitation at the urging of his religious superiors and others.

Father O'Connell continued to live in a residence hall with the students and offered daily Mass for them. He drove a Volkswagen rather than a more impressive vehicle such as members of the previous presidential team thought proper. He was accessible to faculty and students alike. He set out to restore the traditional Catholicism of the school that had given way to a quest "for academic excellence" during the late years of his predecessor. Parents, alumni, and Cardinal Carberry strongly applauded Father O'Connell in this effort. He closed the School of Divinity that had lost its students and should have sealed its door before he took office. O'Connell closed it gracefully. As a result of this obviously necessary step, critics accused him of "retreating from theological reflection."

At the conclusion of his short term, he taught at various universities and made further psychological studies in Germany. The students of Saint Louis University lost an outstanding teacher. The provincial assistant for education of the Missouri Province, Father Edward Drummond, succeeded Father O'Connell for a year, and then Father Thomas Fitzgerald of Fairfield University took charge. He was the first president of the university who came from another Jesuit province. In his term, he emphasized financial stability. A building named for him houses the university's business offices.

Up to that time, customs and regulations had curtailed the work of many "active" sisterhoods. Some could no longer do the work their mother foundresses had set them up to accomplish. As a result, religious women with talent to organize communities, write scholarly books, or serve on boards of large universities, were involved in minutiae that failed to challenge their God-given skills. The Fathers of Vatican II urged religious congregations to look to the spirit and purposes of their founders, and act upon these reflections. During the seventies, the changes brought on by the Ecumenic Council affected religious congregations more dramatically than lay people.

Heeding the call, individual sisters of great talent moved into wider areas. To instance the experience of one congregation, during succeeding years the *St. Louis Globe-Democrat* named seven Sisters of St. Joseph as "Women of Achievement." Among them were Sister Jane Hasset, historian and president of Fontbonne College; Sister Marie Charles who worked for Community Betterment in Carondelet, where a riverside park bears her name; Sister Ann Judith in Social Welfare; Sister Agnes Marie in Humanitarian Concerns; Sister Raymond Joseph in Education; and Sisters Joyce and Anna Rose, experts in deaf education who promoted the physical as well as the academic growth of St. Joseph's Institute for the Deaf.[2] Two other outstanding deaf educators of Irish ancestry worked with them at that time: Sister Rose Antonia Malloy and Sister James Lorainne Hogan. Sister Rosemary Connell, science professor at Fontbonne College, worked with ITEST, the Interchange between Theology and Science. Sister Ann Julia Roddy taught at and directed elementary and secondary schools and then, after retirement from the classroom, worked with the Mayor's Office for the Aging. Sister Donna Gunn excelled as an administrator in the office of Provincial. Other Sisters of St. Joseph and members of other congregations found wider opportunities to use their talents as the Church called them or as they volunteered for new ventures.

Lay women of Irish ancestry, too, came in for acclaim. The students at Saint Louis University named their annual "outstanding teacher award" in honor of Nancy Ring, long-time Dean of Women. So well did Dr. Alice Hayes fulfill her duties as Provost of the University that the Trustees of the University of San Diego invited her to become the first lay-woman president of a Catholic University in America.

Pat Benefield, publisher of the *St. Louis Marketplace*, included Louise (Mrs. John F.) Harris among that magazine's "Women of Distinction."[3] An alumna of St. Mary's College in South Bend, with a graduate degree in Library Science from Columbia University, Louise became Consultant for Catholic Schools with the New York Public Library System. Returning to St. Louis, she reared her family and then returned to library work at Cor Jesu Academy and at Margaret Buerkle Memorial School. She served on the Examining Board of the North Central Association of Colleges and Secondary Schools. In retirement she is an extraordinary minister at St. Cecilia's Parish.

All five of her children have achieved: Dr. Tony Harris as a mathematical consultant for various pharmaceutical companies, Angela as publisher and community college teacher, Sheila as artist and art teacher at Rosary High School in North County, NiNi as Carondelet historian, author, and columnist with the *Senior Circuit*, and Dr. Bernadette, as physician with a private practice in geriatrics and internal medicine after teaching at the medical school of the University of Pittsburgh.

Catherine Patrice Gibbons, a graduate of Rosati-Kain High School who attended various local colleges, pioneered among women in real estate. She was the first woman on the County Real Estate Board. "Miss Gibbons," St. Louis historian McCune Gill wrote, "is undoubtedly one of the better known women in the entire St. Louis area." [4]

Ellen (Mrs. Robert E.) Dolan, one of the most successful writers of juvenile fiction in the St. Louis region, published more than forty hardcover books. She shared her experience and knowledge with other writers at workshops, such as the Metro–St. Louis Writers' Conferences sponsored by the Metropolitan College of Saint Louis University under the direction of Dorothy Mattingly. Miss Mattingly also planned and conducted historic tours to the Enchanted Land of New Mexico and the Civil War battlefields in the South, as well as to closer places of interest, such as New Harmony, Indiana, and Nauvoo, Illinois.

At this time, too, one of the older orders in the Church, the Dominican Fathers, opened their first residence in St. Louis. Father Kevin D. O'Rourke became director of Health Care Ethics in the School of Nursing at Saint Louis University Hospital, and Father Neil McDermott headed the Ministry Office on the Frost Campus. A few years later, during Father Thomas R. Fitzgerald's presidency of Saint Louis University, the Dominicans moved their Aquinas School of Divinity from Dubuque, Iowa, to the former law school building on Lindell Boulevard, and opened a priory for seminarians and faculty members of their order in Jesuit Hall, the former Melbourne Hotel at 3601 Lindell Boulevard. Successive priors were Fathers Frank Quinn, Harry Byrne, and Bede Jagoe. The divinity school soon established itself solidly on the academic and religious scene.

Even though the archdiocese had closed McBride High School, the Marianists remained strong in the region with Chaminade, St. Mary's, and

*St. Louis author Ellen Dolan autographs her latest book,* Susan Butcher and the Iditarod Trail, *at a local bookstore, while her family offers congratulations.*

Vianney High Schools. Though founded by French priest Father William Chaminade and heavily of German ancestry in St. Louis, the congregation numbered Irish members. Among these were Fathers Richard O'Shaughnessy, Paul Ryan, John Manahan, and Brothers William O'Leary, Eugene Fitzsimmons, and William Kinnealy. Father David Fleming guided their central province at the same time another David Fleming of St. Louis led the Jesuits of the Missouri Province.

Vatican II brought many liturgical changes, among them the vernacular in the Mass, and a wider selection of scriptural readings. A host of new songs, mostly Old Testament in orientation, replaced the devotional hymns to the Sacred Heart, the Blessed Mother, and Saint Patrick. The young people of St. Louis, Irish and others, accepted the changes of Vatican II wholeheartedly, occasionally without long-range reflection. Many young Catholics composed hymns. A group of midwestern seminarians, called the "St. Louis Jesuits," brought out a book of songs that carried the name of the city to the horizons of the English-speaking world. Father John B. Foley, leader of this group, composed a Mass and became director of the Center for Liturgy at Saint Louis University.

In mid-February 1970, Joseph B. McGlynn, Jr., a lawyer of Donegal ancestry and a graduate of Notre Dame with a law degree from Saint Louis University, mulled over the possibility of a St. Patrick's Day Parade. Circuit Judge James D. Corcoran, president of the "Sons of the Easter Rebellion"; Richard Ash, an accountant and president of the Notre Dame Alumni Club; and Michael Patrick Dolan, a public relations man, got together and planned it.

The timing was good. People needed a mid-March break in routine. Old Man Winter was doffing his overcoat and spring stood ready to push him into retirement. A Weather Bureau spokesman said that only twice since 1937 had snow fallen on St. Patrick's Day. He reported that the normal high for the day was 55 degrees, and in two out of every three years the mid-March days were

*Honorary Grand Marshal Dick Ford and Joseph J. McGlynn, Jr., lead the St. Patrick's Day Parade.*

clear and crisp. A batting average of .666 sounds great. Even Stan Musial never quite reached that at the old Busch Stadium on North Grand.

The committee invited drill teams, high school bands, business firms, civic groups, labor unions, and the American Legion. The Air Force Band from Scott Field agreed to play "McNamara's Band." Mayor A. J. Cervantes approved the plans and promised the cooperation of appropriate departments. In spite of threatening weather, the planners said: "March!"

At eleven o'clock crews from the Street Department began spraying green paint from Fourteenth down Olive to Broadway and south to the reviewing stand just north of the Old Courthouse. Regional political leaders took part: Missouri's Governor Warren Hearnes, Mayor A. J. Cervantes, County Supervisor Lawrence K. Roos, and Mayor James J. Eagan of Florissant. The "Irish Cavalry" left their horses in the pasture and rode in a convertible. Monsignor Jimmy Johnson, director of Father Dempsey's Charities, wore a green derby that contrasted sharply with his clerical black suit. About fifteen hundred marchers took part in the parade. Forty firms that wanted to enter floats submitted their applications too late.[5]

"It snowed on their parade," Patricia Rice wrote in the *St. Louis Post-Dispatch* on Sunday, March 22, "but it didn't bother the Irish."[6] St. Louisans of many ancestries—German, Bohemian, Italian, Jewish, African, French, Croatian, Anglo-American, Scotch, Lebanese, Ruthenian, Greek, Spanish, Slovene, Scandinavian, Russian, Serbian, Ukranian, Bulgarian, Slovak, and others–joined the Irish in wearing green parkas and wind-breakers. Often during the day people heard such remarks as "My grandmother was Irish," and "Our pastor is Irish."

Five hundred guests attended the party at the Gold Room of the Jefferson Hotel, sponsored by the Notre Dame Alumni. They talked of a parade in 1971 and predicted sunny weather for the celebration. Buddye Kaye's band provided the music and the O'Sullivan Dancers from Metro-East entertained.

Joe McGlynn and his wife Helen decided to take a needed rest—and went to Ireland. He deserved it for his careful planning and brilliant execution. Later that year, the St. Louis Irish named McGlynn the "Irishman of the Year." John M. "Jack" Keane, national vice president of the Ancient Order of Hibernians, presented the plaque to the honoree.[7]

In planning for 1971, the committee decided to hold the parade on the Saturday before St. Patrick's Day and invited one of the most distinguished of all Irishmen, Prime Minister John M. Lynch. Senator Thomas Eagleton, Attorney General John Danforth, and Aldermanic Board President J. Joseph Badaracco joined the other dignitaries and three thousand other marchers on the bright sunny day. Unlike 1970, the "Irish Cavalry" rode their mounts from the Bubbling Springs Ranch in Fenton, Missouri. As in the previous year, a dance followed the parade. On Sunday morning, Cardinal Carberry invited

Prime Minister Lynch to serve as lector at Mass at the Old Cathedral. Five hundred worshippers filled the church.

Each year the parade grew. More and more floats took part, more bands, and more paraders. The organizing committee always invited a dignitary from Ireland to preside. In 1972 Erskine Childers, Ireland's Deputy Prime Minister, presided. His father had represented the Irish people, along with Michael Collins, in negotiating with England's Prime Minister David Lloyd George relative to the establishment of the Irish Republic. In a letter of appreciation for the warm St. Louis welcome, the younger Childers wrote to Chairman McGlynn from his office in Dublin, "You set a standard of hospitality and kindness I believe will never be excelled. I only wish your talents could be employed in this country in the direction of trying to influence the Unionists in the North so that they would realize how well they would be received if they joined us."[8]

Michael O'Higgins, the mayor of St. Louis's Sister City Galway, led the contingent in the 1973 parade. In 1974 Senator Eagleton marched with Michael Keaveney, lord mayor of Sligo. Children from St. Elizabeth's School in Crestwood presented a Chinese New Year's–style dragon dance. The United States Navy Drum Band from San Juan played and marched. The Missouri Botanical Garden's float proudly announced "Shaw's Garden Wears Green Every Day."[9] The parade was getting bigger and becoming more and more a people's celebration on the occasion of the Irish festival.

In 1975, Richard Burke, Ireland's Minister for Education, came. The River des Peres Yacht Club had a float that suggested a steamboat wreck on the Mississippi. Since there were no yachts on the River des Peres, in fact no water in the river, this mythical organization drew attention. In 1976, the Committee began to make awards. The best float award went to the Young Ireland Club, and the best band plaque to the Marissa (Illinois) Marching Meteors. In honor of the nation's bicentennial year, George G. Clough, parade chairman, spoke about the events of two hundred years before. He pointed out that more than 40 percent of George Washington's soldiers who fought for freedom from Britain were Irish.

As national president of the Ancient Order of Hibernians, a few years later Clough gained national attention by standing up for the Order's right to exclude unwanted participants in the parade in New York. The case went to court. A young woman judge of Puerto Rican background sustained the Hibernians' right to welcome whom they wished in their St. Patrick's Day Parade. St. Louis would never have any conflict about who should be in the parade. Those in charge specified the rules, and floats and participants met these sensible standards. Things went well.

In 1977 John J. McGuire of the *Post-Dispatch* rated the St. Roch's Catholic School's All-Kazoo Band as the best marching unit. Senator Eagleton strode along with St. Louis Mayor John H. Poelker. In 1979 the planners added another treat to the program. They invited marathon runners to have a St. Patrick's Day five-mile run. Dan Reinke won. Mayor James F. Conway greeted the winners. The weather was off and on, generally cool and crisp, but fair.

In 1980, fifteen hundred runners entered the five-mile race, and many of them in costume. One of the additions for the 1981 parade was a unit of smartly groomed Irish setters. The Riverview Gardens High School Band played an excellent "When Irish Eyes Are Smiling" to the joy of Superintendent Edwin Benton. By this time, people planned well ahead of St. Patrick's weekend for participation. They thought of new costumes to wear—even the joggers. In 1982, five high school students and their teacher from Okawville, Illinois, jogged together dressed as a six-pack. A young lady from Arnold, Missouri, Barb Menner, remarked, "This is the best holiday of the year. We plan months ahead for this day." After the parade, Irish and non-Irish headed for McGurk's Pub at Twelfth and Russell, Maggie O'Brien's on Market at Twenty-Second, Crown Candy Kitchen on St. Louis Avenue, or Ted Drewes frozen custard stand on Chippewa.

In 1983, the committee selected Dennis P. Long, president of Anheuser-Busch, as Honorary Parade Marshal, a custom that endured.[10] Paddy O'Toole of the Irish Ministry of Forests and Fisheries sat on a reviewing stand that was bedecked with large shamrocks.

In the spring of 1983, Saint Louis University School of Medicine recognized a distinguished alumnus of its class of 1932, Dr. Emmet Kelly. Early in his medical career, Kelly chose occupational medicine over private practice and became medical director for the Monsanto Chemical Company. Among other accomplishments, he developed industrial hygiene facilities to monitor the work environment. Dr. Kelly married Ursula Maloney and the two raised six children.

Following the simply stated adage, "When you die, the only thing you hold in your hand is what you have given away," Dr. Kelly set aside much time for a variety of activities. President of the Alumni Association, he volunteered his services as an assistant professor of internal medicine and community medicine. In community affairs, he served on the board of directors of the St. Louis Heart Association and as chairman of the medical advisory committee for the National Agricultural Chemical Association. Active in the Church, he accepted the invitation of Cardinal Carberry to serve on the Archdiocesan Development Council. The cardinal's successor at his retirement in 1980, Archbishop John L. May, named him general chairman of the Archdiocesan Development Appeal in 1983. The drive brought in a record sum under his leadership.[11]

# XXXIII

# A Two-Parade City

I n the meantime, the Ancient Order of Hibernians wanted
to invite representatives of the North Irish Aid Committee,
supporters of the Irish Republican Army, to take part in the
St. Patrick's Day Parade. Commander-in-Chief Joe McGlynn
knew that the North Irish Aid Party made a political statement
that pointed in a confrontational and militant direction. The
leaders of the Ancient Order decided to have their own parade.
They invited the present author to be honorary marshal. He
declined with a reminder of the great need of Irish—unity of
purpose and effort.

   The Hibernians had a parade in Hazelwood on the Sunday
before St. Patrick's Day. Later they held an annual parade on
St. Patrick's Day in St. James Parish on Tamm Avenue, a few blocks

*The Cardinal Glennon
Division of the Ancient
Order of Hibernians
marches down
Broadway on
St. Patrick's Day.*

south of Forest Park. The pastor of St. James, Father Dave Rauch, invited all participants to Mass at ten that morning before the parade that began at noon. He invited a classmate, Father John Costello, pastor of Holy Cross in Baden, to preach on the occasion. What a far cry from the nationalistic days of Father O'Connor at St. James and Father Peter Wigger at Holy Cross.

The lord mayor of Killarney, Paudie O'Connor, represented Ireland in the citywide parade of 1985. A float representing St. Louis's Sister City in Germany, Stuttgart, featured dancers with shamrocks festooning their dirndls and lederhosen. In 1986, even in a crowd of thousands, Jeff McSorley stood out. He chased ten green snakes on a homemade platform.

In 1987, David Kennedy, the chief executive of *Aer Lingus*, the Irish airline, said, "This parade is definitely better than New York's. It's the best I've ever seen."[1]

Leading a squad of St. Louis police officers, Colonel James Hackett said of the 1989 parade, "This is the biggest crowd we have ever had."[2] He estimated the attendance at 350,000. An Irish business executive, Howard Kilroy, of Dublin, attended the 1990 parade, and he admitted it was an emotional experience. "In Ireland," he said, "we don't have this many people at one place at any one time."[3] Sheriff James Murphy again was pleased all went so well.

While the parade was the major Irish event, the Irish were busy in other ways. The St. Louis Irish community boasted of several recognized writers. Sister Marcella Holloway composed prize-winning poetry. Bernadette McCarver was a nationally syndicated columnist. NiNi Harris wrote five books on St. Louis neighborhoods, among them Carondelet and University City, and prize-winning articles and columns for various journals. One feature in the *Senior Circuit* opened the local discussion of urban sprawl. Many Jesuit priests

*Paudie O'Connor, lord mayor of Killarney, Ireland's representative in the 1985 parade, talks with Jim Mulloy, president of Jefferson Smurfit, while past grand-marshals (left to right) Robert Staed, Robert Kerr, Joseph McGlynn, Jr., Andy Walsh, George Clough, and Robert Muldoon prepare to march.*

wrote books. Father Jules Brady, of an old St. Louis family, on the faculty of Rockhurst College, authored several successful books in philosophy. His colleagues, Fathers Frank Cleary and John Kavanaugh, authored books and weekly columns, the first on Sacred Scripture, the second on a variety of religious concerns. Monsignor Timothy Dolan wrote a life of Archbishop Edwin O'Hara of Kansas City, Missouri. With a historian's vision, Blanche Touhill described the growth of the University of Missouri–St. Louis. Shortly after that, the authorities of the school wisely recognized worth at home and invited Dr. Touhill to be chancellor of the university. Kevin Madden wrote for the *Labor Tribune*, and Patricia Rice covered the wide local church scene as Religion Editor of the *St. Louis Post-Dispatch*. St. Louis's surviving daily paper had a number of sport writers with Irish surnames, among them Dan O'Neil. Jake McCarthy wrote for a labor paper in the 1950s and, almost a half century later, continued to put out a column in a local weekly.

Saint Louis University Professor of Law Gerald T. Dunne wrote extensively on legal matters. Two of his best works were *Hugo Black and the Judicial Revolution* and *The Missouri Supreme Court from Dred Scot to Nancy Crusan*. A colleague on the law faculty, Francis M. Nevins, Jr., published in two quite different métiers: scholarly law and intriguing mysteries. Both *Missouri Probate: Intestacy, Wills and Basic Administration* and *The Ninety Million Dollar Mouse* came from this versatile wordsmith. Other distinguished Irish professors at Saint Louis University included Thomas Michael Ruddy and Edward Maguire in History, William Monahan in sociology, David Murphy in Russian literature, William Shea in theology, Eileen Searls in the Law Library, and Helen Mandeville in English studies.

A popular radio special, "Donnybrook," features several Irish participants: Chair Martin Duggan, Anne Keefe, Charles Brennan, and Scotch-Irish Bill McClellan.

Attorney Edward C. Cody gathered a group of fellow members of the Galway–St. Louis Sister Cities Committee at McGurk's on Twelfth at Russell to support a writing project of this author on the post–Civil War career of the famous priest of St. Louis and Dublin, Father John B. Bannon, whose name appeared in several earlier chapters. St. Louis author Dr. Philip Thomas Tucker had already won the Douglas Southall Freeman Award for the best work in Southern History with his book on Father Bannon's efforts as a Southern chaplain and later as a Confederate agent in Ireland. The University of Alabama Press published that book in 1962 under the title *The Confederacy's Fighting Chaplain*. Father Bannon's later years deserved recalling.

A generous grant from the committee, abetted by the owners of McGurk's, Nick Carter and Jim Holloran, allowed the author of the present book to visit Ireland. In the company of a successor to Father Bannon, the Jesuit home-missionary Father Kevin A. Laheen, he visited the places where the great orator preached. The result was a 110–page book published in 1994 titled *The Fourth*

*Career of John B. Bannon, St. Louis Pastor, Southern Chaplain, Confederate Agent, and Irish Jesuit Orator.* Father Laheen later wrote more about Father Bannon's preaching in his book *The Jesuits of Killaloe.*

In 1995, the St. Vincent de Paul Society celebrated the 150th anniversary of the establishment in St. Louis of the first American unit of the society. Robert J. Reilly, II, became president. A memorial booklet told the inspiring history of the society in the United States.

In local church affairs, Archbishop John May submitted his resignation for reasons of age and health. Bishop Edward O'Donnell guided the St. Louis Catholics for fourteen months until Pope John Paul II appointed Justin Rigali archbishop. A priest of the archdiocese of Los Angeles, Archbishop Rigali had served for twenty years in the diplomatic service of the Church. He continued the strong stand for pro-life that his predecessors had taken, set out to improve the financial situation of the archdiocese, and authorized an updated edition of *Dream by the River,* the history of the archdiocese. He invited Pope John Paul II to visit St. Louis.

Shortly after the coming of the new archbishop, Pope John Paul II sent Auxiliary Bishops Terry Steib, Edward O'Donnell, and Paul Zipfel to be bishops elsewhere, and Fathers Michael Sheridan, Joseph F. Naumann, and Edward K. Braxton became auxiliary bishops in St. Louis. Another enterprising Sheridan, Paul, a Jesuit, won wide support for a program called Boys Hope. It spread from St. Louis into Latin American countries.

The area of business saw an interesting development at this time, too. The editors of the magazine *Irish America* put out a special supplement called the *Business Hundred.* While a disproportionate number of wealthy Irish-Americans in the pre–Civil War era, as well as at the turn of the century, conducted business in

*Mary Ann Haven and Dolores Muffler congratulate Bishop Edward O'Donnell on his appointment as auxiliary to Archbishop John May.*

St. Louis, by the 1990s the editors of the *Irish America* magazine placed only one St. Louis–based business leader among the hundred listed in the supplement. He was Michael J. Roarty, director of marketing for Anheuser-Busch Company. Most of the "Hundred" were third-generation Irish-Americans of County Kerry or County Cork ancestry who lived in either New York, Massachusetts, or Illinois. None were natives of St. Louis or educated there. Roarty was one of eight who merited a full-page tribute, especially for his work developing the Budweiser Irish Derby and opening European markets to his firm.[4]

As the 1990s rolled on, more people came to the parade. By that time it ranked high among the events of the city's year. The banquet the evening before welcomed more and more distinguished people. The Hyatt Regency at Union Station planned an Irish cabaret before the parade in 1994. They invited John McNally, one of Ireland's finest tenors, to sing, and comedian Billy Kelly to entertain.

Every year, one or another band stood out. Often it was the blue-clad Mater Dei high schoolers from Breese, Illinois, or Hazelwood Central from North County. Budweiser began to sponsor the St. Patrick's Day Run; it drew six thousand runners, and many of them wore costumes. Each year a dignitary of Ireland came, often from Galway, St. Louis's Sister City, or from the national

*Six thousand runners received a special blessing from the Honorary Grand Marshal in the St. Patrick's Day race on a sunny Saturday in March 1998.*

government. By the time Parliamentarian John Hume, leader of the Socialist Labor Party in Ulster, came in the mid-1990s, the Jefferson-Smurfit Company sponsored a luncheon the day before the parade. At the luncheon John Hume rightly predicted better times for the North. In 1998, close to four hundred thousand spectators greeted Dr. David McDaid of Donegal, Commissioner of Tourism and Sports for all Ireland. Six thousand contestants again ran in the race on that sunny day with the blessing of the honorary marshal.

As significant as it was, the annual parade shared the Irish story with other individuals and events. A group of Civil War buffs from the area of High Ridge in neighboring Jefferson County, led by Stan Prater, set out to reenact the glorious story of the green jackets of the Eighth Missouri Volunteer Infantry from Civil War days. They took part in reenactments at Lafayette Park, where the Eighth Missouri had drilled before moving south with General Grant, and in a commemorative ceremony at the Museum of the Western Jesuit Missions that recalled the career of Father Thomas Sherman, S.J., son of the other great Union general.

On the newly beautified campus of Saint Louis University, Father Terrence Dempsey opened the Museum of Contemporary Religious Art (MOCRA), the first in the country. Father John Kavanaugh won the "Great Preacher Award" from the Aquinas Institute of Divinity. Father Timothy Dolan of the archdiocese became the director of the North American College in Rome. He returned to the city to give the homily at the Mass on the 150th anniversary of the Church of St. John the Apostle and Evangelist. Priests of the archdiocese took over the staffing of Kenrick Seminary, long a ministry of the Vincentians.

The St. Patrick's Center developed in the vicinity of the old St. Patrick's Parish, where Father Dempsey worked so generously early in the century. It began in 1983 to help poor residents in the area and soon expanded. Shortly it became a multifaceted organization with programs to help the poor, the homeless, and the mentally ill make permanent and positive changes in their lives. It recruited a professional staff and called on three thousand volunteers

*The Honorary John Hume, leader of the Socialist Labor Party in Northern Ireland who worked tirelessly for peace, visited St. Louis with his wife Pat in the mid-1990s.*

who provide services to an average of four hundred persons a day. These include basic needs, counseling, education, and housing. Well supported by Irish and other individuals and groups, it offers even greater promise for the future.

In the spring of 1998, the local Irish and all St. Louisans found themselves caught up in a home-run derby at Busch Stadium. Traditional Cardinal scoring had been based on singles and doubles, hit-and-runs, base-stealing, bunting, and squeeze plays. Coupled with good starting pitching and unbeatable "closers," it brought low-scoring victories. Home run-hitting characterized the New York Yankees, who over the years featured Babe Ruth, Joe DiMaggio, Mickey Mantle, and Roger Maris, who broke Babe Ruth's long-standing home-run record. The Cardinals had beaten the Yanks with Ruth in 1926, DiMaggio in 1942, and Mantle and Maris in 1964.

A different Cardinal team took the field in 1998. Manager Tony LaRussa, who had developed winning teams in Oakland, California, brought a new style of play to the Cardinals that featured home-run hitting, with mighty Mark McGwire leading the way. While the team had trouble staying in the win column because of various weaknesses, McGwire obviously was hitting beyond his average. Pursued by Sammy Sosa of the Chicago Cubs, he challenged Maris's record of sixty-one. Every stadium in every city filled when McGwire came to play. He reached sixty-one, and, with Sosa still coming fast in the stretch, went on to set a new record of seventy homers.

St. Louis and all of America had a new sports hero, Mark McGwire. And he was Irish.

*A group of Irish St. Louisans gather at the Hibernians Hall to welcome the Donegal soccer team of 1986–87 and team physician, Dr. David McDaid, who as Minister of Sport and Tourism, returned as special guest for the St. Patrick's Day Parade in 1998.*

# Epilogue

T he overall effects of the Irish on the St. Louis community were a brightness of spirit, such as Mayor John Darby found among the early French, an enthusiasm to undertake new tasks, an appreciation of the freedom of the country, a concern for spiritual values, a willingness to sacrifice for religious causes, and a rejection of stark materialism—traits so well described by Archbishop John J. Glennon in a 1908 speech.

In recent years, some Irish in other parts of the country have begun to define their "Irishness" in cultural rather than in religious terms. They no longer feel that to be Irish one has to be Catholic. Recent issues of Irish magazines published in New York reflect this. To those editors and writers, Irishmen are Irish even if they have never seen the inside of St. Patrick's Cathedral.

Few St. Louis Irish share this new attitude. When statistics showed that the percentage of Irish in Missouri surpassed that of the great states of New York, Pennsylvania, Illinois, Michigan, and Ohio, the Irish of the city were baffled. Only Massachusetts, New Hampshire, and three states that touched her southern borders outdid Missouri. The urban percentage was generally similar to that of other big cities. The outstate Irish of other religious denominations made the difference. Some St. Louis Irish Catholics adjust only slowly to the fact that some Irish are Protestants.

As Ireland won its rightful place among the nations, the vision of the "distressful country" their ancestors left gradually faded. Instead, the St. Louis Irish visited an attractive land of fine towns and cities, of neat, well-kept farms, and friendly people with whom they shared a common language, common songs, and common memories. Ireland was a fine place to visit. As historian Lawrence McCaffrey of Loyola University wrote: "They [present day Irish Americans] know more about Ireland, its history, literature, and geography than previous generations, even immigrant parents or grandparents."[1] On their visits to Ireland, many go to Dublin Archives to learn more about their ancestors.

Dancers and singers come regularly to St. Louis, where Irish traditional music and dance interest more people than in Ireland itself. There, as Professor McCaffrey points out, "the popular music fads seem to be rock and country western."[2] Helen and Patrick Gannon, relatively recent immigrants from Ireland, have nurtured excellent Irish dance teams and music groups, whose participants model their costumes from artwork in the *Book of Kells*. The Gannon group takes part in the annual International Festival at Faust Park. The Kavanaugh family singers, among others, lure the crowds with traditional and contemporary Irish music. *Riverdance* and *The Chieftans* play to full houses at the Fox Theatre.

"If Irishness in the United States [and therefore in St. Louis] is to survive as something more than St. Patrick's Day parties and parades," Professor McCaffrey points out, "Irish-American leaders must act quickly to guarantee the presence of Irish history and literature in the curricula of Catholic and non-Catholic colleges and universities, particularly in metropolitan areas where their people are concentrated."[3] Fortunately, Chancellor Blanche Touhill of the University of Missouri–St. Louis has taken an initial step along this path, with substantial help from Jefferson Smurfit Company, aimed at endowing a chair of Irish Studies.[4]

Such action will prove the present-day Irish worthy of their pioneer St. Louis ancestors, the Mullanphys, the O'Fallons, and the many others who found freedom and opportunity in the terraced city along the great river.

The Irish in St. Louis kept a strong identity, as they moved into the third millennium, the fourth century of their presence the St. Louis area. Various factors played their part. First, there was continual immigration to St. Louis, unlike the French, few of whom came directly from France at any time.

Even though there was a split in the Irish community during the days of the Know-Nothings, the 1850s, those Irish Protestants who no longer identified with the Irish Catholics rarely identified themselves as Irish. Some of them were Scotch-Irish, some of them of Scots background whose ancestors had come to Ireland. They never opened a Church of Ireland parish here. Instead they attended mainline Protestant churches, and they coalesced with the Anglo-American community. Thus, the Irish, at first unified nationalistically, later unified religiously. This unity of belief and national background continued.

The main schools Irish Catholic young men attended down through the years endured, Christian Brothers College and Saint Louis University. The older St. Louis schools for young women, the Convent of the Sacred Heart and the Visitation continued down through the year, holding the loyalty of their students, many of whom were Irish-Catholic in background. Many other religious orders started schools and academies that held the loyalty of the people.

Through much of the two hundred years the Irish community had outstanding leaders: laymen like John Mullanphy and Julius Walsh in the nineteenth century, and Raymond Tucker and Michael Shanahan in recent times, and churchmen like Archbishop Peter Richard Kenrick and Bishop Patrick Ryan in the nineteenth century, and John Cardinal Glennon and Chancellor William Drumm in the twentieth century.

In this century the concern for the welfare of the mother country never waned. Long after the people of Eire had gained full independence and had put out of their minds the past indignities they had suffered from the British, the memories remained strong in the American people. Then, when the new problems arose in Ulster in more recent times, the concern of the Irish-American for the mother country grew and united Irish-Americans even more strongly. The search for roots brought many tourists back, not simply to see the beautiful country where people spoke their own language and were so hospitable, but also to check the records and find out a little bit more about their ancestors.

The institutions they formed, like the Hibernians and the societies they formed with others, such as the St. Vincent de Paul Society, the Knights of Columbus, and the Holy Name Society, have continued an identity all down through the years. The St. Patrick's Day Parade Committee sponsors a parade that welcomes all nationalities, and reflects the fact that the Irish are an accepted and welcomed part of the community. They have had good leadership such as Robert O'Reilly of the St. Vincent de Paul Society. As national president of the Hibernians, local Hibernian George Clough fought for the right of the Irish in New York to choose who should walk in their own parade. An unusually talented organizer, Joseph McGlynn, Jr., chaired the St. Patrick's Day Committee. They were great leaders of a devoted people.

# End Notes

### I. Creating a French Colonial Community

1. Charles J. Balesi, *The Time of the French in the Heart of North America, 1673–1818* (Chicago: Alliance Française Chicago, 1992), pp. 282–85.

2. John Darby, *Personal Recollections* (St. Louis, 1880), pp. 12–13.

3. W. B. Faherty, "James Maxwell," in *Dictionary of Missouri Biography*, edited by Lawrence O. Christensen, et al. (Columbia: University of Missouri Press, 1999), pp. 523–24.

4. *Record of Catholic Marriages in St. Louis, 1774–1840* (St. Louis: St. Louis Genealogical Society, 1872), passim. The St. Louis Genealogical Society has made the records readily available. Hereafter R.C.M.

5. Menard Family Records, in possession of Ruth Menard, Red Bud, Ill. See also, Kaskaskia Church Records, April 24, 1810.

6. *Catholic Baptisms, St. Louis, MO, 1765–1840* (St. Louis: St. Louis Genealogical Society), p. 88. Hereafter C.B.

### II. Gauls Welcome Gaels

1. Robert E. Parkin, *The Reconstructed 1776 Census of St. Louis* (Genealogical Research and Productions, 1993), p. 5. Hereafter, 1776 Census.

2. R.C.M., July 18, 1797.

3. Flynn, St. Louis, to McCordell, November 8, 1806, quoted in Paul Schulte, *The Catholic Heritage of Saint Louis: A History of the Old Cathedral Parish* (Saint Louis: The Catholic Herald, 1934), p. 73.

4. Idem.

5. C.B., passim.

6. *Missouri Gazette*, January 13, 1810. Hereafter *M.G.*

7. Ibid., July 10, 1810.

8. Ibid., December 28, 1809.

9. Thomas Scharf, *History of Saint Louis City and County* (Philadelphia, 1883), p. 903.

10. Ibid., pp. 192–93. The *M.G.*, August 15, 1811, stated: "Brady & McKnight have just received from Baltimore and Philadelphia in their store opposite Gen. Wm. Clark a handsome and extensive assortment of merchandise, which they will sell unusually low

for lead, Beaver, Beeswax or cash."

### III. The "Chief Irish Settlement in the U.S."

1 Lawrence J. McCaffrey, *The Irish Diaspora in America* (Washington: Catholic University of America Press, 1997), passim. This excellent book contains a superb bibliography of the Irish heritage and the Irish in America.

2 Kerby A. Miller, *Immigrants and Exiles: Ireland and the Irish Exodus to North America* (New York: Oxford University Press, 1985), p. 556. Miller presents a fine picture of the Ireland the immigrants left. The St. Louis Irish experience differs totally from the "central thesis" of University of Missouri Professor Kerby A. Miller's book after the arrival of the Irish in America. Miller begins the concluding chapter of his book with these words: "The central thesis of this book has been that Irish-American homesickness, alienation and nationalism were rooted ultimately in a traditional Irish Catholic worldview which predisposed Irish emigrants to perceive or at least justify themselves not as voluntary, ambitious emigrants, but as involuntary, non-responsible 'exiles' compelled to leave home by forces beyond control, particularly by British and landlord oppression."

3 McCaffrey, p. 9.

4 Ibid., p. 192.

5 Ibid., p. 1.

6 Ibid., pp. 6–7.

7 Ibid., pp. 1, 10. On page 72, McCaffrey writes: "When Irish Catholics, totally unfamiliar with urban life, moved into sections of New York, Boston, Philadelphia, Chicago, or New Orleans, others fled." Resources show that this was not the experience of Irish Catholics in St. Louis.

8 Miller, p. 556.

9 McCaffrey, p. 2

10 Idem.

11 David March, *The History of Missouri*, vol. 1 (St. Louis: Lewis Historical Pub. Co., 1967), p. 529.

12 George Potter, *To the Golden Door: The Story of the Irish in America and Ireland* (Boston: Little, Brown, 1960), p. 202.

13 Idem.

14 Entry of Father De La Croix, May 16, 1822, in *Baptismal Records* of St. Ferdinand's Church, Midwest Jesuit Archives. In his Diary, a young Jesuit, Father Felix Verreydt, who knew both Father Delacroix and John Mullanphy, wrote that Father Delacroix had borrowed twenty thousand dollars from Mr. Mullanphy to build the brick St. Ferdinand's Church. When the priest pleaded that he could not pay, Mullanphy cancelled the debt. Father Verreydt may have been correct, but no contemporary evidence supports this assertion.

15 R.C.M., passim.

16 Elihu Shepard, *The Early History of St. Louis and Missouri* (St. Louis, 1870), p. 89.

17 William Clark Kennerly, *Persimmon Hill: A Narrative of St. Louis and the Far West, as Told to Elizabeth Russell* (Norman: University of Oklahoma Press, 1948), p. 81.

18 Elihu Shepard, *Autobiography* (St. Louis, 1869), p. 106.

19 Annabelle Melville's life of *Louis William Du Bourg, Bishop of Louisiana and the Floridas, Bishop of Montauban, and Archbishop of Besançon, 1766–1832* (Chicago: Loyola University Press, 1986) presents a fine account of this many-faceted, at once attractive and annoying churchman, whom one might have expected to find guiding his flock in Lyons or Bordeaux rather than on the American frontier.

20 *Du Bourg's Financial Papers*, in St. Louis Archdiocesan Archives. Hereafter SLAA.

21 William Barnaby Faherty, S.J., *Saint Louis University and Community, 1818–1968* (St. Louis, 1968), pp. 8ff.

22 Anthony Doyle, Missouri Territory, to Brother and Friends, May 31, 1819, in Missouri Historical Society Files. Hereafter MHS.


## IV. Irish Business After the War of 1812

1 Mary B. Cunningham and Jeanne C. Blythe, *The Founding Family of St. Louis* (St. Louis: Midwest Technical Publications, 1977), p. 147.

2 R.C.M., passim.

3 Frederick Billon, quoted in Scharf, p. 198. Recent studies by Dorothy Garesche Holland show that "15 to 20 European Frenchmen" had come from the French West Indies. See Dorothy Garesche Holland, "St. Louis Families from the French West Indies," in *The French in the Mississippi Valley*, edited by John Francis McDermott (Urbana: University of Illinois Press, 1965), pp. 41–48.

4 Ibid., p. 195.

5 M.G., July 13, 1816.

6 Patrick Corish, *The Irish Catholic Experience: A Historical Survey* (Dublin: Gill and Macmillan, 1985), p. 124.

7 Glen Holt, *The Shaping of St. Louis, 1763–1860* (Chicago, 1975).

8 Emily Ann O'Neill, *Joseph Murphy's Contribution to the Great American West* (Ph.D. dissertation: Saint Louis University, 1947), passim.

9 Richard C. Wade, *The Urban Frontier: Pioneer Life in Early Pittsburgh, Cincinnati, Lexington, Louisville, and St. Louis* (Chicago: University of Chicago Press, 1959), p. 270.

10 Ibid., p. 277.

11 Ibid., p. 278.

12 Ellen Dolan, *The St. Louis Irish* (St. Louis, 1967). Also *Post-Dispatch*, February 20–21, 1971. Hereafter *P.D.*

13 Shepard, *Autobiography*, pp. 101–2.

14 Shepard, *The Early History of St. Louis and Missouri*, p. 166.


## V. Three Scintillating Celts

1 John Darby, *Personal Recollections* (St. Louis, 1880).

2 Ibid., p. 73.

3 Ibid., p. 80.

4 Kennerly, p. 80.

5 Gilbert C. Garraghan, S.J., *Saint Ferdinand de Florissant* (Chicago: Loyola University Press, 1923), p. 72.

6 Potter, p. 202.

7 Alice Lida Cochran, *The Saga of an Irish Immigrant Family: The Descendants of John Mullanphy* (St. Louis, 1958).

8 Scharf, p. 344.

9 Idem.

10 Darby., p. 149.

11 W. B. Faherty, S.J., *Dream by the River: Two Centuries of St. Louis Catholicism, 1764–1998* (St. Louis: Piraeus, 1998), p. 64 ff.

12 Darby, pp. 273–74.

13 Walter B. Stevens, *Centennial History of Missouri*, vol. 1 (St. Louis, 1921), p. 994.

14 Ibid., p. 996.

15 Idem.

16 Idem.

17 Scharf, II, p. 1643. For an evaluation of Kenrick as a theologian, see S. J. Miller, "Peter Richard Kenrick, Bishop and Archbishop of St. Louis," in *Records of the American Catholic Historical Society of Philadelphia* 84, nos. 1–3 (March, June, September 1973).

## VI. Irish Help Irish—And Others

1 Lemont K. Richardson, "Private Land Claims, Part III," in *Missouri Historical Review* 50, no. 4 (July 1956): 387–400.

2 Ruth Cunningham, R.C.S.J., *Anna Shannon, R.C.S.J.* (St. Louis, 1991), pp. 17–32.

3 *St. Mary's Mission, Diaries and History*, p. 167.

4 Quoted in Laurence Kenny, S.J., "The Mullanphys of St. Louis," in *Historical Records and Studies* 14 (May 1920): 95.

5 *Patient Register*, St. Louis Hospital, Archives, Daughters of Charity Archives, Normandy, Mo. Hereafter D. of C.

6 Rosati, St. Louis, to Mother Augustine, November 28, 1828, Ibid.

7 Van Quickenborne Account Books, in Midwest Jesuit Archives. Hereafter MJA.

8 *Missouri Province Catalogues*, 1830.

9 An Irish Jesuit historian, Thomas Morrissey, has written an excellent life of the famous Jesuit, *As One Sent: Peter Kenney, S.J.* (Dublin: Four Courts Press, 1996).

10 Daniel T. McColgan, *A Century of Charity*, vol. 1 (Milwaukee: Bruce, 1951), p. 57.

11 Ibid., p. 77.

12 Ibid., pp. 116–17.

13 Ibid., p. 121.

14 Ibid., passim.

15 Darby, p. 310.

16 Ibid., p. 311.

## VII. Celts Teach, Learn, and Care

1 *Catholic Almanac*, 1840, passim.

2 Society of the Sacred Heart, National Archives, *List of Students, 1836–60*.

3 RSCJ, *Catalogues*, 1829–1860.

4 Corish, p. 215.

5 Thomas Cahill, *How the Irish Saved Civilization* (New York: Doubleday, 1995), passim.

6 Corish, p. 203.

7 James J. Schild, *Houses of God: Historic Churches and Places of Worship of the St. Louis Area* (Florissant: Auto Review, 1995), pp. 30, 32, 120.

8 *Visitation Cash Book*, 1845, in Visitation Academy Archives.

9 Bernard Joseph Code, *Dictionary of the American Hierarchy* (New York: Longmans, Green, 1940), passim.

10 John O'Hanlon, *The Irish Emigrant's Guide for the United States* (Dublin, 1851).

11 John O'Hanlon, *Life and Scenery in Missouri* (Dublin: S. Duffy & Co., 1890).

12 John O'Hanlon, *Irish-American History of the United States* (New York: P. Murphy & Son, 1907).

13 David J. Doherty, *Catholic Schools in Missouri*, unpublished manuscript in SLAA.

14 Glencoe Archives, Christian Brothers.

15 Lloyd P. Jorgensen, "Historical Origins of the Nonsectarian Public Schools, the Birth of a Tradition," in *Phi Delta Kappa* (June 1963): 407–8.

16 *Catholic Almanac*, 1855, passim.

17 Wade, p. 248.

18 Ibid., p. 264.

## VIII. Expanding Neighborhoods Welcome a Windfall

1 Census, 1850, I, 380.

2 Census, 1860, I, xxxii. Gottfried Duden, a civil servant from Cologne in the Rhineland, came to Franklin County, Missouri, in the 1820s and wrote glowing reports of the area to his countrymen. As a result, many Germans, Catholics and Evangelicals, came from the Rhineland and settled in the city, in Clinton or Monroe Counties in Illinois, and in Franklin or Gasconade Counties along the Lower Missouri. In 1838 a group of Saxon Lutherans began Holy Trinity Parish in Soulard, and a seminary and settlement in Perry County. The Germans in the city resided on the southside or the far northside. Others had small vegetable farms at the edge of the city and brought their produce to city markets.

After 1848, the "Year of Aborted Revolutions," in Europe, "Free-thinking" immigrants from various German states arrived in St. Louis. Many of these looked upon the *turnverein*, or gymnastic society, as the center of their social life. They affiliated with no church, and in some instances, were hostile to religion. All the Germans were Free-Soilers and staunch Unionists. They brought to St. Louis strong interests in music and science.

3 John Hogan, *On the Mission in Missouri* (Kansas City, 1892), p. 38.

4 Russell M. Nolen, "The Labor Movement in St. Louis Prior to the Civil War," in *Missouri Historical Review* 34, no. 1 (October 1939): 29.

5 *Daily Missouri Republican*, June 25, 1854.

6 Henry Shaw's Papers, *Workers' Account Books (1854–56)*.

7 Henry Shaw's Papers, *Receipts, Bills, 1849*.

8 Hogan, pp. 88–89.

9 Idem.

10 *Du Bourg's Account Book*, passim.

11 Ibid., March 7, 1820.

12 Patrick Coleman, *Irish Journeys to Iowa* (Minneapolis, 1996), pp. 12–13.

13 *Kenrick's Account Books*, pp. 34–37.

14 Ibid., p. 71.

15 *The Catholic Almanac*, 1859, passim.

## IX. Bigotry and Blunders Break the Bond

1 Ray Allen Billington, *The Protestant Crusade, 1800–1860: A Study of the Origins of American Nativism* (New York: Macmillan Co., 1938), p. 1.

2 Ibid., p. 6.

3 Ibid., p. 9.

4 *Observer*, September 3, 1835. Professor Jasper Cross explained the career of "Elijah P. Lovejoy as an Anti-Catholic," in *The Records of the American Catholic Historical Society of Philadelphia* 62, no. 3 (September 1951): 172–180.

5 Ibid., October 15, 1835.

6 Ibid., December 31, 1835.

7   Ibid., August 10, 1836.

8   *Native American Bulletin*, June 14, 1842.

9   Idem.

10  *Shepherd of the Valley*, November 22, 1851.

11  P. R. Kenrick, St. Louis, to Purcell, March 7, 1854, in the Manuscript Collections of the University of Notre Dame.

12  James Neal Primm, *Lion of the Valley: St. Louis, Missouri*, 3d ed. (St. Louis: Missouri Historical Society Press, 1998), p. 178.

13  William Hyde and Howard Conard, *Encyclopedia of the History of St. Louis*, vol.4 (St. Louis, 1899), p. 2046. Hereafter H & C.

14  On page 5 of his book, *The Irish Catholic Diaspora in America*, Professor Lawrence J. McCaffrey looked on this local experience as widespread. He wrote: "In the late eighteenth- and early nineteenth-century America, there was some community of feeling and interests between Irish Catholics and Protestants. But . . . when American nativists, frightened by waves of Irish immigration, focused on Irish Catholics as the main target of their anxieties, Irish Protestants disassociated themselves from Irish Catholics."

## X. The Camp Jackson "Affair": Blessing or Bane?

1   Stevens, I, p. 711.

2   Ibid., p. 712.

3   Ibid., p. 706.

4   Ibid., p. 712. Major Sweeny saw intense action at Corinth, Mississippi, in the fall of 1862, where he again faced the "Minute Men" from St. Louis in the First Missouri Confederate Brigade. Sweeny had to pull his men back early from the fierce thrust of the First Missouri. But the Southerners on the left attacked late. Sweeny was able to rally his men. The Union counterpunch drove the Confederates back with severe losses to Texans and the St. Louis Irish in Gray. A month after the battle, on November 29, 1862, Sweeny rose to the rank of Brigadier General and led a division in Dodge's Corps in the Atlanta campaign. He retired from the army in 1870 and had no further relationship with St. Louis. Confer *The Photographic History of the Civil War*, vol. 2 (New York: The Review of Reviews Co., 1912), p. 152.

## XI. St. Louis Irish in Blue and Gray

1   Carol K. Coburn and Martha Smith, *Spirited Lives: How Nuns Shaped Catholic Culture and American Lives, 1836–1920* (Chapel Hill: University of North Carolina Press, 1999), p. 63. Hereafter Coburn & Smith.

2   Idem.

3   *Boyce Papers*, MHS.

4   Albert C. Danner, "Father Bannon's Secret Mission," in *Confederate Veteran* 27 (March 1919): 116.

5   "Deeds of Valor," from *Records* of the Archives of the U.S. Government (Detroit, 1906), p. 193.

6   Robert J. Rombauer, The Union Cause in St. Louis in 1861 (St. Louis, 1909), passim.

7   David Roediger, "Racism, Reconstruction, and the Labor Press: The Rise and Fall of the St. Louis Daily Press, 1864–1866," in *Science and Society* 42, no. 2 (summer 1978): 156–77.

8   Marx to Meyer to Vogt, April 9, 1870, in Marx and Engels, *Letters to Americans*, pp. 77–80, quoted in Roediger, p. 162.

## XII. Reunited St. Louis Irish

1   *Boyce Papers*, MHS.
2   "Deeds of Valor," p. 197.
3   Winter, p. 139.
4   Ibid., p. 126.
5   For a fuller examination of the Cummings case, see Chapter 3, "The Ironclad Oath," in W. B. Faherty, S.J., *Rebels or Reformers? Dissenting Priests in American Life* (Chicago, 1987), pp. 21–30.
6   McCaffrey, p. 117.
7   Kenrick to people of St. Louis, August 30, 1865, quoted in John Rothensteiner, *History of the Archdiocese of St. Louis*, vol. 2 (St. Louis, 1929), pp. 459–60.
8   Roediger, p. 163.
9   Ibid., passim.
10  Darby, p. 274.

## XIII. Irish Carry On in a Changed Community

1   Census, 1870, I, 389.
2   *Republic*, August 25, 1889.
3   Faherty, *Dream by the River*, p. 94.
4   Idem.

## XIV. Women of Distinction in Post–Civil War St. Louis

1   A. McAllister, *Ellen Ewing: Wife of General Sherman* (New York: Benziger Brothers, 1936).
2   *The New Catholic Encyclopedia*, vol. 13, p. 174.
3   Testimony of Archivist Sister Genevieve Kuesenkothen, D.C., January 15, 1999.
4   Coburn and Smith, p. 88.
5   Quoted in Hasia Diner, *Erin's Daughters in America: Irish Immigrant Women in the Nineteenth Century* (Baltimore: Johns Hopkins University Press, 1983), p. 89.

## XV. And Still They Came!

1   Census 1880, Compendium, pp. 548–49.
2   H & C, passim.
3   *Edmund Faherty Family Records*, compiled by Adrienne Faherty, El Segundo, CA.
4   *Globe-Democrat*, November 10, 1907. Hereafter *G.D.*
5   H & C, IV, 2061–62.
6   Russell M. Nolen, "The Labor Movement in St. Louis, 1860 to 1880," in *Missouri Historical Society Bulletin* 34, no. 2 (December 1939), p. 158.
7   Arlen Dykstra, "St. Louis Mourns the Untimely Death of Phelim O'Toole," in *Missouri Historical Society Bulletin* 31, no. 1 (October 1874): 32–40.
8   dem.
9   Quoted, idem.
10  *G.D.*, December 17, 1877.
11  Ibid., January 16, 23, 1878.

## XVI. Irish Parishes, Organizations, and Colleges

1 Rothensteiner, II, passim.

2 James Robinson, *A History of Soccer in St. Louis* (St. Louis, 1965).

3 Marshall Snow, *Circular on Higher Education in Missouri* (Washington, D.C., 1901), p. 165.

## XVII. The City's Most Popular Irishman?

1 Logan U. Reavis, *St. Louis: The Future Great City of the World* (St. Louis, 1879), p. 358.

2 Ibid., p. 360.

3 *Irish Catholic Directory*, 1869, p. 379.

4 Quoted by Stevens, I, p. 995.

5 H & C, p. 1746.

6 G.D., December 17, 1877.

7 Idem.

8 Ibid., December 23, 1877.

9 *Western Watchman*, June 14, 1844. Hereafter *W.W.*

10 Ibid., August 23, 1884.

11 U.S. Congress, House, *Investigation of Labor Troubles in Missouri, Arkansas, Kansas, Texas, and Illinois*, House of Representatives Report 4174, 49th Congress, 2d Session, 1887, pp. 468–69. See also W. B. Faherty, S.J., *Rebels or Reformers? Dissenting Priests in American Life* (Chicago: Loyola University Press, 1987), p. 34.

12 Gerald P. Fogarty, S.J., *The Vatican and the American Hierarchy from 1870 to 1965* (Wilmington, Del.: Michael Glazier, 1985), p. 39.

13 Henry J. Browne, *The Catholic Church and The Knights of Labor* (Washington, D.C.: Catholic University of America Press, 1949), p. 222.

14 Terence Powderly, *The Path I Trod*, edited by Harry Carman, et al. (New York: Columbia University Press, 1940), p. 380. See also Faherty, *Rebels or Reformers*, pp. 31–38. Father O'Leary toured Ireland for several years until Kenrick passed away. He then served as assistant pastor at various parishes in the Archdiocese of St. Louis until, at the turn of the century, he became pastor of a new church, Notre Dame, in Wellston. He died by accident when a tornado struck a railroad station at Mineral Point, Missouri.

## XVIII. Twilight of the Lion

1 Rothensteiner, II, p. 572.

2 *W.W.*, March 8, 1896.

3 *American Catholic Quarterly Review* 21 (1896), p. 425.

4 *W.W.*, September 9, 1894, p. 4.

5 SLAA, St. Leo's Parish.

## XIX. New Irish Names Surface

1 See Chapter XV.

2 G.D., May 29, 1896.

3 Faherty, *Dream by the River*, pp. 132–34.

4 The editor was Arthur Preuss of the *Fortnightly Review*, the most prominent lay theologian of the time. In general, the presence of two strong nationalities, Irish and German, strengthened the Catholic community of St. Louis in a way unknown to the eastern seaboard cities, where Catholicism was Irish Catholicism. The leading Irish pastors were public figures like John B. Bannon and Patrick Ryan, or social activitsts like Cornelius

O'Leary or, in the years ahead, Timothy Dempsey. The leading German pastors tended to be scholarly men like Francis Goller and Frederick Holweck. The St. Louis German Americans took the lead early in the century in the fields of art glass, mosaics, and liturgical worship. Leading German pastors and laymen continually expressed appreciation of their Irish archbishops, especially for the breadth of development they allowed.

A St. Louis historian, Elaine C. Tillinger, made a fine study of German-Irish relationships in the Spring 1990 issue of *Gateway Heritage*, titled "German Church, Irish Church: Late Nineteenth-Century Inter-Ethnic Rivalry in St. Louis' Catholic Community," pp. 45–53. In spite of its localization in the title, the article covers the wider American Catholic community.

In his book, *The Irish in America* (Baton Rouge: Louisiana State University Press, 1956), p. 183, historian Carl F. Wittke makes much of German-Irish neighborhood fights in St. Louis. He gives no contemporary studies to substantiate this. The present author uncovered evidence of occasional fights in one small Irish-German neighborhood on the near northside in the 1930s. One in the southwestern section of the city pitted Germans, Irish, Slavs, and one Italian against a team from "the Hill," in 1929. When fights did occur, they usually stemmed from team rivalries in fire-fighting in the nineteenth century and sporting events in the twentieth. Often fights were within one nationality. Such fights rarely had an ethnic aspect, but stemmed from club camaraderie.

5  Fogarty, p. 181.

6  Ibid., p. 187.

7  Census, 1900, I, p. 776.

8  Mercy Archives, St. Louis.

9  Rothensteiner, II, p. 621.

## XX. St. Louis Irish Writers

1  *Cambridge History of American Literature*, vol. 2 (New York, 1944), p. 390.

2  *The Mirror*, August 25, 1904.

3  Clarence Miller, "A Patchwork Portrait," in *Missouri Historical Society Bulletin* 17 (October 1960), p. 50.

4  Orrick Johns, *Time of Our Lives: The Story of My Father and Myself* (New York: Stackpole, 1937), p. 170.

5  Max Putzel, *The Man in the Mirror: William Reedy and His Magazine* (Columbia: University of Missouri Press, 1998), pp. 290–91.

6  Ibid., x.

7  Ibid., xi.

8  Ibid., p. 86. Reedy called Archbishop Kain a "Tittlebat Titmouse Torquemada," in *The Mirror*, June 24, 1897.

9  Ibid., p. 143.

10  J. P. Curtiss, ed., *American Catholic Who's Who* (St. Louis: Herder, 1911), p. 204.

11  Anne Andre Johnson, *Notable Women of St. Louis* (St. Louis, 1914), p. 55.

12  Ibid., pp. 252–53.

## XXI. An Amasser of Money and a Martyr for Justice

1  Primm, p. 376.

2  Putzel, p. 14.

3  Ibid., p. 83.

4   Primm, p. 376.

5   *P.D.*, June 14, 1914. The *Cathedral Records* for July 1895 show a gift of $1000 from James B. Campbell, in SLAA.

6   Ibid., June 14, 1914.

7   Primm, p. 381.

8   L. A. O'Donnell, *Irish Voice and Organized Labor in America* (Westport, Conn.: Greenwood Press, 1997), p. 132.

9   *Missouri Report*, Bureau of Labor Statistics, 1910, p. 280; Statistics, *35th Annual Report*, 1913, p. 675.

10  "Washington Avenue Garment District," in Rose Feurer, ed., *St. Louis Labor Tour* (St. Louis, 1994), p. 10.

11  Ibid., p. 11.

12  *St. Louis Labor*, November 12, 1909.

13  Ibid., July 16, 1909.

14. James Cassedy, "A Bond of Sympathy: The Life and Tragic Death of Fannie Sellins," in *Labor's Heritage* (winter 1992): 34–46.

15  Ibid., p. 45.

16  Ibid., pp. 34–36.

## XXII. World's Fair and World War

1   W. B. Yeats, Dublin, to James Reardon, 8 April 1904, quoted in *The Collected Letters of W. B. Yeats*, vol. 3, edited by John Kelly (New York: Oxford University Press, 1994), p. 569.

2   W. B. Yeats, Dublin, to Cornelius Weyandt, 22 June 1904, quoted, Ibid., p. 612.

3   W. B. Faherty, S.J., *Deep Roots and Golden Wings* (St. Louis: River City Publishers, 1982), p. 118.

4   The bulk of the material in this section is taken from the author's *Dream by the River: Two Centuries of St. Louis Catholicism, 1766–1973*, part 4, pp. 149–85.

5   Census 1910, II, 1128.

6   Harold McAuliffe, S.J., *Father Tim* (Milwaukee: Bruce, 1944), p. 56.

7   Ibid., p, 60.

8   Ibid., p. 65.

9   Christopher Tibbs, *The Great Silent Majority: Missouri's Resistance to World War I* (Columbia: University of Missouri Press, 1988).

10  Marion Reedy, "Still Hope for Peace," in *Mirror* 26, no. 1 (January 5, 1917).

11  Reedy, "Reflections: Don't Drum Up Hate," Ibid., 26, no. 2 (May 4, 1917).

12  McAuliffe, p. 83.

## XXIII. The St. Louis Irish in a Melting Pot

1   Census 1920, I, p. 78.

2   Census 1930, II, p. 331.

3   Ibid., p. 281.

## XXIV. Irish St. Louisans on the Political Scene in Washington

1   Alice Anne Thompson, *The Life and Career of William L. Igoe: The Reluctant Boss, 1879–1953* (Ph.D. dissertation, Saint Louis University, 1958), in the Pius XII Memorial Library, St. Louis.

2   David McCullough, *Truman* (New York: Simon & Schuster, 1992), p. 206.

3  Ibid., p. 209.
4  Ibid., p. 293.
5  Ibid., p. 871.
6  Interview with Father Laurence Kenny, S.J., September 18, 1945.

## XXV. Noted Irish Clerical Personalities (1920–1940)

1  Joseph Donovan, C.M., "Is this the Long-Looked For Society?" in *American Ecclesiastical Review* 86 (March 1932), pp. 245ff.
2  Cecily Halleck, *The Legion of Mary* (New York, 1950), p. 101.

## XXVI. St. Louis Irish in Education

1  Jane Kehoe Hasset, C.S.J., *As Strong as Granite* (St. Louis, 1999), p. 18.
2  Faherty, *Better the Dream*, p. 282.

## XXVII. St. Louis Irish in Labor Leadership

1  *Bibliographical Dictionary of American Labor Leaders*, edited by Gary M. Fink (New York, 1974), pages 140–41, 273–74, and 297.
2  Ibid., p. 140.
3  *Dictionary of American Biography*, VII, 544–45.
4  Idem.
5  Will Faherty, to author, December 17, 1936.
6  Fink, p. 273.
7  Ibid., p. 297.

## XXVIII. Irish Clergy and a German-American Archbishop

1  Church historian Gerald Fogarty pointed out that "Late in 1939, Spellman had been assured that he and Archbishop John Glennon of St. Louis were to be elevated to the purple." Fogarty, p. 311.
2  Interview with biographer Lisa Mulligan, May 18, 1965.
3  Sister Mary Mangan, S.L., "Sisters of Loretto in St. Louis, 1847–1947," in *Gateway Heritage* 18, no. 3 (winter 1997–98): 26 ff.

## XXIX. St. Louis Irish in Sports

1  *The Baseball Encyclopedia* (New York: Macmillan, 1993), passim.
2  *The Official NBA Basketball Encyclopedia* (New York: Villiard, 1994), p. 316.

## XXX. St. Louis Irish and the Black Community

1  W. B. Faherty & Madeline Barni Oliver, *The Religious Roots of Black Catholics of St. Louis* (St. Louis: St. Stanislaus Historic Museum, 1977), p. 4. Hereafter *R.R.*
2  W. W. Butts, St. Louis, to Glennon, December 14, 1927, in MPA, Markoe file.
3  McAuliffe, p. 121
4  *R.R.*, p. 56.
5  Ibid., p. 16.
6  Cody, St. Louis, to priests, August 25, 1947, in SLAA.
7  Glennon, St. Louis, to Molloy, December 7, 1943, copy in MPA.

8   Father George Ryder to author, September 18, 1946.

9   Barrett, St. Louis, to Cicognani, September 23, 1947, in SLAA.

10  Ritter, St. Louis, to Priests and People, September 20, 1947, in SLAA.

11  Barrett, op cit.

12  Hamilton, St. Louis, to Ritter, September 18, 1947, in SLAA.

13  Helmsing, St. Louis, to Ryan, September 21, 1947, in SLAA.

14  Ivan James, *The History of Black Catholics in St. Louis*, undated. A copy is in the Midwest Jesuit Archives.

15  Privileged sources.

16  Robert Donner, "Cardinal Ritter: Welcoming the Future," in *The Sign* (March 1963): 17.

17  Faherty, *Dream by the River*, p. 188.

### XXXI. Moving into the Sixties

1   *The St. Louis Labor Tribune*, September 15, 1960, p. 1.

2   *Ibid.*, p. 2.

3   Ibid., October 27, 1960, p. 2.

4   *The Baseball Encyclopedia* (New York, 1993), passim.

5   *Sports Illustrated*, XXV (December 12, 1966), p. 24.

### XXXII. The Tentative Seventies

1   William B. Faherty, *Journal of Georgetown Pilgrimage* (August 15, 1969), in author's files.

2   *G.D.*, passim.

3   Joan Selzer, "Successful Women in St. Louis" in *The Marketplace: A Forum* 3, no. 3 (fall 1985): 32.

4   McCune Gill, *The St. Louis Story*, p. 1273.

5   *P.D.*, March 22, 1970.

6   Idem.

7   *Hibernian Digest*, November–December 1970.

8   Childers, Dublin, to McGlynn, 24 March 1972, in *Parade Scrapbook*, in McGlynn file.

9   *P.D.*, March 17, 1974.

10  *The Irish American News*, June 1983, p. 28.

11  *St. Louis Review*, 1983, passim.

### XXXIII. A Two-Parade City

1   Quoted, in *Parade Scrapbook*, March 1987.

2   Ibid., March 1989.

3   Ibid., March 1990.

4   *The Irish America Business 100* (New York, undated), p. 25.

### Epilogue

1   McCaffrey, p. 198.

2   Idem.

3   Ibid., 199.

4   Touhill to Faherty, St. Louis, October 17, 1998, in author's files.

# Index

Mulhall, Zach, 102

Mullanphy, Bryan, 31, 33, 35–38, 63, 65, 118, 165; befriends John O'Hanlon, 39, 46; criticizes McIntosh lynching, 63; cut from father's will, 38; emigrants' home named for, 38; leaves his fortune for immigrants, 39; shares in sisters' wills, 38; Traveller's Aid stems from will of, 39

Mullanphy, John, 8, 11, 18, 25, 143; aids Daughters of Charity, 26, 44; contributes to brick cathedral, 13–14; daughters of, 11–12; described by Mayor John Darby, 26; estate of, 51; gives property to Mother Duchesne, 32, 41; granddaughters of, donate property to St. Laurence O'Toole Parish, 49; offers financial help to Jesuits, 33; omits son Bryan from his will, 38; purchases property, 31; small charities of, 26

Mulligan, Colonel James, 77–78

Mulligan, Lisa, 195

Murphy, Lieutenant David, 73

Murphy, Reverend Eugene, S.J., 178

Murphy, Joseph, 21–22, 35

Murphy, Joseph P., 213

Murphy, M. J., 102–3

Murphy, Myles J., 154

"Murphy Wagons," 21–22

Murray, Senator James, 169

Museum of Contemporary Religious Art, 230

Myers, George S., 67

National Office of the Propagation of the Faith, 194

*National Rip-saw*, 160

Nativism, 61, 65–67, 127, 205

Nerinx Hall, 182

Nevins, Francis M., Jr., 227

"Night Refuge," 52

Noonan, Mayor Edward Aloysius, 92, 103, 126–27

Noonan, Robert, 102

Notre Dame University football, 113, 199–200

Nugent, Daniel C., 154

O'Brien, Henry D., 86

O'Brien, Reverend Patrick, 48

Obverstolz, Mayor Henry, 92

O'Connell, Reverend Daniel, S.J., 119; characteristics of, 218; president, Saint Louis University, 218

O'Connor, Mother Mary Anne, 32, 36

O'Dea, John, 83

O'Donnell, Very Reverend Edward, 228

O'Fallon, Dr. James, 27

O'Fallon, John, 11, 19, 25, 33, 55, 65, 67, 91, 118–19, 143, 165; builds medical buildings, 65; builds mansion called Athlone, 28; builds O'Fallon Technical Institute, 67; comes to St. Louis, 11; described, 27; praised by Mayor John Darby, 28; praised by historian Thomas Scharf, 27; president, "Friends of Ireland," 35; supplies military posts, 19; supports Eliot Seminary, 67

# Photo Credits

Arteaga Photos Ltd., 74, 96, 129, 156, 159, 167, 174, 176, 185, 193, 202.

Frank Borghi, 91.

Library of Congress, 148.

Bob Merz, 171, 212, 221, 225–26, 229–31.

Missouri Historical Society, 3–4, 9, 14, 19, 20, 25, 27–28, 31, 34, 38, 41, 44–45, 48, 55, 64, 69–70, 72, 106, 108, 112, 131, 135–36, 144, 153, 170.

Midwest Jesuit Archives, 50, 58, 78–79, 81–82, 94, 114, 116, 118, 121, 139, 155, 175, 181, 184–85, 190, 195, 216, 220, 223, 228.

Dr. William and Joan Monahan, 199.

Saint Louis University, sports information, 87.

# About the Author

illiam Barnaby (Barby) Faherty, S.J., has written about numerous aspects of the city of St. Louis: its history, its spirit, its schools, its churches, its people, its world-famous botanical garden, its mosaic-adorned cathedral, its incredible arch. In all, he had published twenty-six books, all but six of them—one on space exploration,two on woman's role, and three novels—about St. Louis subjects. MGM adapted one of his novels, *A Wall for San Sebastian*, for filming

He subscribed to magazines about the Irish in America, but he could find nothing about St. Louis and its people. In books about the Irish, he found an unflattering picture that failed to match what he had learned of his fellow Irish in St. Louis. Little wonder then that in his mid-eighties he set out to tell their story. He visited archives in Ireland and America to learn all the facts.

He had the background for it. His father's parents, William Faherty and Ellen McDonough had come from County Galway to O'Harasburg (later Ruma), Illinois, in 1851, at the invitation of William's grand-uncle, Edmund Faherty, an Illinois pioneer. In the 1890s, the author's father moved to St. Louis to study business administration at Christian Brothers College and became a heating contractor.

Faherty's mother, Angeline Barby, a

native of St. Louis of Alsatian-German ancestry claimed that "she admired the Irish so much, she married one of them." She was as vibrant and talkative as her husband was a quiet listener.

Sparkill Dominicans taught Faherty and sister Louise and brother Dan at Epiphany School in southwest St. Louis. The pastor, Father Joseph English, a native of Cork, emphasized the importance of St. Patrick's Day by giving the children a three-day holiday—March 17–19—every year. Between 1927 and 1931, Faherty attended Saint Louis University High School. In 1931 he entered the Jesuit Seminary at Florissant.

Faherty pursued the traditional Jesuit course of studies from 1931 to 1944. After his ordination to the priesthood, he finished his history doctorate at Saint Louis University. He taught at Regis College in Denver for eight years and later as full professor at Saint Louis University. He spoke on the Sacred Heart Program for fifty years and gave a hundred spiritual retreats. In recent years, he has directed the Museum of Western Jesuit Missions in suburban St. Louis and the Midwest Jesuit Archives. He speaks regularly on "Catholic St. Louis," a weekly feature on radio station WRYT.

He twice served as president of the Missouri Writers' Guild and of the Historical Society of St. Louis County. The latter association named its annual plaque the William Barnaby Faherty Award. Rockhurst University conferred on him an Honorary Doctorate in Humane Letters.

A member of the St. Patrick's Day Parade Committee and of the Ancient Order of Hibernians, Father Faherty served as Honorary Grand Marshall of the Parade in 1998.